THE BOOK OF INFLUENCE

BASED ON THE WORK BY DALE CARNEGIE

CREATED BY MULTI #1 INTERNATIONAL BEST-SELLING AUTHOR & AWARD WINNING SPEAKER ON HABITS

ERIK "MR AWESOME" SWANSON

THE BOOK OF INFLUENCE

CREATING ALIGNMENT

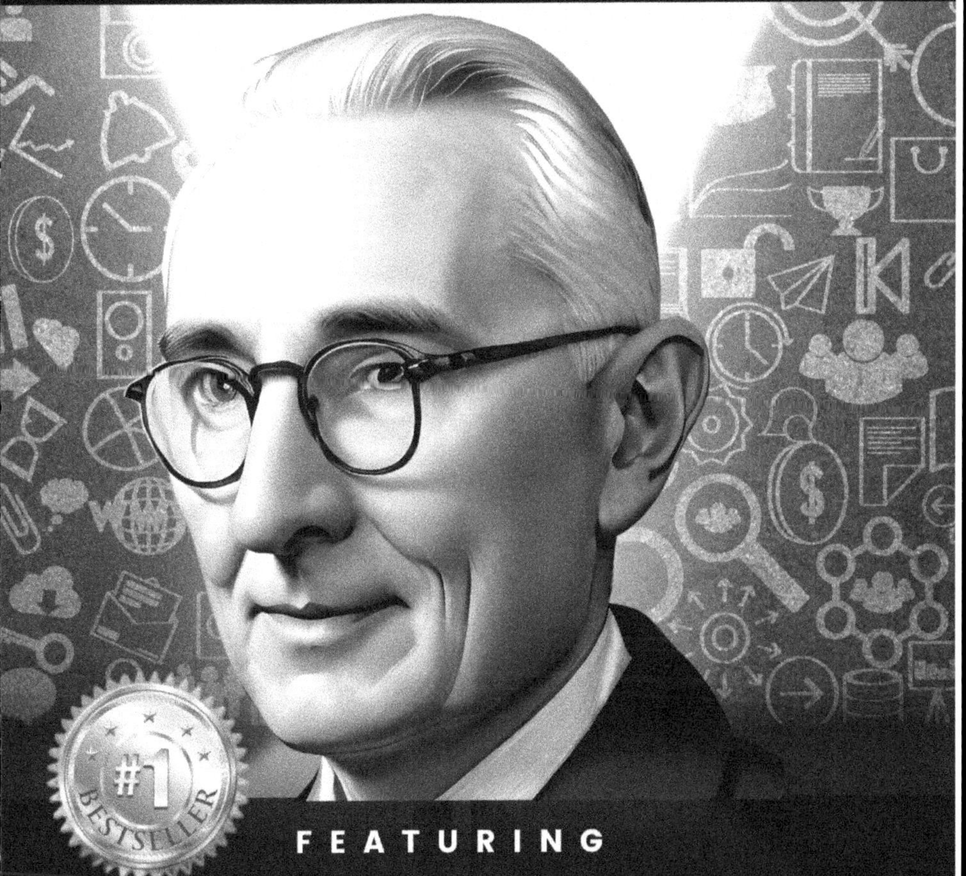

FEATURING

ERIK SWANSON

DAN CLARK ~ DANELLE DELGADO ~ JAMES DENTLEY

FOREWORD BY BRIAN SMITH ~ FOUNDER OF UGG® BOOTS

Orders by U.S. trade bookstores and wholesalers.

Email: *Info@BeyondPublishing.net* and *Team@IntegrityPub.com*

Manufactured and printed in the United States of America and distributed globally by Beyond Publishing and Integrity Publishing.

Library of Congress Control Number:
Hardback ISBN: 978-1-964330-90-7
Paperback ISBN: 978-0-9894136-9-5

The Book of Influence TESTIMONIALS

"Classics are here for a reason. This is exactly the case when it comes to the books and trainings by Dale Carnegie. What an honor to join Erik Swanson and so many other leaders in a modern-day book series bringing the principles into today's era."

Brian Tracy ~ Author, Speaker, Motivator ~ BrianTracy.com

"If you want the best information from the top influencers from around the world - look to International #1 Bestseller Erik Swanson and the team of influencing authors. I am honored to be among those collaborating to give the most important steps in how to influence in today's world. This book series must be in your library and among your top reads! It's important for today's world of connectivity and trust to be filled with rich information you can implement right now for your success!"

Jill Lublin ~ International Speaker, Master Publicity Expert and Best-Selling Author ~ JillLublin.com

"What an honor to join such leaders from around the world in sharing our secrets, techniques, and principles of success in building relationships based on like and trust. Dale Carnegie has had either a direct or indirect influence on everyone throughout the world. Allow these 4 books, in this soon to be a future classic series, to change your life and your relationships forever."

Erik "Mr. Awesome" Swanson ~ Multi Time #1 International Best-Selling Author, Award Winning Speaker, Featured on Ted Talks and Amazon Prime TV, Founder & Creator of Speaker Hearts International ~ SpeakerHearts.com

"What a classic book Dale Carnegie wrote in 1936. *How to Win Friends and Influence People* has changed so many lives in business and in personal relationships throughout the world. It definitely changed my life. Grab this book series and hold on tight, as it will take you from so-so to hero in your relationships if you put the techniques into practice."

Alec Stern ~ America's Startup Success Expert, Entrepreneur, Keynote Speaker, Business Startup Mentor, Investor ~ AlecSpeaks.com

"Having been a student of life-long learning and self-development and following the teachings of the late, great Dale Carnegie, it is my honor to be included in this profound body of work of Erik Swanson's *The Book of Influence.* The messaging in this series will impact people from all walks of life because of it's simplicity and applicable principles."

Bob Donnell ~ Founder of Everything Next Level, Human Behaviorist Author of *Mastering Your Inner Game, Connectology, The Art Of Intervention, 30 Days To Your Next Level, The 13 Steps to Riches* ~ EverythingNextLevel.com

"What an honor to be included in this beautiful series produced by my ever-inspiring friend Erik Swanson! These books offer a fresh view on influence and the work of Dale Carnegie, who's subjects are as relevant today as when they were first published back in 1936. Every book in this series is a must read!"

Jessica Radetsky ~ Founder of Broadway Hearts, 21 Year Broadway Performer on Phantom of the Opera, Breathwork Trainer ~ BroadwayHearts.org

"As a big believer and implementer of the principles of Dale Carnegie's work in *How To Win Friends And Influence People*, I highly recommend diving into this book series so that you can deepen your knowledge and understanding of the power of influence. Erik Swanson has created a masterpiece in highlighting modern-day examples of true influence."

Jon Kovach Jr. ~ International Motivational Speaker, Founder of Champion Circle, Habitude Warrior Mastermind Team Lead, #1 Best-Selling Author ~ SpeakerJonKovachJr.com

"Becoming fully self-authentically expressed leads to a peaceful sense of gratitude, that leads to clarity, that is the bridge to untold riches. What you are is conscious of being! "

Sir James Dentley ~ Entrepreneur, Best-Selling Author, Speaker, Business Strategist, Philanthropist ~ JamesDentley.com

"This is a collaboration of greatness! If you are ready to become an asset to every room you enter this book series is for you. Strategy, truth and principles that will endure for ages fill these pages. Dive in and get ready to rise!"

Danelle Delgado ~ Millionaire Maker, Business Strategist, Co-Founder of Engage Corporate Training ~ DanelleDelgado.com

"The definition of friendship, influence, leadership, and selling is the 'Transference of Trust.' Learning why and how to positively persuade others to redefine what's possible and to think, feel, act, follow, and buy is the most significant and valuable tool we can acquire in life. What an honor to join such influential leaders and honor the late, great Dale Carnegie."

Dan Clark ~ Speaker Hall of Fame & NY Times Best-Selling Author ~ DanClark.com

"Bravo, Bravo, Bravo! Growing up in Italy with our family values and traditions was so important to learn and to bring into my adult years. We need to continue to teach these principles to our youth of today."

Sir Bruno Serato ~ Philanthropist, Founder of Caterina's Club, CNN Man of the Year, Best-Selling Author, Owner and Chef of the Anaheim White House ~ AnaheimWhitehouse.com

"A MUST-READ for anyone looking to build long-lasting relationships and becoming an influence to the world."

Greg S. Reid ~ Award Winning Best-Selling Author, Filmmaker, Speaker ~ GregReid.com

"The privilege of being alive and able to learn and grow is one of the most profound gifts we've been given. What an honor to write a chapter in this series and share in this profound conversation about how we expand what we do and become more kind, skilled, and effective communicators."

Jason W. Freeman ~ Author, Impediment Busting Speaker, Imperfect Best Mentor ~ JasonWFreeman.com

NOW OVER 9,703,000 COPIES SOLD
HOW TO WIN FRIENDS AND INFLUENCE PEOPLE
BY DALE CARNEGIE

Global Speakers Mastermind & Masterclass

Join us and become a member of our tribe! Our Global Speakers Mastermind is a virtual group of amazing thinkers and leaders who meet twice a month. Sessions are designed to be 'to the point' and focused, while sharing fantastic techniques to grow your mindset as well as your pocket books. We also include famous guest speaker spots for our private Masterclasses. We also designate certain sessions for our members to mastermind with each other & counsel on the topics discussed in our previous Masterclasses. It's time for you to join a tribe who truly cares about ***YOU*** and your future and start surrounding yourself with the famous leaders and mentors of our time. It is time for you to up-level your life, businesses, and relationships.

Global Speakers Mastermind
& Masterclass
Habitude Warrior Mastermind & Global Speakers Mastermind
Surround Yourself with our Planet's Leaders and Mentors!
www.DecideToBeAwesome.com

For more information to check out our Masterminds
Go to: www.GlobalRideAlong.com
& Text the word INVITE to 619-304-6268

BECOME AN INTERNATIONAL #1 BESTSELLING AUTHOR & SPEAKER

Habitude Warrior International has been highlighting award-winning Speakers and #1 Bestselling Authors for over 25 years. They know what it takes to become #1 in your field and how to get the best exposure around the world. If you have ever considered giving yourself the GIFT of becoming a well-known Speaker and a fantastically well known #1 Best-Selling Author, then you should email their team right away to find out more information in how you can become involved. They have the best of the best when it comes to resources in achieving the bestselling status in your particular field. Start surrounding yourself with the N.Y. Times Bestsellers of our time and start seeing your dreams become reality!

For more information to become a #1 Bestselling Author & Speaker on our Habitude Warrior Conferences

Please text the word AUTHORS to 619-304-6268

And also go to:

www.DecideToBeAwesome.com

Acknowledgement to Dale Carnegie

I am honored and would like to acknowledge and thank Mr. Dale Carnegie for his dedication and influence to millions throughout the world. From his mentorship, leadership, philanthropy, and commitment to worldwide learning and education, Carnegie's legacy is unmatched.

We would like to pay tribute to his ongoing and continuous training, including his 1936 classic in self-improvement and interpersonal communication, *How to Win Friends and Influence People*, as well as the other legendary books and training programs he had created throughout the years. His influence reaches beyond the millions upon millions of students who have all taken part in his training around the world.

For this, I thank you Mr. Carnegie, from the bottom of my heart and the top of all our connections and relationships. Thank you for inspiring us all to build stronger connections, better trust, and genuine experiences with those who we serve. Let us all use our power of influence for the betterment and service toward others and make this world an amazing place to live!

~ Erik "Mr Awesome" Swanson & The Awesome Team of Authors
Multi #1 International Best-Selling Author & Award Winning Speaker

CONTENTS

Introduction to The Book of Influence

BASED ON THE WORK BY DALE CARNEGIE

For the first time ever in history, 33+ professionals, celebrities, mentors, and authors are brought together by Multi #1 International Best-Selling Author and Award Winning Speaker, Erik "Mr. Awesome" Swanson, to share modern-day examples, stories and applications in this book series based on the work by Dale Carnegie. The Book of Influence series consists of four books in which all of the book volumes dive deep into four vitally important classic areas.

In this National Best-Selling series of The Book of Influence, each of the four volumes in the series will cover the following topics:

Book Volume #1 - AUTHENTIC COMMUNICATION

In the training by Dale Carnegie and in his classic NY Times Bestseller, *How to Win Friends and Influence People*, Carnegie focuses on the fundamental techniques in connecting with people. Volume #1 of The Book of Influence discusses and shares many principles and strategies in connecting with others in such an authentic way through modern core values.

Book Volume #2 - LIKABILITY FACTOR

In *How To Win Friends and Influence People*, Carnegie addresses the importance of building like and trust. Being likable and utilizing our modern-day techniques are paramount in building long-lasting relationships and foundations with others. Learn the secrets to becoming 'likable' so that the world finds you irresistible, magnetic and people seem to be drawn to you.

Book Volume #3 - CREATING ALIGNMENT

A big part of Dale Carnegie's training is on influence. He taught how to influence others and gain their cooperation: avoid arguments, show respect for others' opinions, never say "you're wrong," admit your mistakes, begin in a friendly way, get the other person saying "yes," and let the other person do most of the talking. This volume in the series will highlight lessons, stories, and teachings from our authors in this universal law with counsel on creating alignment for success.

Book Volume #4 - WIN-WIN THEORY

Dale Carnegie's trainings always consisted of lessons in how to become a leader. In volume #4 of The Book of Influence - Win-Win Theory, our readers are taught to create Win-Win relationships through various theories and philosophies of professionals who have use time-tested techniques that always begin with praise and honest appreciation.

The Book of Influence emphasizes the importance of treating people with respect and dignity, building positive relationships, and creating win-win outcomes in an authentic way. This National Best-Selling Book series provides practical advice and counsel derived by experience to improving one's communication and social skills. It can be used by anyone looking to improve their personal and professional relationships for success.

FOREWORD BY BRIAN SMITH FOUNDER OF UGG® BOOTS

It's a profound honor to contribute the foreword to this exceptional series, a testament to the transformative power of alignment in the realms of business and personal development. *The Book of Influence* series paves the way for readers to embark on a journey of self-discovery, empowerment, and, most importantly, influence. As we delve into this third volume, *Creating Alignment*, I'm reminded of the countless lessons and trials encountered on my own entrepreneurial journey with UGG® Boots, lessons that resonate with the themes and wisdom encapsulated throughout this volume.

Creating alignment, as I've learned, is not just a business strategy; it's a lifeline that connects your vision to your audience's heart and soul. It's about finding that resonant frequency where your message, your product, or your service harmonizes with the needs, wants, and values of your community. My journey with UGG® Boots—a journey of alignment, misalignment, and realignment—offers a vivid testament to this truth.

When I first introduced UGG® Boots to the American market, I envisioned transforming Californian footwear with the warmth and comfort of Australian sheepskin. However, the initial response was anything but warm. Surf shops, not shoe stores, became the unexpected cradle for UGG® Boots, aligning with surfers who knew the value of warmth after a cold surf session. This was my first lesson in alignment: understanding and connecting with your true customer base, not the one you initially imagined.

I bought 500 pairs of my UGG® Boot designs from Australia to prepare for this vast push I would make in the American retail market. When I went out and did our sales run through the surf shops, I got turned away by all the shoe stores, and they couldn't understand sheepskin in California. But we went to the surf shops because so many surfers had been to Australia and they were familiar with UGG® Boots. In our first year, the sales for December were only 28 pairs, which was disappointing. However, I still grinded it out for two years. I got a summer job to make ends meet. Then, the following year, I thought like any young entrepreneur would, "Okay, I'm gonna do some advertising." So I hired two models, a guy and a girl, and posed them at the beach at Wind & Sea in La Jolla, California.

Then, there was perfect clothing, hair, and sunset, and the boots were front and center in the ads, and the sales that next year went to about $6,000. I couldn't understand it. It should have been way more than that, so I got another summer job, and the following fall, I said, "I'm going to hire better-looking models and a more expensive photographer." And we did the same thing. We again posed them on the beach by the Wind & Sea with the perfect hair, clothing, and tall white boots, which were the ad's primary focus. And the sales that season went a little over $10,000. And again, I needed help figuring out how to breach this setback in sales.

What was going wrong? And so, the following year, I decided I would get out of business. You know, I'm just going to eliminate all the inventory.

I had been developing relationships with all the surf shop owners and retailers, and I had 30 or 40 surf shops dinking along in sales—they were hardly selling anything. But the following year, I decided to get out of business. However, the first big storm hit the coast, and all my retailers started calling me in a frenzy.

They'd say, "Hey, Brian, everyone's in the store wanting your UGG® Boots today. Do you have any? I've run out." I couldn't go out of business if people were demanding more products. So, I had to call up Australia, order a boatload more of UGG® Boots, and restock all the retailers. That year, I knew I had to advertise in the surfing and action sports magazines, but I still knew something I was doing must be wrong. The models I used, the perfect angles, the cameras, and the hair weren't working. Still in my mind was the question, why?

So I had a beer with one of my buddies at the South Coast Surf Shop in San Diego, and I was explaining my advertising dilemma. He said to me, "Oh, shut up, Brian, and listen." And then he called out to about half a dozen young 12, 13-year-old grommets. They stored their boards in the shop. My buddy said to them, "What do you guys think of UGGs®?" And they all expressed, "Oh, man, those UGGS® are so fake. Have you seen those ads? Those models can't even surf."

It was at that moment of honesty and feedback that I realized I was sending the wrong message to my target market. And it was when I saw my ads through their eyes it was absolutely embarrassing. I was cringing at how bad these ads were. And so, as every entrepreneur does when you hit a wall, I called up another buddy of mine and, with lateral thinking, I connected with this guy running a scholastic surf team in Orange County. I said to my buddy, "Hey Pete, do you have any young kids about to go pro soon?" He connected me with Mike Parsons, Ted Robinson, and a few young and well-known surfer kids. So, I just went surfing at Black Beach in La Jolla and Trassel's up in San Onofre, and these are walks that are a mile long, with fantastic surf at the end. I had figured that all the kids who read *Surfer Magazine* would die to go surf those spots. And even more, they would die to be walking down those beaches with Mike Parsons and Ted Robinson.

So, I ran a couple of photos in the next set of ads. I had just used my camera, and it was nothing too fancy like the prior modeling shoots. I ran those ads in October, November, and December, and to my amazement, my sales totaled $220,000. When I analyzed what I'd done, I'd been ruining my image for three or four years because I was not in alignment with what my target market actually wanted.

They wanted credibility, reality, and to be part of the cool inner sanctum of surfing. In those first four years, I was showing these fluffy, horrible ads that didn't represent what my target market wanted. I finally dialed it in, and that's why the sales went through the roof soon after. And it never stopped after that. I figured out how to do the same thing in the snowboarding and ice hockey markets back east, where they don't have surf. And it was that identification of alignment with my target market that was instrumental in building the business of UGG® Boots. Alignment is critical.

The path to alignment was fraught with missteps and learnings. Early advertising efforts, featuring models on sunny beaches, failed to resonate. Sales languished because the ads didn't align with the authentic surfer lifestyle. It took candid feedback from young surfers and a shift to using real surfers in our marketing to truly align our brand with our audience. The result? Sales skyrocketed from a measly $10,000 to $220,000 in a single season. This was a stark reminder that alignment with your target market is not just critical; it's everything.

Another critical aspect of alignment I learned was within the retail space. Observing a potential customer's interaction with our boots, and the retailer's inability to effectively communicate the value of UGG® Boots, was a turning point. Implementing the Six-Pair Stocking Plan, where store owners and managers became product advocates, transformed our retail strategy. This alignment between product, retailer, and customer was pivotal in scaling UGG® Boots to new heights.

Throughout these experiences, the importance of perseverance, vision, and, above all, alignment has been my guiding star. Challenges and setbacks were abundant, but the relentless pursuit of aligning our brand with our audience's expectations and values was what ultimately defined our success.

This volume of *The Book of Influence* is a treasure trove of insights on creating such alignment. Each chapter, meticulously curated, provides invaluable guidance on navigating the complex landscape of influence. It's a manual for aligning your vision with your actions and your actions with your audience's deepest needs.

I'd be remiss if I didn't acknowledge Erik "Mr. Awesome" Swanson, a dear friend and a monumental figure in my speaker journey. Erik's unwavering support and the opportunities he's provided to share my story with inspired audiences have been nothing short of transformative. His dedication to fostering a community of growth, learning, and empowerment through the Habitude Warrior community, events, and masterminds is a testament to the power of alignment in creating impactful, lasting change.

As you read *The Book of Influence, Volume 3: Creating Alignment*, I share my story and insights as a beacon of hope and a guidepost. The path to influence is paved with the stones of alignment—between your vision, your actions, and the hearts of those you wish to reach. May this volume enlighten, inspire, and guide you toward creating your own alignment, in business and in life.

With heartfelt gratitude,
Brian Smith
Founder of UGG® Boots

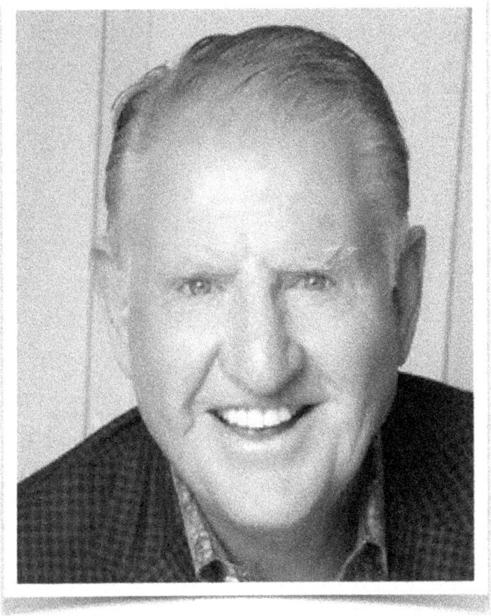

BRIAN SMITH

Brian is Australian born and was raised with an enduring passion for surfing and the surf culture. In his youth, he enjoyed the epic waves on both coasts of his home country. He was educated at the Institute of Chartered Accountants Australia, where he received his first of many business credentials.

After ten years as a public accountant, Brian felt a burning desire to do something that would fit his passion for surfing while looking for a business idea that would allow him to support himself. He turned in his resignation notice, got on a plane to the States, and became a regular at the classic surfing destinations up and down the southern California coastline. He called Malibu, Cardiff-by-the-Sea, and Swami's Beach his "office."

One day, while pulling on his sheepskin boots after a cold surf session, he realized there were nothing like them available in California. He and a surfing buddy shipped six pairs from Australia to show them around, in search of interested takers. It was at this moment that the UGG® brand was born.

Brian called on every surf shop up and down the California coast, enthusiastically showing prospective retailers the UGG® prototype. Most of the shop owners would deliver the same disappointing reaction: "Brian, we sell flip flops, not boots." Not willing to give up his idea, he then embarked on a laser-focused effort to gain endorsements and support from the surf community of which he was becoming a respected member. Finally, with two young Pro-surfers on "the UGG® team", a new cult was born and "UGG®" became the cool word on California campuses and beaches alike.

Had he not diligently stuck to his vision, the idea of UGG® Boots would never have come to fruition. Undaunted by the surf shop owners' initial rejections, Brian forged forward with his dream and we all now enjoy our much loved and favorite casual footwear—our UGG® boots.

After 17 years, Brian sold his company and the brand to Decker's Outdoor Corporation. With their resources, the "casual comfort" segment of the footwear industry came to life and the UGG® Brand now garners more than a billion dollars of sales per year, year after year.

Having developed the art of storytelling throughout the years, the stage became the perfect place for Brian to present to business owners the ups —and downs—of being an entrepreneur. He found that he not only enjoyed giving these talks, but his audiences were responding in wide embrace to his stories like he never could have imagined. The size and scope of the audiences grew and now he is one of the most sought after speakers in the world today. He brings a magical mix of real world street smarts, kindness, compassion and respect for the entrepreneurial drive—all of which fits business of any size. And, yes, he still continues to surf when he's not on tour.

www.BrianSmithSpeaker.com

ERIK SWANSON

THE ALIGNMENT FACTOR

Principle 3 in How to Win Friends and Influence People:

"Arouse in the other person and eager want. When we want someone to do something, we must relate the request to what is important to them. By taking the time to understand what is important to someone and framing our needs with their desires, we make it easy for that person to actually want to do something. The only way on earth to influence other people is to talk about what they want and show them how to get it."
~ Dale Carnegie

Influence

Influence is not merely about having power or authority; it's about the ability to create alignment among diverse individuals, teams, and communities toward a common goal. Whether you're leading a business, a social movement, or simply striving to make a difference in the world, understanding how to foster alignment is crucial. In this chapter, we'll delve into the principles and practices that can help you become a true influencer by creating alignment.

Understanding Alignment

Alignment occurs when people are united in purpose, vision, and values. It's the state where individual actions and objectives are synchronized with overarching goals, leading to collective progress. Without alignment, efforts can become fragmented, leading to inefficiency, conflict, and ultimately, failure to achieve desired outcomes.

Factors Influencing Alignment

To create alignment, you must first articulate a compelling vision and purpose that resonate with others. This vision should answer the questions: What are we working toward? Why does it matter? A clear and inspiring vision provides direction and motivation, drawing people together in pursuit of a shared goal.

Authentic leaders who embody integrity, empathy, and transparency naturally attract followers. By being genuine and true to themselves, they build trust and credibility, essential ingredients for creating alignment. People are more likely to align with leaders they perceive as authentic and trustworthy.

Communication plays a pivotal role in fostering alignment. Leaders must communicate their vision, goals, and expectations clearly and consistently. Moreover, they should encourage open dialogue, actively listen to feedback, and address concerns promptly. Effective communication builds understanding and alignment among stakeholders. Understanding the perspectives and needs of others is crucial for creating alignment. Leaders who demonstrate empathy and inclusivity foster a sense of belonging and unity, enabling diverse individuals to come together despite differences. By valuing and respecting every voice, leaders can create a culture of alignment and collaboration.

Alignment is strengthened when individuals share common values and operate within a supportive culture. Leaders should cultivate a valuesdriven culture that emphasizes integrity, accountability, and mutual respect. When values align, people are more likely to work together harmoniously toward common objectives.

Strategies for Creating Alignment

Involve stakeholders in the goal-setting process to ensure buy-in and alignment. By soliciting input and co-creating objectives, you empower individuals to take ownership of the collective vision.

Inspire others by sharing stories, anecdotes, and examples that illustrate the impact of collective action. Motivate individuals by highlighting the significance of their contributions and celebrating milestones along the way.

Demonstrate alignment through your actions and decisions. Be consistent in upholding shared values and principles, serving as a role model for others to emulate.

Establish clear roles, responsibilities, and performance metrics to hold individuals accountable for their contributions. Encourage accountability not as a form of control, but as a means of ensuring alignment and driving results.

Stay flexible and open-minded, willing to adapt strategies and approaches based on feedback and changing circumstances. Alignment is an ongoing process that requires continuous refinement and adjustment.

Nelson Mandela and the Power of Alignment

Nelson Mandela, the iconic leader of the anti-apartheid movement in South Africa, exemplified the power of alignment in bringing about transformative change. Despite enduring 27 years of imprisonment, Mandela emerged as a unifying figure who sought reconciliation and unity among the country's diverse population.

Mandela's vision of a democratic and inclusive South Africa resonated with millions, transcending racial and ideological divides. Through his unwavering commitment to justice, equality, and forgiveness, he inspired a nation to overcome its turbulent past and embrace a future built on unity and reconciliation.

Key Lessons from Mandela's Leadership

- **Visionary Leadership:** Mandela's vision of a democratic South Africa served as a rallying cry for millions, uniting people across racial, ethnic, and political lines.
- **Inclusivity and Empathy:** Mandela's inclusive approach to leadership emphasized empathy, reconciliation, and forgiveness, fostering a sense of belonging and unity among disparate groups.
- **Strategic Communication:** Mandela's ability to communicate his vision and principles effectively helped galvanize support and mobilize action toward common goals.
- **Resilience and Perseverance:** Despite facing immense adversity, including imprisonment and personal sacrifice, Mandela remained steadfast in his commitment to creating a more just and equitable society.

Becoming an influential force in the world requires more than just wielding power; it demands the ability to create alignment among diverse stakeholders toward a common purpose. By embracing principles of vision, authenticity, communication, empathy, and shared values, you can cultivate alignment and inspire collective action. Like Nelson Mandela, true leaders harness the power of alignment to drive positive change and leave a lasting legacy.

The Personal Touch of Alignment

I strive to align with everyone I come in contact with. As a professional speaker in the self-development industry for over 25 years, and a #1 published author in more than 30 books, I have found that it's much easier to survive and thrive in this world by aligning and surrounding yourself with other individuals who are changing the world as well.

Many people surround themselves with individuals who simply complain throughout their life. Decide for yourself that you will be different. Decide that you will gain new habits of learning the process to align with others and create new friendships and partnerships of growth. Seek out those who are leaders in their fields, and reach out to them. Connect with them. Align with them!

Once you see the magic of creating a life of true alignment, you will start to see your life improving in so many different ways. People will start to gravitate towards you simply because they feel your true, and authentic alignment with them.

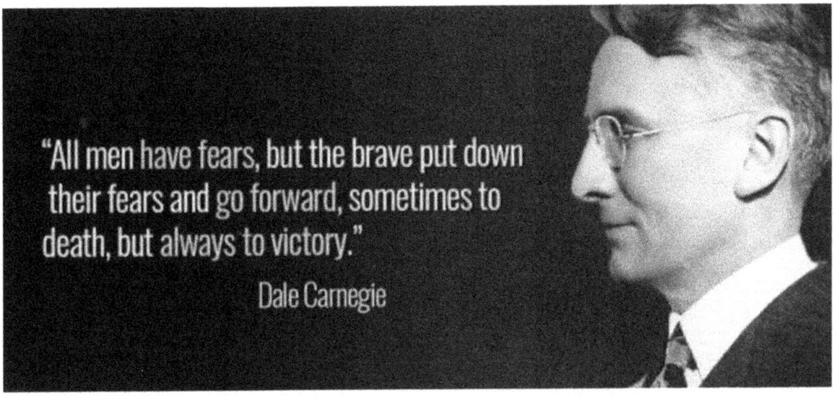
"All men have fears, but the brave put down their fears and go forward, sometimes to death, but always to victory."
Dale Carnegie

ERIK SWANSON

As an Award-Winning International Keynote Speaker and Multi Time #1 International Best-Selling Author, Erik "Mr. Awesome" Swanson is in great demand around the world! He speaks to an average of more than one million people per year. Mr. Swanson has the honor to have been invited to speak to many schools around the world including the prestigious Harvard University. He is also a recurring Faculty Member of CEO Space International as well as an Alumni Keynoter at Vistage Executive Coaching. Erik's speeches can be found on Amazon Prime TV as well as joining the Ted Talk Family with his latest speech called, "A Dose of Awesome."

Erik got his start in the self-development world by mentoring directly under Brian Tracy. Quickly climbing to become the top trainer around the world from a group of over 250 handpicked coaches, Erik started to surround himself with the best of the best and very quickly started to be invited to speak on stages alongside such greats as Jim Rohn, Bob

Proctor, Les Brown, Sharon Lechter, Jack Canfield, Lisa Nichols, and Joe Dispenza—just to name a few. Erik has created and developed the super-popular Habitude Warrior Conference, which has a two-year waiting list and includes 33 top-named speakers from around the world. It is a 'Ted Talk' style event which has quickly climbed to one of the top 10 events not to miss in the United States! He is the creator, founder, and CEO of the Habitude Warrior Mastermind and Global Speakers Mastermind. He is also the creator and publisher of *The 13 Steps To Riches* book series as well as *The Principles of David & Goliath* book series. His motto is clear: "NDSO!": No Drama – Serve Others!

www.SpeakerErikSwanson.com

JAMES DENTLEY

LIKABILITY THROUGH GENUINE LISTENING & CONVERSATIONS

It's fascinating how what you focus on is what you manifest. God promised to give you the desires of your heart. Let's say you don't desire to have all these bills, but all you focus on are the bills. "I've got to pay these bills. I have to pay these bills. I can't pay these bills." On the other hand, you have this promise: "One day, I want to be successful, rich, and debt-free." Well, you're confusing yourself subconsciously because you're sending mixed messages.

The profound journey of self-discovery and influence lies in life, where dreams and reality converge. My path, etched with trials, triumphs, and timeless lessons, mirrors the collective human quest for purpose, impact, and alignment. This chapter unfolds through the lens of my experiences and the wisdom of Dale Carnegie, a beacon of influencing through understanding and empathy.

The Power of Focus & Manifestation

"Whatever you focus on is what you manifest." This principle, a guiding light in my journey, underscores the magnetic power of focus. It's a simple yet profound truth that what occupies our thoughts shapes our reality. As I navigated life's ebbs and flows, from the nights spent in my car under the cold embrace of a comforter in Atlanta, Georgia, to moments of undeniable victory, the essence of focus remained constant.

Carnegie, too, championed the art of steering one's attention, advocating for a directed, empathetic approach to understanding and influencing others.

Communication: The Bridge to Influence

Everything in the universe communicates. Know that first. So, when you're communicating with yourself and others, are you saying things that empower and inspire or tear you down? You're so worried about what could happen again, letting your imagination run wild over something that hasn't even occurred yet, essentially counting God out because you're focused on the potential demise of your dreams, expectations, and aspirations.

Communication, the very heartbeat of influence, demands authenticity, clarity, and purpose. My mantra, "Empower and inspire," resonates with Carnegie's ethos of winning hearts and minds through genuine interest and appreciation for others. It's about elevating conversations and transforming them into channels of mutual growth and understanding. As we navigate our interactions, let us choose words that build rather than break, for every word uttered carries the weight of our intentions.

You get to choose what you focus on. Even amid bills, I was homeless, sleeping in my car. I remember pulling into a Holiday Inn parking lot in Atlanta, Georgia. I pulled the comforter over my head in the front seat and went to sleep with a smile. At that moment, I knew how the end would be. Stephen Covey said it best: "Begin with the end in mind." For human achievement, clarity is key. Get crystal clear on what you want. Focus on what you want, not what you don't want. Always look for the good news.

Now, bad things can happen, and challenges will arise. But they're there to build you and give you a sense of appreciation and gratitude for your origins. So often, people get to the other side and forget what they went through, forget the people who were there with them through it all. They either return to the same situation or live an empty and hollow life because they fail to include gratitude and acceptance in everything.

Clarity & Vision in Achieving Goals

"Begin with the end in mind," a pearl of wisdom from Stephen Covey, has been a cornerstone in my pursuit of clarity and achievement. Despite the immediate reality of bills and uncertainties, the vision of a debt-free, successful life propelled me. Clarity in our goals acts as the North Star, guiding us through the stormiest of nights. Carnegie's teachings echo this sentiment, emphasizing the significance of clear, actionable objectives in influencing outcomes and fostering meaningful connections.

Acceptance means that you don't get to control the world. The world will operate without your intervention. You don't get to play God. Imagine being God for a day—you wouldn't sleep a wink, trying to get everything you ever wanted. But the problem is, the next day, you're not God anymore, and that's when your life really starts to suffer because it's no longer about you; it's about someone else.

So, do the best you can with what you have. Surround yourself with people, read books like *Think and Grow Rich* or *What Makes the Great Great*. These are stories of people who've gone through difficult situations and emerged victorious on the other side.

Take Oprah Winfrey, who was abused as a child and struggled with self-esteem issues, even going through depression. Now, she owns the letter 'O'. Or Colonel Sanders, who, at 65 years of age, was rejected by 1,008 people before finding success with his recipe for fried chicken. Most people would give up after a handful of rejections, but he persevered.

Your perception of reality is unique to you. Hold on to what you know is true, even if it isn't manifest. Consider Ray Kroc, who sold milkshake machines at 54 and struggled until he met the McDonald brothers and revolutionized their business, eventually creating a global empire.

Remember, everything you do creates your brand, which you're known for. You can shift this by simply being aware and taking action. But having mentors and surrounding yourself with the right people is crucial.

Consider Wilma Rudolph, who was told she'd never walk but went on to win gold medals. Or Madam C.J. Walker, who built a mansion in the same community as the Rockefellers at a time when women couldn't even vote.

When adverse things happen to you, know there's a way out because you've prepared by reading and learning about the journeys of achievers. Strive to be the best in everything you choose to do. You don't have to be the best, but you can be the best version of yourself. That becomes a habit, deeply ingrained in your being, making you show up big everywhere you go.

When it's time to play the game for real, to go for your personal Super Bowl, you'll be ready because you've done the work. You've been through the fire and have emerged with your story.

Remember, by making a difference in the lives of others, you gain all the things that money can't buy. So, follow those dreams and pursue them with haste. Your life, the only one you'll get, is too precious and fleeting to waste. Be faithful, be loyal, and all your days through, the dreams you follow will keep.

Gratitude, Acceptance, & Resilience

Gratitude and acceptance, the twin pillars of a fulfilled life, have anchored me in humility and perseverance. The journey to influence is paved with trials, yet each challenge is a catalyst for growth, a reminder of our strength and potential. As Carnegie advocated, embracing life's vicissitudes with gratitude enriches our narrative, transforming obstacles into stepping stones toward greatness.

Every setback, hurdle, and moment of doubt is an opportunity to rise above and showcase the resilience within each of us. In these challenging times, we discover the depths of our character and the true extent of our capabilities. With gratitude as our compass and acceptance as our shield, we can navigate life's uncertainties gracefully and determined. Remember, not the absence of challenges define us, but our response to them shapes our journey toward success. Embrace each obstacle as a chance to learn, evolve, and ultimately become your best version.

Learning from Achievers & Mentors

The stories of Oprah Winfrey, Colonel Sanders, and countless others who turned adversities into triumphs have been a wellspring of inspiration. They exemplify the relentless pursuit of excellence, a testament to the indomitable human spirit. With their reservoirs of wisdom and experience, mentors illuminate our path, guiding us toward our zenith. In this journey, we stand on the shoulders of giants, drawing from their lessons to forge our legacy.

Oprah Winfrey's journey from adversity to success reminds us that we can carve our path to greatness with unwavering perseverance and a steadfast vision. With his recipe for fried chicken and a dream, Colonel Sanders proved that age is just a number when pursuing your passion.

As we navigate the complexities of our paths, mentors serve as beacons of light, offering guidance and wisdom to navigate the twists and turns of life. Their insights and experiences pave the way for us to reach new heights and fulfill our potential.

Standing on the shoulders of giants, we embrace past lessons to shape our future. With each step we take, we honor the legacy of those who have come before us and pave the way for those who will follow. In this journey of self-discovery and growth, we find strength in our shared humanity and the power of resilience.

Action, Impact, & the Legacy of Dreams

Action, the bridge between the possible and the achieved, is the essence of influence. It's about embodying the change we wish to see, making an indelible impact through our deeds and words. "Follow your dreams, pursue them with haste," for our life is too precious to be squandered. Carnegie's principles of influence, rooted in empathy, respect, and genuine interest, align with this ethos, advocating for a life of purpose, integrity, and impact.

It is in the choices we make and the determination we show that we shape our destinies. Every step taken with purpose and passion brings us closer to our goals, and every word spoken with sincerity and conviction can inspire others. As we navigate the intricate web of life, let us remember that our actions carry the potential to create ripples of change that extend far beyond our immediate surroundings. By embracing Carnegie's timeless wisdom and living with empathy, respect, and a genuine desire to make a difference, we enrich our lives and contribute to a more compassionate and harmonious world. Let us forge ahead with courage, for in each moment lies the opportunity to leave a lasting legacy of positivity and transformation.

The Convergence of Influence & Alignment

As our narrative unfolds, the symbiosis of influence and alignment becomes evident. We sculpt our destiny through the amalgamation of focus, effective communication, clarity, gratitude, mentorship, and action. Influencing with integrity, guided by the timeless principles of Dale Carnegie and the lessons etched in my journey, we pave the way for a legacy of impact, a testament to the power of dreams pursued with unwavering conviction.

In this journey of growth and self-discovery, we navigate the intricate paths of our aspirations with steadfast determination. Drawing inspiration from the wisdom of those who have paved the way before us, we learn the art of balancing influence and authenticity. Our words carry the weight of sincerity, our actions speak volumes about our commitment to our dreams.

As we immerse ourselves in the tapestry of life, we understand that true success lies not just in achieving our goals but in the positive impact we leave behind. Each interaction, each decision, shapes the legacy we are building. It is in the moments of mentorship, where we uplift others and, in turn, elevate ourselves, that we truly embody the essence of leadership.

With gratitude as our compass and clarity as our guiding light, we embrace the power of intentional action. Every step we take is a brushstroke on the canvas of our destiny, painting a picture of resilience, determination, and unwavering belief. As we tread the path less traveled, we honor the lessons of the past and the dreams of the future, knowing that our journey is not just our own but a testament to the enduring spirit of human potential.

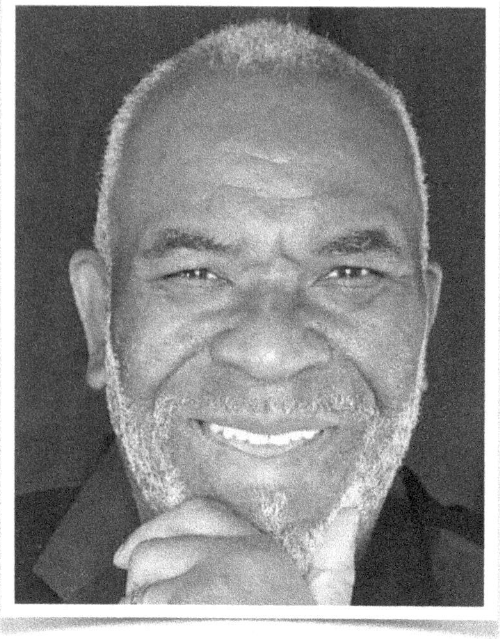

JAMES DENTLEY

Sir James Dentley is best defined as a Change Catalyst because his interventions create results in record times. His speaking style quickly engages audiences and individuals to change and think differently. His presentations are thought-provoking, entertaining, insightful, and straight to the point. Participants in his events are always left with a strong urge to take action. He is a master in the art of anticipation. An avid trend hunter ready to identify new opportunities on the horizon for individuals and organizations.

James has been speaking and training since 1982 and has spoken with hundreds of thousands of individuals in over 750 cities in 34 different countries. Simply, Google his name and you can see the value of bringing him into your next event. He works with Total Life Changes and a wide range of global organizations, and provides them with a competitive edge based on his unique understanding of the world.

His success is based on his belief that behavior is an outcome, not an input. He understands that to bring individuals into action you need to change their belief system. And that requires a very specific approach. James' knowledge & methodology can quickly nudge old habits into new behaviors providing the spark needed to reset the mindset of your organization.

James Dentley is an entrepreneur, best-selling author, philanthropist and one of the nation's top Life and Business Strategist. As one of the world's most renowned motivational speakers, James Dentley is a dynamic personality and highly-sought-after resource in business and professional circles for Fortune 500 CEOs, small business owners, non-profit and community leaders from all sectors of society looking to expand opportunity.

James hosts and speaks at events all over the world! He is the best-selling author of 'The Frequencies of Top Performers' and 'MLM Mastery.' He created the #1 speakers and communication program 'Inspired2Speak: Action Camp.' James' passion for coaching and mentoring speakers has transformed "good speakers to great speakers and great speakers to legendary. He has spent over three decades working with start-ups to major global brands to help them increase sales, productivity, and overall success.

James' message will inspire your audience to take action and turn passion into success! As a philanthropist, James has received the Icon award from 'U4G (Unite4: Good)', and the first prestigious Legacy Award from The City Gala just to name a few. Both companies are dedicated to building a sustainable social good movement. It's James' personal goal to get people around the world active in spreading good by partnering with United for Good, and The City Gala.

James has funded numerous programs to help homeless people, seniors, veterans and provides the educational tools and resources for inner city children. He believes it is our duty to give back and help those in need.

www.JamesDentley.com

DANELLE DELGADO

WIN ON REPEAT: THE 7-STEP SEQUENCE TO BUILDING INFLUENCE QUICKLY

People do life, business, and anything with those who increase their odds of winning. People avoid life, business, and everything with those who don't. This is the softest I can put it friends, but you paid for this, so I owe you my truth this directly.

If you don't choose to win on a daily basis, no matter the task, people notice and step back. You lose your temper, that's behavior they know will repeat and avoid. Set goals and quit on them, yes people catch on to that too. The same is true with winning. Set goals, hit them, people want to play with you. When things are going bad and you can be great, people will walk through fire with you.

Win more moments, you will uncover your most aligned, opportunity attracting self. That is what I am here to show you how to do today and that will scale everything else.

So, how does one learn the habit of winning repeatedly and aligning with their most elite self?

It all starts with believing the most foundational truths that most adults forget.

We were born to ascend. It's our natural inclination every single day to advance. Think of the natural process: we are born, then we learn to roll, then crawl, then walk, then run. Born to progress. No one just stops and says, as a young kid, "No thanks mom, I'd rather roll to school."

They naturally advance. Those who continue the evolution, train and can become world-renowned athletes, whom the world knowns their names. Most find challenges along the way and replace this foundational truth with I quit. Winners, hold to the truth, "I am born to ascend." That is foundational truth.

Again, we naturally progress to communicate. We are born, we make noises, learn words, then speech and how to connect. Those who train become the great orators of our times or platinum recording artists. That same longing for advancement is inside us all. Victory is in our veins; it's our make-up, and, outside of that, it's noticed when we aren't victorious.

Those who are shy and stop communicating stop advancing. Those who stop moving develop disease and discomfort with their health. Our minds, bodies and aptitudes are meant to constantly advance.

When we don't advance, it's painful because it is not in alignment with how we are wired. We are 100% wired to win and taught to quit. This world will train you with trouble and critique you with your response. I promise, the first step, is cling to the truth, influence yourself, we are born to ascend and anything outside of that, just won't fit.

When you begin to live with this truth at your core, you can begin to win, begin to believe, and begin to achieve in a way others will want to watch. Repeat this long enough and you not only master influence of self, but you will also master attention and collaboration of others.

Yes, I know it sounds easier than it is, but I promise it works.

I travel the world speaking and people always ask me how to stop the struggle, how I overcame divorce, cancer, and financial ruin to build all this because, yes, my story is inspiring, but that's the wrong question. It's not how I overcame the hard parts, it's how I guarantee I can finish what I started even when it's hard. It's saying to myself, "I know I am born to win—wh at is the system to make sure I do?"

Well, here it is friends, in 7 simple steps. Master these daily, and you'll master your truest, most aligned and influential self. It's then and only then you will gain influence over everything else.

Step 1: Influence Yourself

While most of the world tries to be consistent, we have eliminated the word. Instead, we say daily. If it is important to do, it should be done daily. And if you want to influence yourself, which is key to influencing anyone in your future, you must build your foundation daily.

This is the time, this is the place, you are the person.... for what is for you NEXT. It's time for you to know the truth about your capabilities and eliminate everything else.

TO do so, first, mold your mind with facts, not feelings. Most people spend their life feeling instead of facting. They overthink, question, doubt and it stops them in their tracks. But those who run with the facts drain all that right out.

So, let's begin with the facts. Make a list of 90 things you love about yourself. DO ITTTTT! It may be easy for some and extremely challenging for others. Do it anyway. You can list physical features, skills and abilities, moments you loved, achievements... just stick to the truth. Make it as long as you need to truly see how incredible and capable you are. Then put it up to see it daily and start each day with the facts; fill up your mind to have only room for that.

Second, if you have been known to find yourself in the pit full of doubt, make another list of all the things you believe hold you back, including limiting beliefs. Dig deep, think big thoughts and get them on paper...if they are feelings, cross them out. If they are real facts, you simply have to antidote them out. Here is an example what I mean:

Limiting fact: "I don't know how."

Write three ways you could learn.

1. Study from the three best experts on the craft.
2. Take a class to learn.
3. Practice until I can't get it wrong.

When I write facts on how to be the opposite, I am no longer the doubt, I am the difference.

These two lists build a foundation on truth and actions to take to live by them. They eliminate the feelings that lie to us or break our foundations down. Build on truth and drown out the doubt; it's critical to being able to influence yourself.

Step 2: Know Your Value

When building your life, business, and relationships on truth, you will start well. When knowing your value and living it, you finish well. No one should have the power to change a life and not execute on it. You wouldn't stand watching another die and say oops I'll help next time. If someone is choking, you would try to help. We each have skills, thoughts, and abilities that are meant for a good purpose and when we live on truth, we act on it, too. It's human nature to use our skills to serve. We just need to spend more time talking about what we are valuable for and making sure we never, not even on one day, forget it.

So, make another truth-filled list of your 10 greatest skills, your abilities you love to use, the abilities others see in you, how you serve yourself, others and the true impact you make (or want to make) in the world. Focus on the value you live, the value you deliver, the value you have built, and the things no one can ever take away from you. This list is your key to walk those dreams out.

Make the list, then next to each item, write every area of life to which you can use those skills in. I am a connector: I use those skills online, at church, in business (I would write more specifics, as the more specific the better use they can be). Do this for the entire list of 10 and you are prepared to unleash that value on others.

List the facts and live them. This value will not be denied.

Step 3: Shout it from the Rooftops

When your value is known, it will be needed. It will make them look!

Yes, you heard me correctly: know your value and shout it from the rooftops! I believe 2Pac said it best, “All eyes on me!” Be anything but quiet. The quiet ones can never help. We are only as valuable as we market ourselves to be. If you know your skillset, you’ll use it, you’ll offer it; it will be called upon. It will not be ignored. Share you wins, as they inspire others. Share your service projects, as they remind others to help. Share the testimonials of your impact, and others will begin to reach out. The world needs you, but can only find you if you help. SHARE IT ALL and never quit.

Side note: People always tell me they are worried about people saying they are bragging. I say, “Who says that?” It is usually followed by Aunt Joyce, or Father-in-law, Bill. I say, “Oh, is that who you were born to help?” NOOOOO. Be louder and prouder of yourself and get used to praising others for their value, too. Cheer for people, get loud with winners. The winners all know each other because their brave moves set them apart.

No, they don’t do life like others; yes, they sometimes get called out by those doing less, but it’s a moment in time they learn to not think much about. The more I learned, the less I bled, ya know what I mean…the more I saw I was to make a difference, the less I cared about those who questioned it.

Winners are busy making a difference and they find others willing to go this brave route. They enjoy doing life, work, and impact together. If you really want alignment with your best, be your biggest fan and share it—it really does help everyone out.

Step 4: Go deeper, CONNECT.

So, you're now living on truth, best friends with your value, you live it daily and it greatly attracts. The world is now your oyster, people are seeing you, so what will you do with it? You'll connect. That's right, this is where the lazy skip and move too quick and the brilliant take just a few more steps.

Make eye contact, show people you see them. Ask questions, one or two more than anyone else. Remember things, check in with people. Notice what others miss. Help, follow up, have a strategy to connect at depth—to those you care about, those you meet, and those who you'd love to have life, business, or relationships with.

This is the separation factor. Stand outs all have it. It's authentic, practiced, and a sure bet. I call it *uncommon care*. This is the key to truly connect.
They used to call it "the extra mile." I say it's personal respect. I could be like everyone else, but I'm going to be extra, and it's served far more people than anything yet.

Maybe you make a list of your 5 more important in your circle and you start serving there. Maybe it's three heroes you want to thank for the impact they made on your path. Maybe its two new prospective clients, your kids or spouse. Extra phone calls to check in, sending gifts or mementos to make people smile, tickets to an event. It can cost or it can be free, but the impact is worth millions in personal and professional capacity. In the hustle and grind of life, true connection is often a lost art, and it shouldn't be.

Be extra. Make the list and working it your priority. Practice exemplary time to connect with all that matter and watch the butterfly affect.

Some of these moments are pinnacle lifetime moments I'll never forget. Step 4 is building an un-ignorable influence that none can forget.

Step 5: Make Moves and Invite Others

When you activate steps one through four, you will align with your highest self and draw out the highest of performance in others. Humans will not only be impressed and inspired by who you are, by the difference you make, but they will want to make moves with you; THIS IS INFLUENCE. They will ache for the invite. Give them one.

This is when you become part of a smaller circle in life. A circle of big opportunities for the small groups of people who have proven they are winning, progressing, and never going back.

Welcome! Get involved: with your community, with global movements; take part in masterminds, invest in things you believe in, serve at your depth… GO big and NEVER EVER go alone. Bring others along for the ride.

There is rarely an event worthy of my time I don't buy extra tickets for or save a seat next to me. Be the one people are thankful for.

Step 6: You are an Asset: Use It, Don't Lose It

It's important here to realize that influence, alignment, and the extra it requires is a responsibility most will want to quit. It can be heavy, taxing, and tempt you to rest. But if you do, that pain is the biggest—it's called regret.

No one told me about this. They didn't tell me that becoming the one my results required would be challenging as all heck. They said sometimes you will feel alone, sometimes you will think it is too much, but they never told me what to do when it did feel like that.

But I won't leave you like that. It is at these moments I go back through these simple steps. I remake my lists. I write down what I love about myself; I write down what I need to eliminate and give each an antidote, so I keep my progress. I make a list of my skills, note how I've grown, and I have even written down the names of those I've helped. I keep a folder of my testimonials or thank you texts, so on challenging days I remember what I do it all for and I promise it will only take moments to get right back on track.

The tests will come, so be prepared: use the steps, and keep that pain of regret far away from what you know is true, that you were born to ascend, and you will and it will influence you and all who know you, too.

Step 7: The Winner's Ultimate List

This is it, just one last step. It was what changed the game of life for me for good.

Write down what you want. Write it so clearly you could say it in four words or less.

Write down why you want it, what you will do when you have it. So clearly you can taste it.

After that, write down one to three things you could do daily to get you closer to that goal—that if done repeatedly over time you know you get there.

Just these three steps show all human what they want and how to go get it…to which I then ask, why haven't you done it yet?

The lists are usually full of feelings, real ones: I'm scared, it's me, I have tried and failed, and a whole list of selfish things that they focus on far too much and it makes room for losing. Loser thoughts, loser moves, and loser moments never feel aligned; that is why they are so painful.

So, are you ready to eliminate them? Then you have one more list to make:

Make a list of those who matter most to you. Those whom you will help when you win big! Write what you will do for them, how much it will mean to you and to them. Yes, get all in there and teary when you read through your list.

And after reading that list, try and imagine saying to that most important person, by name, the other clear statements you have written, "Here is what I want, here is how I will get it, and I wanted to do this for you, But I can't. I let _____ (fill in the blank with why you haven't done it yet) stop me. That was more important than you."

And immediately you will feel how those excuses are not more true or more important than who you are fighting for. Truth is, if you focus on service, you will no longer focus on self. Your next big win, your most aligned self is one correct thought away from breaking you free.

This life is not about you, it's about **"who loses if you don't win."** When you align yourself with that truth, the lies will cease to exist.

This is the time. This is the place, and you are the person. You were born to ascend. Your value, skillset, connection and service are needed. Your highest most aligned self is where your greatest breakthrough is. And when you live it, you will win on repeat. And people will ache to do life, business, and everything with you.

This is alignment. This is influence. And it awaits only your execution of these seven simple steps.

DANELLE DELGADO

The now serial entrepreneur Danelle Delgado began her journey when faced with raising her three small children on her own.

Forced to make a change she went from working three jobs, 80-90 hours a week, and struggling to survive, to award-winning success in business by persisting her way in to align with some of the world's most renowned business experts and gained them as her personal mentors.

After years of high-level learning with them, she built some of the fastest-growing online business training companies to date. She is a known online influencer and has made a massive impact around the globe from her international speaking career, best-selling book, "I Choose Joy" and her unmatched skills guiding entrepreneurs both online and off to scale their companies to a million and their lives to ultimate fulfillment.

From her renowned elite retreats and online training platforms to her wit and skill training from the stage and in the corporate race, Danelle has become a household celebrity name training humans to become high performers like few ever will.

Her latest company build has the world in awe as she and partner, Mike Draper, are taking the corporate training space by storm. None seem to be able to rival this duo's expertise in human advancement and social media scaling. TeamEngage.com is the one to watch.

Although her work is her heartbeat, her dream is now a reality as she lives blessed beyond measure with her three incredible kids, boy & girl twins age 15 and daughter 16 in Colorado, teaching them to live the life they are capable of as well.

www.DanelleDelgado.com

DAN CLARK

DECISIONS CREATE ALIGNMENT

In the book, *How To Win Friends And Influence People*, the beloved Dale Carnegie states that, "Inaction breeds doubt and fear. Action breeds confidence and courage. If you want to conquer fear, do not sit at home and think about it. Go out and get busy." The longer you dwell on making the correct decision, the more your mind will be consumed by fear and uncertainty. Why?

In my experience, there are only four reasons why people choose to procrastinate and delay making decisions:

- Low sense of self-worth
- Refusal to live in the present
- Complacency
- Focus on the outcome instead of the process

Developing and Enhancing Self-Worth

The implementation process required for you to become a consistent confident decision-maker begins and ends with an up-leveling of your sense of self-worth. The best example comes from the HVAC world of Heating and Air Conditioning.

In every home and office building, thermostats are installed that focus on inside conditions, measuring changes in circumstances that allow us to accurately predict and expect what the temperature will be. A thermostat is a component of an HVAC control system that senses the difference between the actual temperature and desired set-point temperature. The

moment you set the thermostat, it triggers a furnace or air conditioner to run at full capacity until the desired warmer or cooler set-point temperature is reached. Then it shuts off the equipment until it's needed again.
In terms of our human set point, it is always dialed into the level of our self-esteem, sense of self-worth, and degree of personal development.

For example, how many times have we seen someone win 100 million dollars in the lottery only to be flat broke three years later? How many people do we know who go on a faddish diet and lose fifty pounds, but six months later, they have gained all the weight back and more? How often have we seen a wonderful woman do everything she knows how to do to get out of a physically and emotionally abusive relationship, only to jump back into a more devastating relationship with a bigger loser than the bum she just kicked out?

Why is this?

It is simply because of their personal thermostat—the inner-decision-making ability to align with our desires through immediate action. No matter what happens on the outside with money, weight, relationships, promotions of authority, ultimately, our thermostat is going to kick in to bring our outside world to match our internal set point. To accumulate more in the outside world, it is a critical unavoidable fact that we absolutely must become more on the inside. We must realize who we really are and who/what we have the potential and obligated opportunity to become.

A Benevolent Calling

When Louis XVI was forced from his throne and imprisoned, his young son, the prince, was kidnapped by those who overthrew the kingdom. They thought that in as much as the king's son was heir to the throne, if they could destroy him morally, he wouldn't realize the great and grand destiny that life had bestowed upon him.

Consequently, they took him to a community far away and exposed the boy to every filthy and vile thing that life could offer. They exposed him to foods that would quickly make him a slave to appetite, used vulgar language, and constantly exposed him to alcohol, dishonesty, and all things crude, lewd, and unrefined.

For six months, he was bombarded twenty-four hours a day by everything that could drag the soul of a man into wickedness and rebellion. But never once did the young prince buckle under pressure. Finally, his captors gave up on tempting and changing him and asked why he had not submitted himself to partaking of these worldly pleasures to satisfy his most lustful desires that were his for the taking.

With a deep and confident sense of self, the boy looked his captors square in the eyes and proudly proclaimed, "I cannot do what you ask, for I was born to be a king."

We all can become great aligned decision-makers when we stop procrastinating by focusing on the process instead of the outcome, refuse to be complacent, reset our personal thermostats and remember who we were born to be!

Embrace the Present Moment

The reason some people don't live in the present is because their present sucks! So, they medicate or live in the past, which causes pain, depression, regret, or a false sense of accomplishment. We all know someone who is stuck in the glory days, refusing to stop reminiscing when they threw that 40-yard touchdown pass in high school that won the game – "Yep, like Uncle Rico, I was a superstar; give me more nachos and another beer! Burp!"

Why can't they see this and choose to let go and improve? It's because they continue to associate with those who force them to join them in their past. To be a consistent, positive, powerful, effective, efficient, and aligned decision-maker, we must first stop procrastinating. This begins when you tell your procrastinating friends to stop dragging you into their past, reminding them that it's like robbing your old house and you don't live there anymore!

The flip side and other root cause of procrastination is to live in the future, believing that when 'this' occurs, I will be successful; when I do 'that,' I will finally be somebody. No. Living in the future creates worry, anxiety, and stress.

The practical application challenge to this truth is that if you sit around wondering if your glass is half empty or half full, you've missed the point. It's refillable! Thinking positively or negatively doesn't fill up the glass. The pouring does! It's easier to act your way into positive thinking than to think your way into positive action! Is this not decision-making 101?

Avoid Settling for Complacency

As a teenager, I had been a Golden Gloves boxing champion, and Muhammad Ali had been my idol. I emulated everything he did, from tassels on my boots to the Ali Shuffle and taunting jab. With fast hands and a desire to beat everybody, I was known as the "Great White Hope." Each time I fought, instead of chanting, "Danny, Danny," my friends chanted, "Dali, Dali!" Muhammad Ali truly was my hero, and I would have given anything to meet him.

Years later, in 1988, I had just finished speaking to the students of Andrews University in Berrien Springs, Michigan. I was in the Union Building signing books when I overheard some students talking about seeing Muhammad Ali on campus.

I was so excited I could hardly ask where. They informed me that he was gone, but it was no big deal because he lived there and visited the school often. When I finished the book signing, I immediately excused myself and asked the two gentlemen who were driving me around to grab a camera and take me to Ali's home. They told me I was fooling myself if I thought I could meet him.

But at that moment, I decided to at least try. Leaving no regrets is always a powerful motivator. So is a sense of urgency: I will never get this chance again! They stopped at the big white wall and giant iron gate at the edge of a long, curving driveway. The gate was open, and the sign didn't say 'No Trespassing.' Instead, it said 'Welcome,' so I decided to get out and walk the hundred yards to his beautiful home. His eighty-eight acres had previously belonged to the Chicago gangster Al Capone, and "Muhammad Ali Farms," as Ali called it, was an amazing sight.

With my heart pounding, I took a deep breath and knocked on the front door. A woman answered. I knew from photographs that she was his lovely wife. She asked, "May I help you?" I said, "Yes, ma'am. Is Muhammad in?"

She asked, "May I tell him who is calling?" Sheepishly, I replied, "Yea, Dan Clark." She walked away, and within seconds, an imposing six-foot-three-inch, 225-pound world champion, world peace ambassador, advocate of human rights, living legend, and idol filled the entire doorway. Muhammad simply smiled his famous smile and invited me in in his quiet, breathy voice. I excused myself for a minute, sprinted to the garden to where my friends could see me, and wildly waved my arms and whistled for them to come in.

In 1988, Muhammad's Parkinson's disease had not yet taken away his speech and mobility. For the next five hours, we sat in his living room and watched his greatest fights on his big screen, with his own personal commentary, jokes, and stories. He fed us and even performed his favorite magic tricks.

At the two-hour mark, I had realized that I needed to leave to catch my flight, but I made the decision to briefly excuse myself to reschedule my flight, so I could return to this once-in-a-lifetime experience! I'm so grateful that I did.

As we were leaving, Muhammad asked if I had any questions. I replied, "Yes. You are the three-time world heavyweight champion, which means you got beat twice. Over your career, you lost a total of five times, all to inferior opponents. Why?"

Muhammad's answer taught me the number one cause and only solution to eliminating complacency in our lives, "When you start looking at yourself as the competition and attempt to live off your past laurels and successes, you lose your competitive advantage and eventually lose the fight. Once the fight begins, you no longer hold the title but have put it up for grabs. You must do everything in your physical, mental, emotional, and spiritual power to win it back. Every time you climb in the ring, you must be brilliant at the basics, having outworked and out-prepared your opponent as a hungry, fiercely focused warrior willing and able to fight as hard as you did the first time you won the title—throwing every punch with power and purpose to do whatever it takes to win the title back!"

A paraphrased Theodore Roosevelt quote reminds us, "It is not the undecided critic or complacent who count. The credit belongs to the one who has decided to continually enter the arena, whose face is marred by dust and sweat and blood; who strives valiantly, errs, and comes short again and again, because there is no effort without error and shortcoming; who at best knows the triumph of high achievement, and who at the worst, if he fails, at least fails while daring greatly, so that his place shall never be with those cold and timid souls who neither know victory nor defeat."

Focus on the Process Versus the Outcome

Stay In Process—exchanging your focus on future outcomes for an extreme focus on the present action steps that will make the projected event and desired result probable.

Stop acting as if life is a rehearsal. Live this day as if it is your last. Whatever the present moment contains, accept it like you chose it, and work with it, not against it. Realize deeply that the present moment is really all you have. Excellence and greatness are achieved when you make Now the primary focus of your life!

Instead of fixating on the future outcomes, stay in the process and do those things at the moment that are necessary to achieve the projected outcome. Then, when you do, your desired results will come!

We saw this Decision-Making ability illuminated and in action on the same weekend during the National Football League Divisional Playoff

Games, in which four playoff games came down to the very last play. Think about that. From an actuarial sense, the odds against that are immense to have every game come down to the final play.

Do you remember the game between the Buffalo Bills and the Kansas City Chiefs? A combined 25 points were scored in the game's last two minutes! Bills quarterback Josh Allen battled it out with Patrick Mahomes.

With 1:54 left to play in the game: The Bills take their first lead since the first quarter. DECIDING to go for it on a fourth down and 13 to go—Allen throws a touchdown pass.

Score: Bills 29 - Chiefs 26.

Buffalo's Center Mitch Morse said: "I wish you could have been in that fourth down huddle. It was just a lot of love. Guys saying they loved each other, 'Let's execute, let's do this for each other.'"

1:02 to go: Chiefs quarterback Mahomes DECIDES they need to march 75 yards down the field to score. In five plays that took only 52 seconds, Patrick finishes by DECIDING to throw a 64-yard touchdown pass to retake the lead. Score: Chiefs 33 - Bills 29.

0:13 to go: Allen DECIDES to drive his Bills 75 yards in 6 plays, throwing a touchdown pass to get within seconds of advancing to the AFC title game. Score: Bills 36 - Chiefs 33.

With 13 seconds left on the clock, Mahomes DECIDES to drive his Chiefs 44 yards on 19 yards and a 25-yard pass. Kicker Harrison Butker (who had missed the previous kick) DECIDES to tie the score with a 49-yard field goal. Score: Bills 36 - Chiefs 36—the game goes into overtime.

Bills quarterback Allen never gets another chance as Mahomes & Co. DECIDE to drive 75 yards in 8 plays, with Patrick throwing an 8-yard touchdown pass to win the game and Divisional Championship! Final score: Chiefs 42 - Bills 36.

After the game, Chiefs All-Pro receiver Tyreek Hill said: "Nobody panicked. Nobody was like, 'Oh, the game is over with 13 seconds left.' We just went out and DECIDED to make plays, and the rest is history. We have a great head coach, a great offensive coordinator, and obviously a great quarterback and playmakers. All of us made critical DECISIONS that allowed us to win!"

What's important in life is resilience. It's the ability to bounce back. It's the ability to have reverses. And then an inherent sense of optimism. Can you see the light at the end of the tunnel? If there's a barn filled with defecation and pony poop, can you imagine there's a pony in there somewhere?

The ability to be resilient and take the inevitable reverses that life throws at all of us is key. It's simple and nothing more than Decision Making 102—preparing yourself so you can positively respond to rapid change!

At the end of the day, in every industry, every profession, and every personal and professional circumstance, you don't rise to the occasion under pressure. You fall to the level of your training. This means the pressure is not something that is naturally there. It's created when you question your own ability. When you know what you've been trained to do, there is never any pressure. That's why you continuously train, prepare and practice so hard!

The Solution

Seek counsel, not opinions. When it comes to making important decisions, let us never forget: some things are true whether you believe them or not; everybody is entitled to an opinion, but nobody is entitled to the wrong facts; you shouldn't believe everything that you think! Who do we trust in our world of fake news, with multiple contradicting opinions causing confusion and uncertainty? Is trust not at the heart and soul of decision-making? Is trusting ourselves not at the heart and soul of making a decision?

Trusting ourselves begins when we acknowledge that every person born into this world was born with an inherent ability to discern good from evil and recognize right from wrong. We commonly call this ability our conscience, which means our conscience will never fail us. Only our desire to follow it decreases as we continue to do the wrong thing.

To illustrate, you and I were joined by a group of people. We entered a room that smelled so bad that our eyes teared up, and we collapsed into automatic gag reflex. But after only ten minutes in the room, it suddenly no longer smelled. Why? We had become desensitized, and the rank, smelly room was now the new normal. Is this not happening in our world of fake news where everybody with a phone has an opinion?

It's obvious that we become the average of the five people we associate with the most. So, if you hang around five negative, whining, blaming, and complaining people, you will become the sixth. If you hang around with five obese, broke people who refuse to make responsible decisions about health, exercise, nutrition, and staying out of debt, you will become the sixth who can't decide to choose juice over soda and savings over credit card jail!

To become a great, confident, and consistent decision maker—especially courageous enough to make tough decisions that go against the status quo flow—the process is simple—not easy, but clear and doable when we get the facts, the whole complete truth, both the pros and cons. Study and learn everything we can about the subject or case in point. Counsel with unbiased experts. Ponder, and most importantly, stay true to your conscience by staying in tune with your natural intuition. It's called trusting your 'gut,' realizing that most of our significant and monumental decisions are usually our first choice, made quickly and intelligently by listening to our 'still small voice' of conscience, illuminated through intuitive promptings, made possible because of our strong 'thermostat' sense of self-worth, commitment to being present in every moment, refusal to be complacent, and focus on the process instead of the outcome.

DAN CLARK

Dan Clark is the founder and CEO of an International Leadership Development Company; a High-Performance Business Coach; New York Times Best Selling Author of 35 books; a University Professor; a Primary Contributing Author to the *Chicken Soup for the Soul* series; International Podcaster; Gold Record Songwriter; and an Award-Winning Athlete who fought his way back from a paralyzing injury that cut short his football career.

Dan was inducted into the National Speakers Hall of Fame – and has been named one of the Top Ten Motivational Speakers In The World.

Dan has spoken to over 6 million people, in all 50 states, in 71 countries, on 6 continents, to more than 6,000 audiences, including most of the Fortune 500 companies, Super Bowl Champions, NASA, and our Combat Troops in Iraq, Afghanistan, Asia, and Africa.

Dan has appeared on over 500 television and radio shows, including *Oprah* and *Glenn Beck*, *PBS*, and *NPR*, and has been featured in the *Mayo Clinic Journal*, *Forbes*, *Inc*., *Success*, *Entrepreneur*, *Thought Masters*, and *Millionaire Magazines*.

Dan's extraordinary life includes soaring to the edge of space in a U2 Spy plane; flying fighter jets with the Air Force Thunderbirds; racing automobiles at Nürburgring and sailboats in Australia; serving on the Olympic Committee, and carrying the Olympic Torch in the Winter Games, and keynoting the United Nations World Congress.

Dan was named an Outstanding Young Man of America - and has since received the United States Presidential Medal presented by President Ronald Reagan; the United States Distinguished Service Medal presented by the U.S. Department of Defense; he was the national recipient of the prestigious Air Force American Spirit Award, and was named Utah Father of the Year!

www.DanClark.com

ALEXANDER BALL

MY AUTHENTIC PATH TO ALIGNMENT

As I sit down to share my story with you, I'm reminded of the profound journey that has brought me to where I am today—a journey not just of professional achievements but of personal transformation and discovery. I hope this story will resonate with you, no matter where you are in your journey towards creating alignment in your life and work.

It all began with a simple realization—that true fulfillment comes from living an authentic life that reflects who we are at our core. This realization sparked a series of reflective moments that led me to redefine my goals, values, and priorities. With each step forward, I embraced the unknown, letting curiosity guide me toward new opportunities and experiences.

Through the challenges and triumphs, I learned the power of resilience and the importance of staying true to myself even when uncertain. In those moments of vulnerability, I discovered my strength and potential, paving the way for growth and self-discovery.

As you continue your journey, remember that every twist and turn is an opportunity for growth. Embrace the unknown, stay true to your values, and trust in the process. Your story is unique, and the world is waiting to hear it. Let your journey inspire others as you create alignment in your life and work, one step at a time.

Embracing My Authentic Self

For years, I grappled with authenticity, often wondering if the key to success lay in conforming to what I thought the world expected of me. It wasn't until I faced my own set of challenges, from the depths of drug addiction to the heartache of my daughter's cancer diagnosis, that I truly understood the power of being authentically me. These experiences, as harrowing as they were, peeled back the layers of who I thought I should be, revealing the person I truly am. In this revelation, I found my first step toward genuine alignment.

Embracing my authenticity was a journey filled with ups and downs, moments of doubt, and moments of pure clarity. It was a path that required me to confront my fears and insecurities head-on, to strip away the masks I had worn for so long, and to stand vulnerably in my truth. As I navigated through the storm of uncertainty, I discovered a newfound strength within myself - a strength that came from embracing every aspect of myself, flaws and all. In this acceptance, I found a sense of freedom and empowerment I had never experienced before.

No longer shackled by others' expectations, I could chart my course guided by the compass of my authentic self. In that moment of liberation, I realized that true success isn't found in conformity but in the courage to be unapologetically yourself.

Integrity and Honesty: My Guiding Stars

My journey taught me that a commitment to integrity and honesty lies at the heart of likability and trust. It's easy to fall into the trap of portraying an image we think is more acceptable or appealing. However, I've learned that honesty and upholding my promises are the foundation of lasting relationships and success. This principle has guided me professionally, from a company's operations to the deep, personal connections with my clients and partners.

I strive to be authentic and transparent in every interaction, building trust and fostering respect from those around me. Being true to myself and others allows genuine connections to form, creating a solid network of support and collaboration.

As I continue on my journey, honesty is not just a virtue but a powerful tool for building meaningful relationships and achieving true success. Through this commitment to integrity, I navigate the complexities of the professional world with a sense of purpose and fulfillment.

The Courage to Be Myself

One of the most liberating aspects of my journey has been discovering the courage to be myself. I've realized that our genuine nature is the most magnetic trait we can possess. Standing firm in our authenticity is revolutionary in a world where we're often encouraged to fit molds and meet expectations. This authenticity attracts the right people, opportunities, and circumstances into our lives, creating a circle of influence filled with meaningful interactions and connections.

Embracing our true selves is a powerful act of self-love and empowerment. We honor our uniqueness and permit others to do the same when we dare to show up as we are, without masks or pretense. This ripple effect of authenticity can positively change our lives and the world around us.

It reminds us that our worth is not tied to conformity but to the genuine expression of our hearts and souls. So, let us continue to shine brightly in our authenticity, illuminating the path for others to follow suit and embrace their true selves with courage and pride.

Navigating Life's Challenges with Alignment

The path to alignment has its challenges. I've faced moments of despair and hopelessness, where everything seemed to crumble around me. Yet, in these moments, the importance of alignment became crystal clear. Aligning my actions with my true self, grounded in authenticity and integrity, gave me a compass through the darkest times. This alignment has been my saving grace and propelled me towards my most significant achievements and most fulfilling moments.

In staying aligned, I've learned that it's not always about being perfect but about being true to yourself. In those moments of uncertainty, our alignment truly shines through, guiding us towards our purpose and passions. Embracing our authenticity and integrity allows us to navigate through challenges with grace and resilience, knowing that we are staying true to who we are at our core. This journey towards alignment is a continuous process of growth and self-discovery, but the rewards of living in harmony with our true selves are immeasurable.

Through this self-discovery and acceptance, we can indeed find peace and fulfillment. The journey towards authenticity is a personal one, unique to each individual. Embrace your uniqueness, honor your values, and trust in your intuition to lead you toward a life that feels genuine to who you are at your core. Remember, the path to alignment may not always be easy, but it is always worth it. Trust in yourself, believe in your journey, and let your inner light shine brightly for the world to see.

As you begin your alignment journey, you are stepping into a realm where self-discovery and growth intertwine. Embrace the path leading to your authentic self, where your values, aspirations, and actions align harmoniously. This alignment is more than just a destination; it's a continuous process of self-awareness and self-acceptance.

Along this journey, remember that each step you take towards aligning with your true self brings you closer to a life of fulfillment and contentment. Embrace the moments of reflection, the challenges that push you to grow, and the joys that come from living in alignment with your deepest values.

As you navigate this journey, surround yourself with supportive, like-minded individuals who uplift and inspire you. Please share your experiences, insights, and struggles with others, as their perspectives can offer new insights and help you stay on course.

Above all, remember that the most significant alignment you can achieve is with yourself. Trust in your intuition, honor your truth, and live authentically. When you align with your inner compass, you pave the way for a life that is not just successful by society's standards but deeply fulfilling and rich in meaning.

As you embark on this alignment journey, may you find the courage to embrace your true self, the wisdom to navigate the twists and turns, and the joy that comes from living a life in alignment with your essence.

Through the lens of my life and experiences, I invite you to embark on our journey of alignment, where success is measured not by external accolades but by the depth of our connections and the authenticity of our actions. In pursuing alignment, we find professional fulfillment and the key to living a life of purpose and meaning.

Establishing alignment goes beyond strategies and principles; it highlights the impact of authenticity, integrity, and self-belief. Reflecting on my life, I encourage you to join me on this alignment journey. Success is about external recognition, genuine connections, and authentic actions. By striving for alignment, we discover fulfillment in our careers and unlock the secret to a purposeful and meaningful life.

ALEXANDER BALL

About Alexander Ball: Alexander J. Ball loves helping business owners reach their real estate investment goals within 1-2 years and tax free through life insurance investment strategies. Whether you are seeking to buy properties within 1-2 years, take advantage of tax free accounts, or keep money liquid while still outpacing inflation and having your money work for you, Alex specializes in helping people from all walks of life.

Alex has work for World Financial Group (WFG) for over 7 years and is currently Marketing Director helping successful business owners and high performers in business take control of their financial futures. Alex loves to give free 30-minute consultations on how to use cash flow and leverage success to build a financial empire, whether that is real estate investments, buying companies, or expanding your own.

Alex's skills include Real Estate Investment, Investment Properties, Life Insurance, Indexed Universal Life Insurance, and Capital Gains Tax. Alex can help people seriously reduce or eliminate capital gains tax on sale of real estate or other large assets.

Author's Website: *www.linkedin.com/in/Alexander-J-Ball-888201137*

Book Series Website: *www.TheBookofInfluence.com*

AMY MINGIN

ALIGNMENT THROUGH EMPATHY & GENUINE INTEREST

In the journey of life, the paths we walk are rarely straight. They twist and turn, and, sometimes, they intersect with the lives of others in unexpected ways, and I've come to understand that these intersections are where the true magic of human connection happens. In these moments, the power of creating alignment—through empathy, genuine interest, and heartfelt communication—can transform relationships and lead to profound personal and professional growth.

Delve into the essence of fostering harmony in personal and professional bonds, as illuminated by Dale Carnegie's teachings. Explore the profound influence of empathy and sincere curiosity in forging connections with others. Ponder the pivotal role of communication and friendliness in constructing resilient relationships.

The Essence of Communicating with Love

The story of T and her father shared in Volume 1: Authentic Communication describes a family's emotional journey as they face losing a loved one. T, Mary, and Jay navigate their grief and communication struggles in a hospital setting. Jay receives advice from a couple in the hospital, learning to connect with his family through understanding and love, leading to a moment of heartfelt communication and reconnection.

Reflecting on a poignant moment of loss, I recall the story of T and her father—a narrative that encapsulates the essence of communicating with love. The regret of unspoken words and the realization that a single conversation, had it been approached with love and understanding, could have changed their relationship is a powerful reminder. Dale Carnegie once taught that understanding, empathy, and genuine connections are the foundation of effective communication. It's not merely about the words spoken but the love and intention behind them. As T learned, the longest journey is from the head to the heart. Communicating with love bridges that distance, creating a space where words are felt, and healing begins.

Reflecting on Dale Carnegie's principles of understanding, empathy, and genuine connection, we can see how they align perfectly with the story of T and her father. This poignant tale is a powerful reminder of the significance of communicating with love. The missed opportunities and regrets stemming from unspoken words highlight the importance of approaching conversations with compassion and empathy.

Dale Carnegie's teachings emphasize that effective communication goes beyond mere words; it involves conveying love and genuine intention. T's story beautifully illustrates how the journey from the head to the heart is the most profound. Communicating with love bridges the emotional distance between ourselves and others, creating a space where healing and understanding can flourish. As T discovered, when we infuse our words with love and empathy, we pave the way for transformative connections and meaningful relationships.

Becoming Likable by Showing Genuine Interest in Others

In our daily interactions, likability is crucial in connecting with others. One key aspect contributing to likability is genuine interest in the people we engage with. By actively listening and asking questions about their experiences, thoughts, and feelings, we value their perspective and care about what they say.

Moreover, empathy is another essential trait that can enhance likability. Putting ourselves in someone else's shoes and understanding their emotions can help us forge deeper connections and build trust. When we show empathy towards others, it creates a sense of understanding and support, fostering positive relationships.

Authentic engagement is also pivotal in being likable. Being true to ourselves and expressing our thoughts and feelings can help others see us as genuine and trustworthy. When we engage with sincerity and honesty, meaningful connections form naturally.

Overall, by incorporating these principles of likability—showing interest in others, practicing empathy, and engaging authentically—we can positively influence our relationships and create a more welcoming and harmonious environment for everyone involved.

Tie these ideas back to Carnegie's emphasis on focusing on others to build rapport and trust. The concept of likability, often misunderstood, is not about altering oneself to fit the expectations of others. It's about showing genuine interest in the people around us, listening to their stories, and connecting on a deeper level. As my daughter humorously demonstrated through a dance intended to teach about relationships, likability stems from authenticity and the joy of sharing moments.

Dale Carnegie believed that becoming genuinely interested in others was the cornerstone of building positive relationships. This principle holds in personal interactions and in fostering professional connections. We create a foundation for trust and mutual respect by expressing genuine interest and empathy.

Strategies for Creating Alignment

By merging my perspectives with Carnegie's timeless principles, we can cultivate a harmonious connection in our relationships and engagements. Practical strategies rooted in empathy, active listening, and genuine understanding pave the way for authentic alignment. By valuing others' perspectives, practicing effective communication, and fostering mutual respect, we can build solid, meaningful connections that stand the test of time. Let us embark on this journey of growth and collaboration, where synergy and cohesion flourish in every interaction.

The role of positive attitude and humor in making connections is more substantial than regular connections. Creating alignment in our relationships and interactions requires more than understanding; it necessitates action. Here are practical strategies inspired by both my insights and Carnegie's teachings:

- **Communicate with Authenticity and Love:** Approach every conversation with the intention of understanding and connecting. Let your words be guided by empathy and compassion.
- **Show Genuine Interest:** Listen more than you speak. Be curious about others' lives, dreams, and challenges. This interest fosters connection and mutual respect.
- **Use Empathy and Active Listening:** Try to see the world from the perspectives of others. Active listening not only shows that you care but also helps in understanding their needs and emotions.
- **Cultivate a Positive Attitude and Humor:** Positivity and laughter are universal languages that break down barriers and make interactions more enjoyable and meaningful.

Personal & Professional Applications

In practice, these strategies have the power to transform both personal and professional relationships. Whether leading a team, building a partnership, or nurturing family connections, the principles of empathy, genuine interest, and love are universal. They enable us to meet others where they are, build rapport, and create a sense of alignment that transcends mere agreement. It's about understanding, respecting, and valuing the unique perspectives each person brings to the table.

Alignment is crucial in shaping leadership, teamwork, and personal growth. By incorporating alignment strategies into our interactions, we can witness a profound impact on the dynamics of our relationships, both in the workplace and in our personal lives. These strategies catalyze empathy, genuine connection, and love, which are fundamental elements in nurturing harmonious relationships. Whether we are guiding a team toward a common goal, forging strong partnerships, or strengthening familial bonds, the principles of empathy and understanding are essential.

Through alignment, we can connect with others on a deeper level, acknowledging and appreciating the diversity of perspectives each individual brings. This mutual respect and recognition of unique viewpoints create a strong foundation for collaboration, communication, and growth. Through alignment, we can transcend mere agreement and cultivate a sense of unity that goes beyond superficial interactions. By embracing alignment in our leadership approach, teamwork efforts, and personal development journey, we can unlock the true potential of our relationships and pave the way for meaningful connections and shared success.

Challenges & Overcoming Them

The journey towards creating alignment is a transformative process that requires patience, empathy, and resilience. It's essential to navigate the obstacles of misunderstandings and preconceived notions with an open heart and a willingness to listen. Past hurts may linger, but approaching them with compassion and a desire for healing can pave the way for deeper connections.

Embracing open and authentic communication is vital in bridging gaps and fostering understanding. We can dissolve barriers and build trust by actively listening to each other's perspectives and being willing to see things from different angles. Through this commitment to empathy and forgiveness, we can strengthen the bonds that unite us and create a harmonious synergy in our relationships.

Every challenge we overcome and every moment of growth we experience along this journey contributes to the tapestry of our collective connection. Each step forward brings us closer together, reinforcing the ties that bind us and enriching the fabric of our shared experiences. As we continue to learn and evolve together, we nurture a sense of unity and solidarity that transcends differences and celebrates the beauty of our interconnectedness.

The power of creating alignment lies in our ability to communicate with love, show genuine interest in others, and practice empathy. These principles, exemplified by Dale Carnegie's teachings and woven through my experiences, offer a roadmap for building more profound, meaningful relationships. As we embark on this journey, let us remember that the most profound connections are forged not by words alone but by the love and understanding that infuse them. In doing so, we enrich our lives and contribute to a world where empathy and genuine connection prevail.

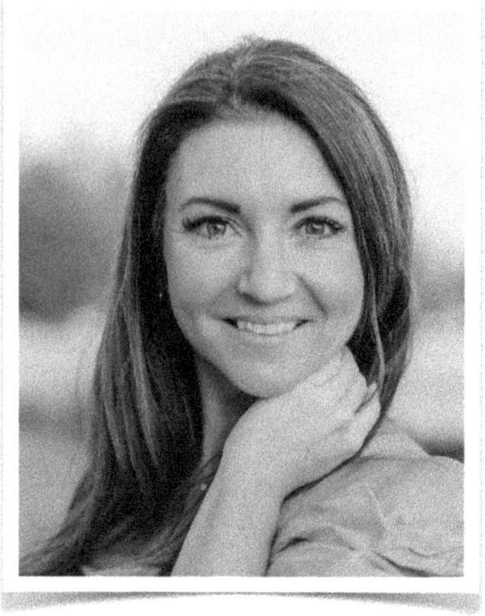

AMY MINGIN

About Amy Mingin: Amy Mingin is a business coach for influencers, best-selling author, speaker, naturopath, yoga & meditation teacher, wife and mum of two, residing on the Gold Coast in Australia.

She has helped thousands of people find their inner spark, access their version of perfect health & scale sustainable businesses over the last 15 years.

She facilitates personal development events, retreats, and quantum healing training for people in Australia and worldwide.

Author's Website: *www.AmyMingin.com*

Book Series Website: *www.TheBookOfInfluence.com*

ANGELA HARDEN-MACK

A HEARTFELT STORY OF FRIENDSHIP: TRANSFORMATIVE POWER OF ALIGNMENT

Have you ever experienced the incredible power of alignment in a close friendship? It's a dynamic force that brings people together, fostering a deep sense of connection, purpose, and fulfillment. Having a best friend has been, and continues to be, a major blessing for me. I want to share with you a story, my story, of friendship with Angela M., my best friend. Our journey is a testament to the transformative impact of alignment and the profound benefits it offers. It is my hope that through our story, you will be inspired to seek and cherish close friendships that embody the essence of alignment.

Finding Alignment—Finding My Tribe

Our friendship began in high school, and over the years, it has blossomed into something truly extraordinary. Angela M. and I, affectionately known as Ann and Ann, share a unique bond built on shared values and a common vision for a happy, healthy, close, and fulfilled family. Our families are the heart and soul of our lives, and we cherish them dearly. Our values encompass faith, wellness, women's empowerment, and love. These guiding principles have aligned our actions and decisions, leading us on a path of unity and purpose.

The Power of Alignment—The Power of Community

Alignment has been the key to our personal growth and progress. By aligning our efforts, we have discovered that we can overcome challenges with resilience and determination. Our shared vision propels us forward, pushing us to exceed our individual capabilities. We achieve more together than we ever could on our own. It's a testament to the incredible benefits alignment brings to our lives.

Deepening the Connection—A friend in Good Times & Bad Times

Alignment nurtures deep and meaningful relationships. In our friendship, alignment has fortified the bond between Ann and Ann, creating a safe space built on trust, respect, and collaboration. We honor and appreciate each other's opinions and perspectives, fostering open and honest communication. Through alignment, we have weathered the storms of life together, providing support and understanding during both joyful and sorrowful moments. Laughter has filled our lives, and tears have been shared. It is a blessing to have a friend with whom we can experience the full spectrum of emotions.

The Joy of Alignment—Joy is Good for the Soul

Alignment brings immense joy and fulfillment. Our aligned vision for our families gives purpose and meaning to our actions. We cherish the quiet moments, cooking together, and pampering our loved ones. We celebrate every milestone, big or small, with love, encouragement, and edification. Our aligned values create a positive and supportive environment, where laughter, love, and compassion thrive. The joy we experience in our girlfriend circle times is an example of the power of alignment in our lives.

Paving the Way for Success—The Friend Cheering You On

Alignment not only brings joy and fulfillment, but it also paves the way for success and achievement. By aligning our actions with our shared vision, we have unlocked our true potential and seized opportunities that have come our way. The young ladies carrying backpacks in high school to the completion of our education and training for careers, we have been in the cheering section for one another. Our collective efforts and shared values propel us toward our desired outcomes. It is through alignment that we live a purposeful and fulfilling life.

Cultivating Alignment—Nurturing the Friendship

Cultivating alignment requires intentional practices and habits. Effective communication is a vital component, where active listening and clear, concise messaging create a strong foundation for understanding and empathy. Ann and Ann often engage in friendly chats, sharing with one another and providing feedback. We have given each other permission to be authentic in our communication, always being loving but honest.

There have been a few quiet pauses in conversations. Something was said, a truth, that required the listener to pause, reflect, and process before answering. Yes, it was a little uncomfortable, but beneficial. Those words and times of reflection and process empowered us to release "things" that were no longer relevant to us. Hmm… many call this pruning. Our commitment to open and honest communication strengthens our friendship and helps us navigate challenges.

Trust is another essential element in our friendship. We prioritize honesty and transparency, fostering a safe space for vulnerability and authenticity. We rely on each other, keeping our commitments and reinforcing trust. Our alignment embraces and celebrates our unique perspectives, creating an inclusive and harmonious environment where mutual respect and understanding thrive.

Embracing Close Friendships

Our friendship beautifully exemplifies the power of alignment. The unwavering bond we share, nurtured through our shared vision and values, has stood the test of time. Through alignment, we support each other's dreams, providing unwavering encouragement and support. We champion one another, creating a strong and fulfilling friendship that embodies the essence of alignment in our daily interactions.

Our journey towards alignment has not only transformed our lives but also had a ripple effect on our families. Our shared vision for happy, healthy, close, and fulfilled families has influenced the way we approach relationships with loved ones. We prioritize quality time, engage in meaningful conversations, and offer support during challenging times. The power of alignment has created a positive impact within our own lives and the lives of those around us. At each high school reunion event, people are excited that we remain close friends.

In a world that often feels disconnected, close friendships that embody alignment are a precious gift. I treasure the gift of friendship with Angela M. It is my hope that you are fortunate to have a best friend. My friendship with Angela M., or Ann and Ann, serves as a heartwarming example of the transformative power of alignment. It has brought us unity, purpose, and boundless love.

As you read our story, I invite you to seek out and cherish close friendships that align with your values and vision. These friendships will enrich your life, bringing happiness, growth, and shared dreams. Embrace alignment in your relationships and experience the profound impact it can have on your own journey of friendship and personal fulfillment.

ANGELA HARDEN-MACK

About Dr. Angela Harden-Mack, MD: Dr. Angela Harden-Mack, MD, is a renowned wellness advocate, international keynote speaker, and Amazon #1 Best-selling Author, and CEO dedicated to empowering ambitious high-performing women. With a focus on personalized self-care and stress relief, she guides women on a transformative journey towards unlocking their full potential and unleashing peak performance. Dr. Angela's expertise in wellness and women's empowerment has garnered recognition from major national television and magazine outlets. With her powerful formula for embracing the wellness lifestyle, she inspires women to release the burdens of the Superwoman mindset and achieve holistic wellness and success in all areas of life. Dr. Angela is a catalyst for change, motivating women to take action and live fulfilling lives by prioritizing their well-being.

Author's Website: *www.AngelaHarden-Mack.com*

Book Series Website: www.TheBookOfInfluence.com

ANGÈLE LAMOTHE

SEEK ALIGNMENT WITH YOUR AUTHENTIC SELF

"Someone who takes the time to understand their relationship with source, who actively seeks alignment with their broader perspective, who deliberately seeks and finds alignment with who they really are, is more charismatic, more attractive, more effective, and more powerful than a group of millions who have not achieved this alignment."
~ Esther Hicks

I once heard the expression, "The key to everything you want and desire in life is creating alignment." But what does it really mean to be in full alignment with yourself and the Universe?

Being aligned with the Universe means that I am in harmony with the energies that surround me, that I am living in a state of flow where everything seems to fall into place effortlessly and through synchronicities. Being in sync with the energies of the Universe has brought a sense of clarity, purpose, and deep personal alignment into my life. It has become a significant building block for how I thrive to live my life and it has offered me an incredible amount of peace, harmony, and deep fulfillment, but it hasn't always been the case.

I am sure you can relate to what I am about to share regarding our culture of performance, perfectionism and finding personal worth through material possessions, accomplishments, and perhaps even status through our ego self. On my path to spiritual growth, I recognized that I had confused alignment with taking control and making things happen in my life. I did not yet understand the difference between inspired action through alignment and ego-based actions that gave me the false sense of power. I was stuck in the doing and living out of alignment with my full truth and I was paying the price and feeling lost.

I was coming from a place of ego and non-alignment and things felt heavy and like I wasn't enough. No matter how hard I tried to control my life, things just didn't run smoothly and go as I planned them in my mind, over and over. We all desire to have control over many spheres in our lives—it's in our nature as humans and it gives us a false sense of security and safety. When life isn't going quite as we had planned it, we are usually tempted to control things so that it goes the way we intend.

But, if you've lived long enough, you recognize that life doesn't always work that way. In more ways than not, it's more difficult to control your life than to simply flow and align with it, and this was a really difficult concept to grasp and accept as the "mover and shaker" of my life. I had been living out of alignment with my soul and it absorbed more of my energy than I realized, and I was running on empty and almost soulless; I was working harder towards something that wasn't aligned with my soul's purpose and the universal energies that are always omnipresent and ready to support.

I am challenging you to rewire that desire and false need to control and to replace it with a desire of alignment. I believe that our need for control stems from ego, lack, fear, and false security.

Alignment, on the other hand, isn't about being in control, it's about flowing with who you are. I have noticed that when I am out of alignment, it's usually a conflict between my head and my heart and if I pause long enough, it never feels good and my gut has a way of telling me if I take the time to listen.

Ego-based thoughts result in ego-based actions and often come from feelings of anxiety, hate, anger, jealousy, or desperation and, therefore, not in alignment with your true self. The ego blocks you from being aligned with the Universe because it directs your attention to separation and individuality, which is aligned with its own smaller desires of safety and low risk. Your ego just wants you to succeed, not the greater world. I started feeling the difference between thoughts that stemmed from my intuition and inspired action and thoughts that came from my ego.

I am not saying that you should take a back seat in life and let it happen to you and live "unconsciously," but what if you recognized that you have a natural rhythm as a human when manifestations can more easily occur from a place of alignment instead of ego?

When I'm not in alignment with my truth and what I'm meant to create in that moment, there's a sense of chaos and discomfort that I feel throughout my body and in every fiber of my soul. Whenever I am feeling disconnected and not on path, it usually is because I am not aligned to my truth in that moment and refuse to surrender to a higher purpose.

To let go of your ego and thoughts that are out of alignment, you have to first have the courage to look at yourself. This takes great strength; it takes time out of your busy life for self-reflection, and it can sometimes be really uncomfortable to look at yourself from under the microscope and perhaps notice things that you don't want to look at. But when you look within and identify what's holding you back from creating deep alignment, you can move through the world embodying your true self and take action with ease and flow, and things just begin to make sense and start working in your favor and it's so much easier!

Our deepest soul desires are aligned with the desires of the Universe—which are always about growth, universal love, and oneness. Alignment is when we listen to our intuition and align with our truth, intuition, and with the energies of the Universe.

Sometimes this happens naturally; something in our life just falls into place. This is usually a time when we take a moment to listen to our true self and not all the noise of life, people, society, culture, and everything in our surroundings.

Living in a state of flow is being in the moment and trusting that everything that's presented to me is meant for me and either aligns with my dreams and desires or it does not. Imagine how simple life would be if we lived moment to moment and simply asked ourselves in every scenario if whatever is presented to us aligns with our truth, our desires, and our intent or if it does not.

Trusting in the Universe means believing that there is a higher power at work, a force that is guiding you towards your highest good and in alignment. When I have faith in the Universe, I let go of my worries and fears and trust that everything will work out in the end for the highest good of all.
That's when we start noticing the synchronicities and coincidences that seem too perfect to be chance, and we trust that they are guiding us towards our next path. It's about being in tune with your intuition and trusting that the Universe is always guiding you down the path of least resistance.

I have surrendered and released my false sense of control by trusting the Universe and believing that everything is happening for me. I now take comfort in knowing that even though things might not make sense at the moment and might feel out of my control, they will eventually fall into place, and it's all divinely planned.

When we are in alignment with the Universe, we start noticing signs and synchronicities that confirm our alignment and choices and live with ease and flow.

When I started trusting the Universe and believing that everything happens for a reason, I really started trusting my intuition and my inner voice that already had all the answers. Things start to flow effortlessly, and everything starts to fall into place and manifesting our goals becomes easier. We start to have a clearer understanding of our purpose and the direction we need to take in life. We experience a sense of calmness and contentment, knowing that everything is happening for a reason, and that life is happening for us; it creates a feeling of inner peace and deep knowing.

We attract people and opportunities that are aligned with our goals and aspirations. We start to notice more coincidences and signs that guide us along our path in the right direction.

Alignment is about listening to the whispers of our souls. Is this giving me energy? Is this bringing me joy? Does this feel like something I genuinely like, or is it something I just want to be in control of? It's important to remember that things don't always go as planned because some things are out of our control.

We're not striving for control—we are striving solely for alignment, and when we align from the heart, the whole Universe conspires in our favor; the right people and opportunities present themselves.We remember to live life on purpose and in alignment, rather than by default.

As you let go of unwanted possessions, commitments, relationships, and things that are no longer serving you, your life becomes more aligned with the truth of who you are meant to be. You become aligned with your authentic self, and inner peace, freedom, and limitless possibilities become reality. You realize the true freedom that comes from living in alignment with your true self and having the tools to realign yourself when you disconnect allows you to quickly and consciously return into alignment.

When your mind, body, and spirit are aligned with your authenticity, you are energized and balanced. You are more creative, more giving; you achieve wellness, and feel you are living a more fulfilling life as you believe things are working out as they should and in alignment with the abundant Universe.

Intentionally seeking alignment with your authentic self is the key to a happy, limitless, and abundant life. When your life starts aligning with this greater purpose of the Universe, then you are at peace, in flow, unstoppable, and things start working out for you as the Universe opens up abundantly and works for you and for the goodness of all.

ANGÈLE LAMOTHE

About Angèle Lamothe: Angèle Lamothe is a high-vibrational leader who lives a heart-centered life and whose mission is to help raise our planet's consciousness so that everyone lives their most abundant life. She is a mom of three, a triathlete, and a soul transformational coach who works with high-performing leaders who are feeling overwhelmed and helps them create abundance, unlock their purpose and develop their intuition to live their richest life. She also has a degree in psychology, a Master's in Health Sciences, training in energy medicine, and has completed leadership trainings. Angèle has worked for 20 years in an acute care hospital. She is obsessed with people's transformational journeys and how the power of the mind creates miracles when aligned with purpose and action. She continues to be inspired by highly motivated individuals who seek opportunities to make changes in their lives, grow through challenges and accelerate transformation.

Angèle leads a high-performance lifestyle and has more joy, energy, and time to do things she deeply enjoys. She can support you in developing tools and strategies to help you connect to your intuition and unleash your full power so that you can lead a balanced and abundant life!

You can find out more about Angèle by visiting:
linktr.ee/AngèleLamothecoaching

Author's website: *www.AngèleLamotheCoaching.squarespace.com/*

Book Series Website: *www.TheBookOfInfluence.com*

BONNIE LIERSE

TO BE ALIGNED OR NOT ALIGNED, THAT IS THE QUESTION

This is the chapter of "Creating Alignment," and it was, honestly, fascinating to see, how many personal perspectives I had on alignment! So much so that this list keeps growing. I will touch on a few. I need a whole chapter for the rest! I truly had to learn many new ALIGNMENTS and I am still growing in these areas daily.

Aligning Interests

I have multiple interests that vary from day to day, and year to year. From my creative interests that definitely change, to now, my passion for graphic writing! There are many techniques in art and I desire and choose to invest time to excel in them! Aligning your interest must be a major focus.

Aligning Concerns

I had many concerns with adapting to family changes and dealing with the loss of my soulmate and spouse in November 2021. I had to learn, as part of my personality, to go with the flow and not worry. It is okay to not worry and to let things fall into place! I am always concerned with those I love and deeply show it to them, whether through quality time or through some kind of mutual ACTION. I know we all deeply share concerns. Are you willing, to share it with colleagues, friends and family, anytime, like I am now?

Aligning True Love

I am still IN LOVE with my husband that passed. However, it is possible to hold onto that love and not need to grieve at the same time! It is also possible to love another differently, if the situation presents itself. You can fall in love again with another soulmate. It is a CHOICE.

Aligning Mastermind & Mindset

I am always around successful entrepreneurship mindsets through masterminds, with, as an example, Erik Swanson and Jon Kovach Jr, as well as my business leadership group because they taught me to read SUCCESS books and study leadership. I also excel in real estate after thirty plus years, due to inspiring platforms and team meetings. Consistency, of any growth, wanting to stretch yourself, is a vital key!

Aligning Focus

I have DISCOVERED I am so charged and totally laser "focused on my passions and priorities"! When I have a "mission" to complete in anything, like my graphic progression, there cannot be distractions! End of subject! I am evolving BIG TIME on this!

Aligning Time Spent Together

Don't take your time or loved ones for granted. You don't want regrets! Time flies; value it; they won't always be there in the physical. Spend quality time with them because things can change in an instant, like when my husband or parents passed away unexpectedly. I would have spent more quality time with them and developed more personal connection. Have no regrets!

Aligning Truth

Will people at times tell white lies? What is your resolution? Sometimes, we are afraid to share a truth because of hurting someone. It is challenging when there is that gray area of truth. Why not just say the full truth? It does not always work. It can still deeply hurt someone you care about or love. White lies have their pros and cons. Be careful. Someone will figure it out. I am now aligned with that.

Aligning "DO NOT STICK YOUR HEAD IN THE SAND"

It is easy to stick your head in the sand and hide from the truth. It is recommended to face the facts upfront. Truth will eventually come out in time.

Aligning Goals

I have multiple goals and passions now. I have them completely aligned now, due to a mission and purpose, as well as a focus.

Alignment with Eavesdropping & Overhearing or Picking Up Wrong Information

It is very easy to eavesdrop, but you can get incomplete information. It can become a rabbit hole, if it is accidentally passed along. Make sure you get the right and complete information and DO NOT ASSUME. Ask questions if you are not sure.

Aligning Passions and Goals

My other love and passion is the ARTS. It is all now aligned, due to my graphic progression in business and creative writing.

Alignment with Lighting

It is difficult to work projects or write when you have poor lighting. The best thing, if it is daylight, is to sit near a window. If it's nighttime, like I am writing now, I know I have access to the light from the computer or phone. Use a blue light screen. Make sure you have better lighting available, so you do not strain your eyes.

Aligning to Understand the Difference Between Sympathy & Empathy

We feel sympathy for someone if they lose a family member or friend from passing away. That is when you need to be sympathetic. Being a humble listener will help others feel your empathy. That is clearly being EMPATHETIC.

Aligning & Understanding What is Platonic Friendship

This is when one person in a relationship believes they are just friends, but the other person, actually, is in love with them. In hindsight, they are not just friends, but one is actually in love. Platonic is rare. Be aware of this, so no one gets hurt.

Aligning Who Truly Cares

This is simple: Do you genuinely and truly know who cares about you and what you need and desire? In most cases, we DO NOT know this. Get clarity and I mean clarity on this truth.

Aligning How to be Your Own Person

I am now my own person who stands up for myself. I let (in the past), others walk all over me, but now I can say to myself, allow or don't allow. I am standing up for myself and others, to protect those I care about and adore, or they will NOT understand who truly cares.

Aligning Priorities

Make sure you have your priorities clear for yourself and others, especially those you love. They will feel it, if they are genuinely loved, and that they are a priority.

Aligning Regarding Control

You DO NOT want to be controlled by anyone—yup, period.

Aligning – Are you a "FREE THINKER?"

Do you need to ask everyone permission regarding your life business and future decisions? If you DO NOT need permission, you are a FREE THINKER. Who controls your decisions?

Aligning FEARS

I have conquered many of my own FEARS by taking action on what I feared the most. As a mentor in leadership, I helped others recognize their fears. They knew then that they needed to take action to conquer that fear.

Aligning Self-Esteem

My self-esteem was always low; I finally conquered that with the journey I am on!

As shown below, there are sooo many more alignments I personally am working on or I am choosing to excel in. It takes major listening skills and creating an aligning mindset.

Aligning - entrepreneurship vs employee mentality.
Aligning - journeys and how fast to reach those goals.
Aligning - who should mentor and coach you.
Aligning - what is health and what is not.
Aligning - how to know to your serving of others platform.
Aligning - time and business organization.
Aligning - how to get facts versus fiction.
Aligning - who you can trust and who will be there for you.
Aligning – heartstrings.
Aligning - meditation and how to relax.
Aligning - how much physical activity and what to do.
Aligning - what dreams mean.

Aligning - personal beliefs.
Aligning - who is on my journey in life and business.
Aligning - who is spiritual and like-minded, like me.
Aligning - true friendships.
Aligning - who I can trust.
Aligning - when to say I am sorry.
Aligning - when to pick up mutual eye contact.
Aligning - awakening your Highest Self, as I did.
Aligning - "Who am I?" Great question to ask yourself, like I did at my "Art of Living Retreat."
Aligning - my relationship and business boundaries.
Aligning - to have a FIO (Figure it out) attitude.
Aligning - about worrying what others think.
Aligning - do you get scared of aging? Will it effect your success? I, at sixty-eight years young, am finally living my almost dream journey.
Aligning - do you let others intimidate you?

We are not all perfect, but long as we are willing to create alignment, we will succeed in love and life!

BONNIE LIERSE

About Bonnie Zaruches Lierse: Bonnie Zaruches Lierse is extremely artistic and creative, with an entrepreneurial bent. Besides that, she is a seasoned agent with more than twenty years' experience in real estate in the New York/Long Island area. She relocated to Northern Virginia in 2012 and continued her real estate career there.

Another passion is creating leaders by working in business leadership development with *Leadership Team Development (LTD)*, marketing products supplied by *Amway.* She was also a member of *The Screen Cartoonist Guild of Motion Pictures* for many years. Also, she did freelance for *Sesame Street* in New York City. In addition, she was a District Director for an interior accessory design company, as her own business.

Bonnie is blessed with five beautiful grandchildren and is very close with her children and family, some of whom are also in Virginia. Her missions are leadership, mentorship, paying it forward, and changing lives one at a time. Her motto is "<u>You</u> be the difference!"

Author's website: *www.amway.com/myshop/SplashFXEnterprises*

Book Series Website: *www.TheBookOfInfluence.com*

CHARLOTTE DELON

YOU WANT PEOPLE TO FOLLOW

Alignment is critical to team success and yet, while it is a foundational ingredient, it is often overlooked. Most rely on their position to draw alignment. It's command control versus inspiring alignment. I'm the boss and you will follow. The problem is, you will never get the best out of those who follow you with this form of leadership. I would question whether, even if they follow you under this form of leadership, is it true alignment.

As a leader, you will know if you have alignment. You will see increased improvements in efficiency, creativity, and commitment to achieve objectives; there will be mutual respect. People are wired to increase pleasure and avoid pain and so there are some key things that must be present to draw alignment.

1. **Start with you.** People buy into the leader before they buy into a vision. Ask yourself:

    - Are you a leader that people want to follow?
    - Are you a leader who has a track record of making sound decisions?
    - Are you excellent at stories and can you enroll people into what you are thinking?
    - Are you Dynamic?
    - Are you a leader who creates psychological safety?
    - Are you a leader who creates trust and instills belief?

You will need to have some of the characteristics to have people buy into you initially. You will need all to sustain the buy-in. I had a leader who was dynamic. She was excellent at storytelling. When she finished speaking, you felt like you could climb Mt. Everest. We felt there was nothing we couldn't achieve as a team. Her actions, however, did not match the energy she was exuding from the stage. She lacked focus. She was quickly identified as someone who was in over her head and wasn't able to make sound decisions. She was unwilling to listen to others. She eventually created division. The buy-in was lost in a moment and there was devastation in the aftermath.

2. **Create a compelling vision.** For a vision to take root, the following should be considered:

- The vision must tug at the head and the heart.
- The vision must allow for everyone to understand their part.
- The vision must be clear and help people to visualize what it will be like when you get to the other side.
- The vision must be delivered across many different channels.

The biggest mistake I see leaders make is they create a vision that they don't buy into themselves, or they share the vision once and hope everyone will get it. You first must buy into the vision and the vision must be repeated over and over again across many channels. Quick action must be taken to help mobilize the team around the vision.

Many years ago, I had a team that would refer to themselves as stepchildren. I quickly realized that if I were going to shift this team from bottom to top, I needed them to believe in me a little to buy into my vision. My vision was everyone in the company would know of this team and want their services. This was a lot to take in considering they were often forgotten.

I would layer them with messages of belief. I would tell them often that they were one of the most brilliant teams I have ever had the pleasure to work with and it was the truth. Visiting with them and getting demos of their work always gave me the booster shot I needed until the next visit. I shared this story repeatedly.

One day during a meeting, I said, embrace these slow days because a year from now, everyone is going to want your time and attention. They chuckled because this was a small team and this company always saved the small for last. I begin creating small wins for the team that led to big wins. I have always said you are only as good as your network, and I gave the team access to mine.

They were empowered, which led to them being on the boat with me rowing in the same direction. Everyone felt they had a contribution to make and they had purpose. We were out to achieve something that had not been done in the history of the company by this team. They bought into the vision.

3. **Take an inventory of your team.** Start with how would the team be if they were functioning healthy? Some of the soft skills that made our list were:

- Curious
- Self-Starter
- Collaborative
- Empowered
- Courageous
- Bold

The list could go on and on and did include hard skills, too. The fundamental realization was, if we didn't change the team, we were not going to be successful. Hold on. We did not let anyone go. We literally changed the team. We shared with the team some of the characteristics we were looking for out them. We had weekly growth accountability conversations to ensure the characteristics were top of mind.

One that sticks out the most is the conversation we had on empowerment versus delegation. I knew we nailed it when our most junior employees were excited. They were used to delegation masking as empowerment where someone would give the assignment and details on how to execute and stand down. Now, we were talking about true empowerment. Everyone was demonstrating courage. Speaking up and challenging each other. We gave awards and recognition to continue to foster the behaviors. The team was innovating. They were training themselves and each other. The team demonstrated a growth mindset learning new ways of working, thinking, and doing. The engagement was off the charts.

In the end, we were able to meet our commitments with our business partners and came in 3 months ahead of schedule. Everyone was counting us out and saying we would not be able to hit our date. We had lost too many months on the front-end of the effort to hit the target. We exceeded the expectations of everyone, and the team received notoriety up to the right-hand man of the CEO. This was a big deal for a team our size.

After everything was said and done, my management team and I evaluated the events that occurred that led to the success. We agreed that it was awesome to watch everything unfold so beautifully. What we concluded was:

1. The foundation was being laid long before this effort started building trust and getting the buy-in from our people. [**Start with you**]
2. We created a vision that included everyone. The new brand this team would have, the notoriety, and the opportunities we could see in the future got everyone excited. [**Create a compelling vision**]
3. Growth included everyone including leadership. Everyone was being stretched. We were in it together. We started with the supporters. The rule was that you did not have to be with, you just could not derail. We respected that some would need to see evidence before deciding if it was safe. The safety of opposition helped them get on board quickly. [**Take inventory of your team**]

These three steps secured a win! We hit the target while maintaining everyone's happiness.

CHARLOTTE DELON

About Charlotte DeLon: Charlotte is a motivational speaker and coach with over 16 years of transformational leadership experience. She helps organizations transform culture for optimal output defining operational tenants and assessing behavioral gaps that can impede or accelerate change.

Charlotte is a Maxwell Leadership Certified Team Member and Certified Advance Behavioral Analysis DISC coach. Through the discovery of DISC results, Charlotte helps individuals define their superpowers and also what can be holding them back from being all that is possible.

Some key highlights: Speaking: Keynote speaker, panel discussions for women in IT providing strategies on how to manage work, family and life, launched leader to leader series discussing Leadership Philosophy's and benefits.

Coaching: Executive leadership coaching to improve organizational health. Career and life coach helping people succeed in career and managing life challenges like fear.

Teaching: Facilitate Leadership Acumen Mastermind series. Train on leadership styles (situational, transformational and servant). Teach how to build Leadership Philosophy's to deliver and drive inner and outer accountability.

Favorite quote: "No one cares how much you know until they know how much you care." - Theodore Roosevelt.

Author's Website: *www.LeadershipByCharlotteDelon.com*

Book Series Website: *www.TheBookOfInfluence.com*

CHE BROWN

CREATING ALIGNMENT THROUGH EXTRAORDINARY TIMES

Life's journey is fraught with unforeseen challenges and disruptions. The COVID-19 pandemic was a stark reminder that circumstances can change rapidly, transforming well-laid plans into chaos. Within this turbulence, however, lies a unique opportunity to learn and apply valuable lessons in creating alignment—lessons that are applicable on personal, professional, and interpersonal levels.

Navigating through the ebbs and flows of life requires resilience and adaptability. While unexpected obstacles may divert our paths, they also present us with a chance to grow and evolve. In the face of uncertainty, it is crucial to cultivate a mindset of flexibility and openness to new possibilities. By embracing change and seeking alignment with our values and goals, we can harness the power of adversity to propel us forward on our journey of self-discovery and fulfillment. Remember, amid chaos, there is always an opportunity for growth and transformation.

A Unified Approach to Overcoming Adversity

Nearly three years ago, my oldest son, Che Brown and Brittanee Brooks faced the ultimate test of their love and resilience when they chose to marry amidst the pandemic. Originally, planning a large, traditional wedding, they quickly realized that adaptability and alignment among all parties involved were crucial due to the shifting landscape.

They transformed their grand wedding into an intimate backyard ceremony surrounded by their closest family and friends. Despite the challenges and uncertainties brought on by the pandemic, Che and Brittanee's love shone even brighter in the simplicity and sincerity of their ceremony.

Their love story had weathered the storm and emerged stronger, a testament to their unwavering commitment to each other. The guests toasted to the newlyweds as they danced under the twinkling lights, celebrating a union of two individuals and a merging of two families. It was a night filled with laughter, joy, and hope for the future.

As Che and Brittanee held each other close, basking in the glow of their love and the warmth of their loved ones, they knew that no matter what challenges lay ahead, they would face them together, hand in hand. And so, their journey as husband and wife began, marked by a love that had conquered all obstacles and emerged victorious.

Embracing Everyone's Role

Much like influence, creating alignment is about rallying people around a shared vision or goal. This was particularly essential in ensuring the safety of all guests from COVID-19. Through concerted efforts and clear communication, we ensured that each participant understood their role in protecting the community's health, fostering a collective safety responsibility.

By fostering a sense of unity and common purpose, we instilled a deep understanding of commitment among all individuals involved. This cohesion led to a successful implementation of safety measures and created a supportive environment where everyone felt valued and empowered.

Through such collaborative efforts, we can overcome challenges and thrive as a community, united in our dedication toward a shared objective.

Collaborative Effort for Safety

The success of this event hinged on seamless coordination and a shared commitment to safety protocols. Demonstrating leadership in times of uncertainty meant guiding with empathy, ensuring that every measure, from mandatory testing to social distancing, was a collective decision, thus uniting everyone in a common cause for health and safety.

The collaborative efforts of all involved underscored the importance of clear communication and mutual respect. By fostering an environment of understanding and support, participants felt empowered to follow the safety guidelines diligently, knowing that their well-being was a top priority. As the event unfolded smoothly, it became evident that a collective sense of responsibility and cooperation could overcome any challenges. This shared journey towards a safer and healthier future was a testament to the strength of community spirit and the power of coming together for the greater good.

Empathy & Understanding in Communication

During such uncertain times, patience and compassion in our communications were paramount. For example, adjusting seating arrangements to comply with health guidelines required sensitivity to guests' feelings and expectations. This approach minimized discomfort and strengthened the sense of community and mutual respect.

Witnessing how a simple act of understanding and empathy could make a significant difference in creating a warm and welcoming environment was heartening. As we navigated these challenges together, it became clear that our ability to adapt and support one another was a testament to our connections' strength. By prioritizing the well-being of others and fostering a sense of unity, we overcame obstacles and built a stronger, more resilient community. In times of uncertainty, these moments of kindness and consideration remind us of the power of compassion and solidarity.

Navigating Through Challenges with Patience

By carefully considering our words and actions, we maintained a harmonious atmosphere, highlighting the importance of patience and empathy in preserving unity and preventing conflict.

We cultivated a culture of understanding and respect by fostering open communication and actively listening to one another. Our commitment to kindness and cooperation served as a solid foundation for building strong relationships and overcoming any challenges that came our way.

With each thoughtful interaction, we reinforced the values of tolerance and compassion, creating a space where everyone felt valued and heard. In this way, we upheld the spirit of unity and set an example for others to follow, inspiring a community bound by shared values and mutual respect.

Innovation & Flexibility as Solutions

The constant flux leading up to the wedding taught us that there is always a solution if we remain adaptable and open to change. This mindset is crucial for creating alignment, as it involves seeking and implementing solutions that accommodate everyone's needs and expectations.

During these times of transition and growth, we truly learn the value of flexibility and openness. Like a beautifully orchestrated wedding, life presents unexpected challenges and opportunities. By embracing change and remaining open-minded, we not only navigate the uncertainties but also pave the way for understanding and harmony. As we move forward, let us remember that our willingness to adapt and seek solutions together strengthens our bonds and creates a shared vision of a brighter future.

Adaptability as a Leadership Quality

Our ability to adjust and creatively solve problems underscored the significance of adaptability in leadership. It's a testament to how being flexible and solution-oriented is essential in guiding others towards a shared objective.

In times of uncertainty and change, a leader's adaptability becomes a beacon of hope and guidance for those around them. By embracing challenges with a problem-solving mindset, leaders navigate obstacles and inspire others to do the same. Adaptable leaders' fluidity and openness to new ideas foster a culture of innovation and resilience within their teams. Ultimately, the ability to pivot, adjust, and creatively solve problems defines effective leadership and paves the way for success in the face of ever-evolving circumstances.

Broadening the Impact: Life & Business Insights

The lessons learned from orchestrating a wedding during a pandemic extend beyond personal milestones. They underscore the power of creating alignment in all facets of life, from navigating global crises to addressing daily business challenges. At its core, creating alignment fosters understanding, empathy, and cooperation to achieve shared goals.

As we navigate our paths, remember that even in the face of adversity, we can unite, demonstrate compassion, and devise solutions. When applied thoughtfully, these pillars of creating alignment can lead us to remarkable accomplishments, even under the most unexpected conditions.

CHE BROWN

About Che Brown: Che Brown is a globally renowned giant in the sales world. He has cracked the once elusive code of entrepreneurial success with a game-changing model that unlocks unlimited financial potential, power, and wealth. In just six short years, he has dominated the sales space, coaching thousands of rising business leaders to achieve exponential growth and success in their industries, to the tune of over $400 million and counting. His acclaimed 7-Figure Sales Team concept has forever erased the outdated notion that generating revenue in business is a sole-source game—instead illustrating it is indeed a team sport.

Che lives, breathes, and sleeps his craft. He has his fingers on the pulse of profit generation and an instinctual insight into why the heart of a flailing business has stopped. Most importantly, he can resuscitate the flow of revenue in any company with just a whiteboard and a conversation. Che Brown is the CEO of EasySalesHub (*www.EasySalesHub.com*), scaling businesses to six and seven figures. This all-in-one solution generates leads, qualifies prospects, books appointments, closes deals and frees entrepreneurs to focus on other business needs. Che was named one of the Top 15 entrepreneurs to keep an eye out for across North America in 2021 by USA Today News.

Che is the Executive Producer of *www.TheMakingOfAnEntrepreneur.com* DocuSeries, Host of the #1 Business Development and Late Night Show In The Country: *The Happy Entrepreneur Show* (*www.HappyEntrepreneurShow.com*), and Founder of Comeback Champion (www.ComebackChampionSummit.com).

Author's Website: *www.CheBrown.com*

Book Series Website: *www.TheBookofInfluence.com*

CYNTHIA GALLARDO

THE ART OF ALIGNMENT AS A LEGACYPRENEUR

Parallels With Renewable Energy

In the realm of sustainable business, the legacypreneur stands as a testament to the power of alignment—melding entrepreneurial drive, intrapreneurial innovation, and a profound legacy vision. This chapter explores how defining and creating alignment is pivotal in a holistic approach to life and business. We draw an enlightening parallel between this and the way renewable energy systems, like windmills and solar panels, harness and convert natural energy into usable power.

Alignment in legacypreneurship means synchronizing various aspects of business—values, goals, strategies, and actions—with a long-term legacy vision. Creating alignment involves integrating personal values with business objectives, aligning team efforts with company goals, and ensuring that business practices resonate with broader societal and environmental concerns.

For a legacypreneur, there is an interconnection between life and business. Business isn't a separate entity but an extension of life's purpose and values. A holistic approach requires balancing financial goals with personal well-being, social responsibility, and environmental sustainability.

Just as windmills and solar panels efficiently capture wind and solar energy, legacypreneurs harness various business resources—people, capital, technology. Renewable energy systems convert natural energy into electricity or some other form of usable power. Similarly, legacypreneurs transform resources into sustainable business outcomes through strategic alignment.

Renewable energy systems are designed for maximum efficiency and adaptability to changing conditions—principles mirrored in effective legacypreneurship. The emphasis on long-term sustainability in renewable energy parallels the legacypreneur's focus on creating a lasting legacy.

Just as precise engineering is critical for energy systems, strategic planning and careful resource allocation are key for business alignment. The ability to adapt to market and environmental changes is as crucial in business as the adaptability of energy systems to varying natural conditions.

Alignment leads to sustainable business growth, similar to the sustainable energy produced by windmills and solar panels. Just as renewable energy systems are built for longevity, aligned businesses are more resilient and better equipped to withstand market fluctuations.

One notable case study that exemplifies the strategic alignment of resources to create a legacy and achieve specific goals is the story of Patagonia, the outdoor clothing and gear company. Founded by Yvon Chouinard in 1973, Patagonia's journey is a prime example of how a business can align its resources, values, and operations to not only achieve commercial success but also make a significant impact on environmental conservation and sustainability.

Yvon Chouinard, an avid climber, established Patagonia with a vision to create the best outdoor gear without causing unnecessary harm to the environment. The company was built on the values of environmental stewardship and ethical manufacturing.

As a legacypreneur, Yvon led his company to create a strategic alignment of resources through product design, corporate culture, and employee engagement (the people), marketing and consumer engagement, and environmental advocacy and community involvement.

First, Patagonia invested in designing durable, high-quality products, aligning its manufacturing resources to reduce waste and environmental impact. They pioneered the use of recycled materials in their products, aligning their supply chain to support environmental sustainability.

Also, Patagonia created a positive corporate culture and employee engagement by fusing communication and education. Patagonia fostered a corporate culture that echoed its environmental values, encouraging employees to participate in environmental initiatives. The company provided resources for employee education on environmental issues and supported their involvement in conservation efforts.

In addition, Patagonia valued marketing and consumer engagement. Patagonia's marketing strategies were aligned with its mission, often highlighting environmental issues and promoting responsible consumption. Campaigns like "Don't Buy This Jacket," aimed at reducing consumerism, reflected an alignment of marketing resources towards their sustainability goals.

Patagonia led by example in environmental advocacy and community involvement. The company engaged in various environmental initiatives, aligning a portion of its profits to support conservation efforts. Patagonia encouraged community involvement in environmental advocacy, aligning its brand with broader environmental movements.

By strategically aligning resources, Patagonia achieved and continues to achieve specific goals, which has allowed it to create a legacy. Despite its unconventional approach, Patagonia achieved significant commercial success, becoming a model for sustainable practices in the industry.

Patagonia's commitment to sustainability influenced other companies to adopt more environmentally friendly practices. Therefore, the company has left a legacy as a pioneer in corporate responsibility and environmental advocacy, proving that aligning business practices with environmental and ethical values can lead to long-term success and impact.

Patagonia's journey demonstrates how strategic alignment of resources towards a core vision and values can create a lasting legacy. By integrating sustainability into every aspect of their business, from product design to marketing and advocacy, they have not only achieved commercial success but also made a significant impact on environmental conservation, setting a benchmark in the industry for responsible business practices.

With Patagonia as an example, each of us as legacypreneurs must embrace alignment for a sustainable future—a lasting legacy.

Next Steps for Legacypreneurs

For legacypreneurs looking to integrate the principles of strategic alignment, sustainability, and legacy creation into their entrepreneurial or intrapreneurial journeys, the following practical steps can provide a roadmap for success:

1. Define Your Core Values and Vision

Understand and articulate the core values that drive you. This could be sustainability, social responsibility, innovation, or any other value that resonates with you. Define what you want to achieve with your business in the long term. Your vision should align with your values and reflect the legacy you wish to leave.

2. Align Business Model with Values

Incorporate practices that reflect your values. If sustainability is a key value, consider how your business can minimize its environmental impact. Ensure that your operations, from sourcing materials to labor practices, align with ethical standards.

3. Cultivate a Strong Brand Identity

Develop a brand message that communicates your values and vision clearly to your customers. Ensure that every aspect of your brand, from marketing to customer service, is consistent with your core values.

4. Foster a Collaborative Culture

Engage your team in your vision and values. Encourage ideas and feedback that support your goals. Create a workplace culture that prioritizes employee well-being and professional development.

5. Build Strategic Partnerships

Form partnerships with other businesses, non-profits, or communities that share your values and can help amplify your impact. Networking is also critical to build strategic relationships. Attend industry events, join relevant groups, and engage with others who can provide support, advice, or collaboration opportunities. One of my favorite words is synergy, the whole is greater than the individual parts. Working together towards a common goal allows legacypreneurs to achieve exponential growth.

6. Implement Sustainable and Scalable Systems

Develop business processes that are efficient, scalable, and sustainable. Use technology to improve efficiency, reduce waste, and enhance customer experiences.

7. Keep Up with Industry Trends, Emerging Technologies, and Best Practices

Be open to adapting your business model as needed and embrace innovation to stay ahead.

8. Measure Impact and Iterate

Define key performance indicators (KPIs) that align with your values and vision. Regularly review your business performance against these metrics and adjust strategies as necessary.

9. Engage with Your Community and Customers

Be active in your community, participating in events or initiatives that resonate with your business values. Actively seek and incorporate customer feedback to improve your products or services.

10. Communicate Your Journey

As legacypreneurs, we each have a story. Share your journey, challenges, and successes with your audience. This helps build a connection and can inspire others. Be transparent about your business practices, learnings, and achievements.

Becoming a successful legacypreneur is a journey that requires dedication, strategic planning, and a commitment to your core values. By integrating these principles into your business, you can create a venture that not only achieves commercial success but also contributes positively to society, leaving a lasting legacy. Remember, the path of a legacypreneur is not just about reaching a destination; it's about the impact you make along the way.

In conclusion, alignment is a key ingredient in the journey of a legacypreneur, drawing an innovative analogy with renewable energy systems. It illuminates how strategic alignment, much like the efficient harnessing and conversion of natural energy, is crucial for creating a sustainable, impactful business legacy.

CYNTHIA GALLARDO

About Cynthia Gallardo: Cynthia Gallardo, your Leading Legacy Lawyer™, keynote speaker, author, business strategist, legacypreneur™, and lawyer. Cynthia is passionate about providing a positive interaction with every person she meets on a daily basis, whether in a personal, professional, or academic setting. Cynthia's creed is "Results. Not excuses." Cynthia is a catalyst that empowers and inspires entrepreneurs struggling to transform a business idea into a vision, and from a vision into the reality of a profitable business by discovering their unique business DNA to launch, build, and protect their legacy.

Cynthia graduated with honors earning her MBA and law degree. Cynthia is a proud graduate of Southern University Law Center. Cynthia is CEO and founder of Cynthia Gallardo Law, LLC and Synergy Solutions PRO, LLC which houses Launch to Legacy Academy™. Cynthia practices immigration law, transactional law, and estate planning. Cynthia takes a holistic approach to business and shares her 5 Step Launch to Legacy™ Blueprint outlining the framework to live and leave a lasting legacy. Cynthia worked in the corporate environment for nearly fifteen years transitioning from front line representative to management roles to a leadership role. Cynthia is a lifelong learner and strives to guide others to become the best versions of themselves personally and professionally.

Cynthia lives in Louisiana with her husband and son where they enjoy spending time together in spiritual activities. In addition, the Gallardo family has four fur babies—three Doberman pinschers and a cat. The Gallardo family is a strong advocate of the foster to adopt program as they have personally taken the foster to adoption journey.
Author's Website: *www.CynthiaGallardo.com*
Book Series Website: *www.TheBookOfInfluence.com*

DANIEL KILBURN

SPEAK THEIR LANGUAGE: COMMUNICATE TO INFLUENCE & CREATE ALIGNMENT

Let's discuss how we can establish or create Alignment based on Dale Carnegie's classic, *How to Win Friends and Influence People*. We are influencing people all the time, good, bad, or indifferent; our mere presence will influence those we come in contact with. Though, pressing on with what we want at the risk of all other considerations may not be the better path to move forward. It can be better to create an ally who is interested in the same goals as we are through alignment.

Having a roadmap for creating an ally through alignment is a valuable tool for accomplishing our goals. By using these tools of appreciation, empathy, clear communication, and active listening, we can navigate the complexities of human interaction and achieve win-win situations.

"The only way I can get you to do anything is by giving you what you want."
~ Dale Carnegie

Understanding Alignment

When thinking about personal and professional relationships, creating alignment can refer to an agreement, balance, harmony, and shared objectives between individuals and groups. However, before creating alignment outside, one must first find and create alignment within. If we fail to align intellectually, morally, ethically, and physically with the goal at hand. It will be impossible to create alignment with others to achieve any objective.

Being internally aligned will assist in fostering cooperation, trust and understanding, because it sets the foundation for collaboration and creates a positive environment. Which can be perceived as a crucial element of a healthy personal and professional relationship.

One key factor to recognize is the unique alignment within oneself. We are who we are 100% of the time. Demonstrating competing values, ethics, or morals will only confuse those around us. By striving for and expressing our internal values, morals, integrity, and a sense of purpose, we will attract those who are aligned with us. And repel those who are not. Quite possibly, we will contribute to a better society as a whole.

On the flip side, being inconsistent with our words and actions can create a level of uncertainty and distrust with those we are seeking to work with. Demonstrating competing values, ethics, or morals will only confuse those around us.

With the COVID-19 pandemic winding down to an endemic, the Great Resignation is on top of mind. Here are some of the top reasons people are quitting:

1. Not Feeling Connected
2. Feeling Devalued
3. High Expectations
4. Low Clarity
5. Lack of Acknowledgement.

The lesson learned is that people do not want to work with or for people they do not like.

(*www.thepremierdaily.com/what-bosses-do-employees-quit/*)

These are just a few of the indicators that a lack of alignment exists in the workplace. If you're in charge and this is happening at work, what's happening at home? These items and many more can be addressed through clear communications. First with yourself, then with the world you are creating.

Perspective on Alignment

I must stress the importance of avoiding criticism when interacting with others. Unless you are a Professional Music, Movie, Food, or Fashion Critic, AVOID IT! Remember, we all are the most important person in our own lives. Casting doubt, dispersion, or disapproval will not ingratiate anyone to us unless they are a person who enjoys pain, such as a masochist. And then you might want to reevaluate that relationship.

The title of Dale Carnegies book says it all. *How to Win Friends and Influence People*. Alignment is crucial to effectively influencing people. In order to persuade and gain support from others, we first must develop a connection by aligning with their values, or discovering if they can align with ours.

Real influence will only come from building a relationship built on empathy, trust, common objectives, and being genuinely interested in others. Demonstrating our ability to listen to their point of view, and finding ways we are more alike than we are different will help us clearly communicate and influence them.

It is true that people are more drawn to others they believe genuinely understand them. By seeking to know others' wants, needs, desires, and challenges, we can authentically communicate in a way that will create an experience for the other that they so deeply desire. The outcome can possibly solidify our connection and place us in a position as someone who genuinely is invested in the well-being of others.

It has been proven that people tend to learn more when playing or being playful. Since you have already discovered what makes them tick, what tickles their funny bone? We are all different and there is still an opportunity to gain more alignment with someone just by playing with them. So go for it—you are never too old to have fun.

A Journey to Alignment

As a former member of the U.S. Army, I define "alignment" in a whole new way. In combat situations, being aligned with my fellow soldiers meant the difference between life and death. I had to put aside my personal beliefs and connect with theirs. The possibility of fighting alongside them, for each other, was more crucial than any patriotic symbol or political ideology.

When deployed to Southwest Asia, I realized that it's crucial to approach unknown and hostile situations with an open mind, clear eyes, and open ears. Understanding the other person's perspective, culture, or group incentive was invaluable to our mission, even if I couldn't totally align with them. And by communicating clearly and respectfully with local counterparts, we were able to avoid life-threatening situations. Shared alignment allowed people to come back home alive. Alignment is key in all situations, every day, all over the world.

"Pay less attention to what men say. Just watch what they do."
~ Dale Carnegie

Challenges in Creating Alignment

The greatest challenge with creating alignment lies within us. There are six reason people will not do something:

1. Vague Goals
2. Do Not Know How to Do it
3. Can Not Do It
4. Are Afraid They Will Make a Mistake
5. Does Not Want to Do It
6. Needs Permission

Achieving alignment requires a proactive mindset and accepting responsibility for our actions. Sometimes we don't know why others are unwilling to align, and sometimes the fault is ours, and these issues can be fixed. By taking ownership of our own lives and actions, we can overcome the barriers preventing us from creating alignment.

For your complimentary copy of the Six Reasons People Will Not Do Something eBook, go to: *bit.ly/srwpwnds*

Or scan the QR Code below, there is no opt-in required.
Applying Carnegie's Principles to Create Alignment

Successful relationships at work and in our personal life depend on our ability to communicate our values clearly and connect with others. It's not just those in positions of power and authority that need effective communication skills, we all hold some level of power in different aspects of our lives. When we communicate with clarity and precision, we foster respect and trust with our loved ones and business associates.

To be a clear communicator and respected leader, there are a few things to keep in mind:

1. Be clear and concise to avoid misunderstandings.
2. Listen actively to understand and show that you value others' perspectives.
3. Practice empathy to build relationships and resolve conflicts.

4. Adapt your communication style to fit the situation and audience.
5. Believe in yourself and what you have to say to earn trust and respect.
6. Be culturally sensitive to prevent misunderstandings and build stronger bonds with others.
7. Avoid criticizing, condemning, or complaining.

In general, effective communication involves a mix of skills, attitudes, and actions that help us connect with and influence others. Keep these tips in mind, and you'll be well on your way to mastering the art of communication and building relationships that last.

As leaders know, effective leadership is created through clear communications. The ability to communicate your intent to the listener in a way that appeals to their self-interest can effectively influence others to your goals. Alignment is a valuable part of being able to influence others. Creating alignment starts from within ourselves, as we must be congruent with our words and actions to establish trust and credibility. Connecting genuinely, listening with intent, finding what makes us alike, communicating clearly, and having fun is a recipe for success. Remember, alignment is not just a concept; it is a journey towards understanding, collaboration, mutual growth, and creating your legacy.

DANIEL KILBURN

About Daniel Kilburn: Daniel Kilburn, America's "5-Star Leadership Coach," will open communications, build resiliency, and develop leadership by preparing you, your family, and your organization to have tough conversations by helping you prepare for inevitable emergencies and natural disasters so you can protect your children and live with a sense of security.

Put a plan in place and act on it. Dream, Develop, and Deliver.

Daniel's passion for disaster management can be traced back to the Loma Prieta earthquake in 1989. It became his mission to learn disaster management to protect his children. As a single father, Daniel raised two beautiful daughters while serving in the U.S. Army.

Daniel has over 30 years of experience training young men and women, foreign nationals, and Department of Defense Civilians to survive on the modern battlefield. Daniel is a retired Training and Operations NCO, Senior Infantry Drill Sergeant, and Instructor at the U.S. Armies Non-Commissioned Officers Academy, including the U.S. Army Sergeants Major Academy. Pairing his instructional background and education in leadership, communication, and disaster management, he specializes in the All-Hazards Disaster Planning approach and acceptable risk aversion.

Daniel has been featured in WFLA News Channel 8, Authority Magazine, Communication Intelligence Magazine, Lifestyles over 50, and Carewell. Daniels BHAG is to successfully impact the lives of 1,000,000 at-risk urban families by 2027.

Author's Website: *www.DanielKilburn.com*

Book Series Website: *www.TheBookOfInfluence.com*

DAPHENE BOOKER-HARRIS &
TODD HARRIS

HARNESSING THE POWER OF INFLUENCE THROUGH ALIGNMENT

The Essence of Mutual Respect

In the previous book in this series, we focused our teachings on the principles of respect. Drawing inspiration from Aretha Franklin's iconic call for respect, our journey in business and personal spheres echoes a profound truth: Influence begins with giving respect, not just receiving it. My husband Todd and I have navigated the intricate dance of fostering respectful relationships for two decades. This journey has been pivotal in nurturing our ventures, community engagements, and personal connections.

As we've learned, respect goes beyond admiration—it's about genuinely valuing others for their contributions, perspectives, and unique qualities. This foundational respect paves the way for meaningful connections, establishing a fertile ground for influence that extends to employees, peers, and the wider community.

Respect fosters a culture of appreciation and understanding, creating an environment where everyone feels heard and valued. Recognizing the diverse strengths and perspectives each individual brings builds stronger relationships and encourages collaboration and innovation. When we embrace the principles of respect in our interactions, we lay the groundwork for a more harmonious and productive community where empathy and kindness are the guiding principles. Let us continue cultivating a culture of respect where every voice is heard, every idea is considered, and every individual is celebrated for their unique contributions.

Cultivating Success Through Respect

Our path to success, marked by the creation of diverse enterprises, is a testament to the power of sustained effort and respect. Despite the occasional hurdles and misunderstandings, our commitment to care has been unwavering, enabling us to overcome challenges and thrive amidst adversity.

As we navigate the intricate landscape of opportunities and challenges, it becomes increasingly evident that our shared commitment to collaboration and empathy has been the cornerstone of our achievements. With every endeavor we undertake, we strive for excellence and foster a culture of inclusivity and support, ensuring that every voice is heard and every contribution is valued.

Together, we transcend boundaries and break barriers, emerging more substantial and more resilient with each shared success. Let us uphold the principles of unity and compassion, for they are the guiding stars illuminating our path toward a brighter, more prosperous future.

The Transformative Power of Attitude & Communication

Our early experiences, especially in our childcare business, underscored the significance of attitude and communication. Embracing the lessons of crucial conversations, we recognized the necessity of listening, engaging, and appreciating everyone we interact with. This shift improved our business operations and reinforced the importance of empathy and understanding in building influence.

This newfound perspective allowed us to foster deeper connections with our clients, employees, and partners. By actively listening and showing genuine appreciation for their views, we cultivated a culture of respect and collaboration within our childcare business. The ripple effect of this approach was profound, as it not only enhanced our day-to-day operations but also positively impacted the overall well-being of everyone involved.

As we prioritized open communication and empathy, we noticed a significant improvement in resolving conflicts and making decisions. By valuing diverse viewpoints and understanding each individual's unique needs, we created a harmonious environment where everyone felt heard and valued.

Our journey in the childcare business taught us that attitude and communication are not just tools for success but pillars of creating a thriving and inclusive community. The power of empathy, active listening, and appreciation cannot be understated, as they lay the foundation for building meaningful relationships and making a lasting impact in the lives of those we serve.

Strategic Relationship Building

Our focus on developing solid and respectful relationships transformed our business and personal interactions approach. By prioritizing connection and mutual respect, we saw remarkable growth and loyalty, underscoring the effectiveness of Carnegie's principles in real-world applications.

Our commitment to fostering genuine and respectful connections enhanced our business endeavors and enriched our interactions. This shift towards prioritizing understanding and respect brought about a significant positive impact, leading to unprecedented growth and unwavering loyalty from those around us. Implementing Carnegie's principles in our daily interactions was a powerful reminder of the profound influence mutual respect and genuine connection can have on both professional and personal spheres. By upholding these values, we achieve success and cultivate meaningful and lasting relationships that are the foundation for a fulfilling life.

The Likability Factor in Influence

As we shared in our previous work in *Volume 2: Likability Factor*, Tim Sanders' teachings on likability have struck a chord with us and guided our actions in forming meaningful connections. We have cultivated a network built on mutual trust and respect by embodying approachability, understanding, and authenticity. Our voyage stands as a testament to the profound impact of likability in nurturing cohesion and establishing a positive sway over others.

Reflections on Growth & Influence

As we navigate through the chapters of our narrative, we are reminded of the profound impact of embracing diversity and fostering unity. Just as Oprah Winfrey's wisdom has illuminated pathways to growth, we stand firm in our commitment to inclusivity and collaboration. With each step forward, we weave a tapestry of shared experiences and triumphs bound together by empathy and compassion. Our journey is not just a solitary path but a collaborative dance of harmony and progress, where every voice is heard, and every perspective is valued. Together, we continue to shape a narrative that celebrates the beauty of difference and the strength found in unity.

DAPHENE BOOKER-HARRIS & TODD HARRIS

About ToDario A. Harris: ToDario A. "Todd" Harris, NAREB, NAR, ABR, CCIM, is the founder and principal broker for Metropolis Real Estate Services. Todd Harris has brokered both commercial and residential real estate sells and lease transactions throughout his career.

As a preschool purchase and lease specialist, Todd Harris has provided clients with insight on how to evaluate a programs value, feasibility of acquisition, and facilities assessments. From start-up to business with real estate purchases, Todd Harris has the experience, skill, and expertise to get you to a desired end.
Mr. Harris has held two offices with the National Association of Real Estate Brokers (NAREB), local board President and Commercial Investment Division's National Treasurer. As the largest minority trade organization in the US, NAREB is an advocate for minority participation in the Nation's Housing Policies.

Mr. Harris attained the prestigious CCIM Designation in 2021. Todd is a graduate of the Fogelman College of Business located on the campus of the University of Memphis. Todd currently holds real estate brokerage licenses in Tennessee and Mississippi. He also consults clients and brokers throughout the United States.

About Daphene Booker-Harris: Daphene Booker-Harris, the Preschool Icon®, is changing the trajectory of children and families throughout the city of Memphis and beyond. As a much sought-after childcare consultant, she launched Global Preschool Consulting, designed to teach new and expanding childcare providers with proven blueprints and principles for building profitable childcare empires. When asked about the foundation of her work, she summed it up by saying, "We are creating achievers who will become leaders," which encapsulates her core philosophy about investing in the value and uniqueness of children, nurturing their intellectual genius, developing their overall health and wellness.

Through her GPS blueprint, Daphene's mission is to transform the childcare industry by empowering new and expanding owners through increased visibility, brand recognition, and profitability. Through any fallacy, Daphene's challenges have helped her become the success story she is today. Daphene Booker-Harris, the Preschool Icon®, is indeed a trustworthy GPS for a childcare business owner.

Authors' Websites: *www.MetropolisRealEstateServices.com & www.GlobalPreschoolConsulting.com*

Book Series Website: *www.TheBookofInfluence.com*

DAWNESE OPENSHAW

CREATING HARMONY IN ALIGNMENT

"Happiness is when what you think, what you say, and what you do are in harmony."
~ Mahatma Gandhi

Harmony…what a beautiful word.

I can hear a beautiful melody play out as I speak the very word harmony out loud or even hear it in my mind. It's a deep resonance that reaches into the core of my being like when hearing an orchestra coming together to play a classical masterpiece. I feel the energetic frequency coming from each of the instruments as they masterfully come together to create the music.

I hear the reverberating sounds of a well-trained and rehearsed symphony orchestra playing, whether I've heard it before in person or on a movie soundtrack. Imagine the sound of all those dozens of instruments (or more) flowing together to create something beautiful, something masterful, something magical. This is HARMONY!

Harmony is the outcome of creating alignment and synergy in any group of people, any team within any organization, including an orchestra, or even within a family. When alignment happens within a group of people, vision and authentic communication flow freely.

Without the harmony that comes through alignment, there is discord.

And what is discord?

Have you ever heard a middle school orchestra play? (I'm trying right now not to cover my ears as I make that scrunchy face of being ever so uncomfortable with the sound.) And if you haven't heard this sound with your ears firsthand, I am confident you can imagine what it may sound like. Maybe you can recall the sound that comes from an instrument being played by someone just beginning to learn how to play. Now imagine that times 40 instruments. This is the sound of discord.

In the symphony of influence, creating alignment is the conductor's baton, guiding disparate elements into a harmonious whole. Just as a skilled conductor ensures every instrument plays in sync, a master leader orchestrates alignment among individuals, teams, and organizations. Vision within an organization is accomplished because it's a symphony with a purpose, enabled through diverse individuals and perspectives harmonizing toward a common goal.

Alignment is the art of channeling diverse energies towards a unified goal, fostering synergy, and maximizing impact.

Alignment is more than mere agreement; it's the alignment of hearts, minds, and actions towards a shared vision. Like tuning a violin, it requires patience and precision, adjusting each string until they resonate in perfect harmony.

Picture a flock of birds flying in perfect formation or a team of dancers moving in sync with the rhythm of the music. In both cases, alignment emerges from a deep sense of connection and mutual understanding.

Creating alignment is not without its challenges, as individuals may resist change or cling to outdated paradigms. For a team to move forward with efficiency and effectiveness, everyone does not have to agree. Some individuals may even speak against what is being proposed. What creates alignment is when every voice and viewpoint gets to be heard and weighed out by the individuals as a whole.

When the team can clearly see the vision of what is being created, the collective vision becomes the lens for people to see what gets to be created to move things forward. Whether in business, politics, or social movements, alignment serves as the North Star guiding teams to their end goal.

When individuals feel they can speak authentically, it creates the kind of space that leads to powerful alignment. And where you create powerful alignment, you create powerful impact and influence.

Authenticity is the tuning fork of alignment, grounding interactions in truth and integrity. By cultivating open dialogue and mutual respect, leaders build bridges that span differences, fostering a culture of trust and collaboration.

The second book in this series, *The Book of Influence ~ Authentic Communication* is a great resource for understanding the benefits of authenticity and how you can incorporate it in your life, your business, on your team, and in your home.

Trust is the currency of alignment.

Trust is a precious commodity that must be earned through honesty, integrity, and reliability. Leaders who prioritize trust cultivate an environment where individuals feel safe to express themselves and take risks, knowing that their contributions as individuals will be valued and respected.

Transparency is the cornerstone of trust, fostering open communication and a culture of accountability. Leaders who embrace transparency invite feedback and collaboration, inviting others into the decision-making process and empowering them to take ownership of their actions.

Five Factors for Team Alignment:

1. **A Clear and Compelling Vision that Serves as the North Star**—the lens for everyone to see the why, how, and what of the organization.

2. **Authentic and Transparent Communication**—open, honest, sincere value-focused communication within team meetings as well as one-to-one conversations.

3. **An Inclusive and Open Environment**—a psychologically safe space where everyone can share their ideas and feel like they are contributing to the team and Vision as a whole, even if they are opposed to what's on the table.

4. **Trust**—everyone is valued as individual contributors and what they have to share and who they are matters.

5. **Responsibility**—each person on the team is 100% responsible for their role on the team and for being present, open, and committed to contributing to the common goal.

As Dale Carnegie communicated in his 7 Steps to Personal Growth, "Only you can take care of your personal development." You get to own your personal and professional growth as an individual and as someone who contributes to a team. Your team is wherever it is you may serve, whether at home, work, or within your church or community.

Something I've learned throughout my life is, if you want to be a great leader of others and create a powerful impact, you get to be a great leader of yourself first. In essence, learn to conduct the conductor.

Creating a harmonious alignment within any group of people or on any team begins with creating harmony within yourself as an individual. Learn to identify what your strengths are (I highly recommend Clifton Strengthfinders for this) and where you may have some weaknesses or blind spots.

How in the world do you create harmony within yourself and what does this even mean? Creating harmony within myself means discovering what my life vision is and living in alignment with that vision and my core life values.

Discovering your vision is a whole other chapter, but knowing what values are most important to you is pretty straightforward. You can generally tell what these are when someone says or does something that "triggers" or "activates" you. Whatever it is underneath that reaction is where your core value exists.

Example:

Parenting my children when they were younger, I noticed how triggered I would get when they would lie to me. No matter the lie, it absolutely drove me bonkers. As I got curious about this and explored what the root of this trigger was, it became clear to me how much I value honesty and integrity.

Once I took a values assessment, it was confirmed. In fact, integrity is one of my top three core values. So, I know that I get to show up in 100% integrity to be in harmony with myself. I also choose to surround myself with people in my social circles and build my business team with those who operate with integrity.

I also choose to be a part of organizations or teams that have integrity as a collective value, otherwise, I find I'm creating conflict within myself and creating discord instead of the resonance of harmony I desire. There are a couple of times I found myself working for an organization where integrity was spoken to be a value, but after a time I could see it was not being lived and knew it was time to gracefully exit.

Creating alignment and harmony within myself (body, heart, mind and spirit) means being congruent in how I show up in all the spaces of my life. When I show up congruently, it leads to me standing in a space of authentic power versus conditional power. The power that comes from this space is much like the resonance and sound of a symphony orchestra playing in beautiful harmony together.

Alignment truly can have a profound impact on our lives and the world around us. Just as a conductor guides a symphony, we too can orchestrate alignment among individuals, teams, and organizations, creating harmony by embracing authenticity, fostering open communication, and cultivating trust and collaboration. You can harness the power of alignment to drive meaningful change and create a future filled with unity, purpose, and possibility. Be a conductor of alignment in your own spheres of influence, leading with compassion, vision, and integrity, and together, let us create a symphony of harmony that reverberates throughout the world.

DAWNESE OPENSHAW

About Dawnese Openshaw: Dawnese Openshaw is a radically authentic John Maxwell certified leadership coach, trainer, and speaker. At the age of 14, her father had her read Dale Carnegie's *How to Win Friends and Influence People* and she has been a student of leadership ever since. With over 25 years of experience in small business and non-profit organizations creating and executing plans for growth, Dawnese offers marketing and strategy coaching for small businesses and training for non-profit boards.

Dawnese Openshaw Coaching expanded in 2020 to include families—supporting emotional regulation, communication, and relationship building. She combines her passion for leadership and commitment with strengthening families as a family empowerment coach, primarily serving families with teens. Dawnese empowers families to heal individually and as a unit, creating harmony in their home. She supports frustrated parents to love their kids again and not just like them.

She has been married to her husband, Scott, for 26 years and they are the parents of three amazing children, Randy, Thaniel, and Olivia, and one doodle named Tigger.

Author's Website: *www.DawneseOpenshaw.com*

Book Series Website: www.TheBookOfInfluence.com

DEE MANUEL CLOUD

THE ALIGNMENT OF INFLUENCE

Reflecting on the many experiences that have shaped my journey, I'm drawn to the pivotal concept of alignment. Dale Carnegie so eloquently discussed this principle, which transcends mere strategic alliances or superficial agreements. It represents a profound harmony between our inner truths and the outer world, between what we believe and how we act, between our soul's purpose and our earthly endeavors.

In essence, alignment is the synchronicity of our thoughts, intentions, and actions with the greater universe. When aligned, we move with a sense of ease and purpose, as if we are flowing effortlessly with the rhythm of life. This alignment allows us to tap into our true potential, unlocking doors to opportunities and experiences that resonate with our deepest desires.

Just like a perfectly tuned instrument produces harmonious melodies, alignment in our lives creates a symphony of fulfillment and joy. It is a powerful force that guides us towards our goals and dreams, helping us navigate challenges with resilience and grace.

As we strive to maintain alignment in our journey, we must cultivate self-awareness, authenticity, and mindfulness. By staying true to ourselves and honoring our values, we pave the way for a life filled with purpose and passion. So, let us embrace the transformative power of alignment and allow it to lead us toward a future brimming with possibility and fulfillment.

Interwoven with this concept, my narrative begins with an introspection triggered by a simple yet profound question: "When you hear the word alignment, what first comes to mind and why?" Instantly, my thoughts gravitate towards GUS—God, the universe, or spirit. This divine trinity, as I like to refer to it, encapsulates the essence of my understanding of alignment. It signifies a harmonious connection with a higher order, guiding me towards a path where everything falls into place.

In my journey of self-discovery, I've realized that alignment is not just a word but a state of being. It's the art of synchronizing my thoughts, actions, and intentions with the greater forces at play in the universe. Just like the celestial bodies move in perfect harmony, alignment beckons me to find my place in the grand orchestration of life.

As I delve deeper into the realms of alignment, I find solace in surrendering to the flow of existence, trusting that every step I take is guided by a wisdom far beyond my comprehension. Embracing this concept brings clarity and purpose to my endeavors and infuses me with a profound sense of peace and serenity.

So, when I ponder the question of alignment, it is not merely a matter of words but a profound realization of my interconnectedness with all that is. It reminds me that I am but a thread in the intricate tapestry of the universe, weaving my story in harmony with the cosmic design. And in the whispers of the wind and the dance of the stars, I find my alignment—my eternal connection with Gus, the divine trinity that shapes my existence.

The journey towards alignment has been challenging. It's been a pilgrimage marked by trials, transitions, and transformations. From the personal revelations of a difficult marriage to the liberating shifts post-divorce, each phase of my life has been a steppingstone toward understanding and embodying alignment.

Each step of the way, I've learned to embrace the lessons hidden within the twists and turns of fate. The struggles have refined me, shaping me into a stronger, wiser version of myself. Through the darkness, I discovered the light of self-discovery and acceptance.

Reflecting on the path behind me, I realize that alignment is not a fixed destination but a continuous journey of growth and self-realization. In these moments of vulnerability and resilience, I have found my true north, guiding me toward a more authentic and fulfilling existence.

With each hurdle overcome and every triumph celebrated, I have come to appreciate the intricate dance of life's challenges and blessings. Through it all, I have emerged as a testament to the power of resilience, courage, and the unwavering pursuit of alignment in all aspects of my being.

Delving into the depths of this concept, I draw upon my experiences and Dale Carnegie's teachings that resonate with the power of creating alignment. With his timeless wisdom, Carnegie taught us that alignment isn't merely a transactional relationship but a fundamental state of being that enhances our influence and impact. It's about aligning with people, energy, objects, theories, and belief systems. This alignment paves the way for meaningful connections, fostering influence and transcending conventional boundaries.

At the heart of my alignment journey is the pivotal role of faith and obedience to a higher calling. This was most evident when I ventured into the world of coaching and speaking, guided by a divine nudge towards serving others through my breast cancer journey. This leap of faith was not about pursuing success in its conventional sense but about aligning my desires with a purpose far more significant than myself. The transformation redefined success as the harmony between my aspirations and divine purpose.

In my coaching and speaking endeavors, I found myself drawn toward sharing my experiences and insights gained through overcoming breast cancer. The struggles and triumphs I faced became a beacon of hope for others navigating their challenges. Through each conversation and workshop, I witnessed the power of vulnerability and authenticity in creating deep connections and fostering growth. In these moments of shared humanity, I realized the true essence of success—not in accolades or material wealth, but in the impact made on hearts and souls. My alignment journey continues to evolve, guided by faith and a commitment to serving others with love and compassion.

Through my varied professional endeavors, I realized that alignment can shift the trajectory of our lives. Each transition from a legal career to adult education and real estate reflected my alignment search. It wasn't until I embraced stillness and listened to divine guidance that I found my true calling. This calling centered around supporting and inspiring others through their battles with breast cancer and illuminated the path of alignment for me. It was a testament to the power of aligning one's passion with one's purpose.

Reflecting on whether we are born with alignment or whether it is cultivated, it's a blend of both. We are born in a pure alignment, untainted by societal norms or expectations. Yet, as we journey through life, external influences may lead us astray, distancing us from our innate alignment. Through conscious effort, personal growth, and a deep connection with the divine, we rediscover and realign with our true essence.

As we navigate the complexities of life, it becomes apparent that the journey toward alignment is not a linear path. It is a continuous process of self-discovery and introspection. We must peel away the layers of conditioning and societal pressures to reveal our authentic selves. We gradually realign with our true essence by embracing our vulnerabilities, acknowledging our strengths, and nurturing our passions.

Cultivating practices nourishing our mind, body, and soul is essential. Whether through meditation, mindfulness, creativity, or connecting with nature, these rituals can guide our path to alignment. Surrounding ourselves with positive influences, supportive relationships, and a community that uplifts us can also aid in our quest to rediscover our innate alignment.

Ultimately, the journey towards alignment is a profoundly personal one. It is about honoring our uniqueness, embracing our imperfections, and finding peace in our authenticity. By staying true to ourselves and listening to the whispers of our hearts, we can navigate life's twists and turns with grace and resilience. Trust in the process, have faith in your inner wisdom, and remember that alignment is not a destination but a way of being.

This chapter, infused with my lived experiences and Dale Carnegie's wisdom, aims to illuminate the profound impact of creating alignment in our lives. It's a narrative of finding one's true north amidst the chaos, aligning with a purpose that transcends individual desires, and the transformative power of living in harmony with one's divine calling.

Alignment is the thread weaving our deepest desires with the universe's grand design. It is the bridge between our earthly existence and spiritual essence, a state of being where our actions, thoughts, and beliefs are in perfect harmony. As I share my journey and reflections on creating alignment, I hope to inspire you to embark on your quest for alignment, discover your unique path, and influence the world in ways only you can.

DEE MANUEL CLOUD

About Dee Manuel Cloud: Dee Manuel Cloud is a two-time breast cancer survivor, Breast Cancer Recovery Strategist, Best-Selling author, international speaker, and owner and CEO of Intentional Living Academy.

As a Breast Cancer Recovery Strategist, Dee helps survivors overcome the fear, trauma and suffering of breast cancer to creating a life of peace, joy, and fulfillment so they can thrive and rebuild their lives even better than before.

Understanding the unique life experiences and goals of breast cancer survivors enables Dee to create an action plan that supports survivors in moving beyond breast cancer to create their best life. Driven by the success of her clients, Dee prides herself on creating a personal and meaningful coaching experience that empowers survivors to achieve their goals and make the rest of their lives the best of their lives.

Dee is the author of *Beauty In The Breakdown, Finding Peace In The Midst of Life's Disruptions*.

Author's Website: *www.DeeManuelCloud.com*

Book Series Website: *www.TheBookofInfluence.com*

DIANA SMITH

MY ALIGNMENT JOURNEY

In my journey through life, I've encountered moments that have not only tested my resolve but also offered profound insights into the essence of human interaction. One such revelation came unexpectedly, stemming from an innocent query about my facial expression, which, unbeknownst to me, broadcasted a message contrary to my inner warmth and kindness. This encounter set me on a path to explore the principles of alignment, influenced significantly by the work of Dale Carnegie, who championed the art of influencing others through understanding and empathy.

"Are you okay? Are you worried about something?" These questions, posed by a stranger, were the catalyst for a profound self-examination. Initially taken aback by the nerve of the question, I soon realized it was a mirror reflecting an aspect of myself I had ignored. My daughter's explanation of my resting expression, which she described with a term I found both shocking and amusing, was a revelation. It underscored a disconnect between my internal state and the image I projected.

Embarking on a quest for alignment, I sought to bridge this gap to ensure my external demeanor accurately reflected my inner self. The challenge was akin to navigating a labyrinth, with each turn offering lessons in self-awareness and the power of non-verbal communication.

I reflected on the memories of my mother and grandmother, both of whom, despite their scowls, were beacons of strength and love in my life. While initially daunting, this genetic inheritance became a puzzle I was determined to solve. How could I honor my lineage while embracing a more open and inviting presence?

The answer lay in Carnegie's principles, particularly the importance of smiling genuinely to create a positive first impression and foster goodwill. This simple yet profound advice guided my efforts to transform my resting expression into one of openness and approachability.

Venturing into public spaces, I observed the myriad expressions of those around me, noting how a smile, a nod, or a spark of warmth in the eyes often preceded moments of genuine connection. These observations underscored the universal language of facial expressions and their impact on interpersonal relationships.

Embracing the concept of "fake it 'til you make it," I consciously adjusted my facial expressions, particularly in social situations. This exercise, though challenging, gradually became second nature. By lifting my cheeks into a slight smile and infusing my eyes with life, I could alter the atmosphere around me, inviting more open and positive interactions.

This journey of alignment, rooted in the desire to harmonize my inner self with my outward expression, taught me invaluable lessons about the power of non-verbal communication. It illuminated the subtle ways we influence others and underscored the importance of empathy, kindness, and genuine interest in the well-being of those around us.

In alignment with Carnegie's teachings, I learned that influencing others begins with understanding oneself. By embracing my unique expression and working to align it with my intentions, I fostered better relationships and cultivated a more profound sense of self-awareness.

As I continue to navigate the complexities of human interaction, I am reminded of the importance of authenticity, empathy, and the pursuit of alignment. These principles, championed by Carnegie and reflected in my journey, serve as beacons guiding us toward more meaningful and fulfilling connections.

Ultimately, my exploration of alignment and influence, sparked by an offhand comment about my facial expression, has been a transformation journey. It has taught me that while we may inherit certain traits, we have the power to shape how we present ourselves to the world. Through intentional effort and an understanding of the principles of human interaction, we can foster environments of understanding, cooperation, and mutual respect.

The alignment journey is ongoing, a perpetual learning, adapting, and growing process. As I reflect on my path, I am grateful for the lessons learned and the opportunities for connection that have arisen from a willingness to explore the depths of my expression and its impact on the world around me.

When we embrace the principles of alignment and influence, we find that the essence of meaningful interaction lies not in changing who we are but in aligning our outward expressions with our inner truths. This alignment, rooted in authenticity and empathy, is the foundation for building more robust, positive relationships, personally and professionally.

DIANA SMITH

About Dinky Diana Smith: Diana suffered many abuses in her childhood, which left her unsure about her own adulthood and trusting others in her life. By 1979, she had two biological daughters. Poverty-stricken and with nowhere to go, she learned to survive in a world of doubt and desperation. In 2011, Diana's youngest child was killed by a drunk driver on her birthday. Diana suffered grief and severe depression for seven long years.

Diana researched mental health to understand the effects on her own mental well-being. She is writing a memoir of her loss and a book on parenting called *If My Brain Had Wheels*. She is a motivational speaker on mental health regarding depression and childhood abuse.

Diana met and married a wonderful man after her move to Colorado. Together, they have five children, four grandchildren, and two great-grandsons. Life has gotten much better for her.

Author's Website: *www.TheFWord.biz*

Book Series Website: *www.TheBookofInfluence.com*

EILEEN GALBRAITH

TRANSFORMING YOUR LIFE THROUGH AUTHENTIC LISTENING

What do the actions you take, the decisions you make, and the way you behave all have in common? They all help to create your core values, your goals, your beliefs, and define your true purpose in life. This, in turn signifies your alignment, not only with yourself, but with others you meet throughout your lifetime. When you are in alignment, there is a sense of **Authenticity and Integrity** in everything you do.

Let's investigate this a little deeper. Your actions and choices reflect the fundamental beliefs and principles that matter most to you. There is a clear correlation between what you believe in and how you behave. Some would classify this as your **Core Values**. It signifies a state of harmony and congruence between your inner values and the way you conduct yourself in the external world.

Some would say that you are **Living with Purpose**. You have a clear understanding of your overarching purpose in life, and your actions are directed towards fulfilling that purpose. Your daily activities are meaningful and contribute to your sense of fulfillment. When faced with choices, you make decisions that align with your values and long-term goals. This ensures that your actions are in line with your higher aspirations.

Most would agree that there is a sense of inner peace and harmony, as there is little to no internal conflict about the choices you make. You have clarity about what matters most to you.

Being in alignment empowers you. You feel confident in your decisions because they are grounded in those core values and beliefs we mentioned earlier. Oftentimes, it leads to a sense of contentment, satisfaction, and a feeling of being on the right path.

Have you ever encountered a moment when you felt you were more effective and productive in your endeavors because your actions were purposeful and directed towards your goals? If so, you've experienced being fully aligned in your purpose.

Let's back up a bit and review what we mean when we hear or read the term Core Values. While there are hundreds of terms one may identify with when they are defining their individual core values, whether it be in their personal or business life, I will speak to the top 30 common Core Values that many people consider important:

Integrity, Honesty, Authenticity, Respect, Empathy, Compassion, Accountability, Responsibility, Fairness, Equality, Trustworthiness, Dependability, Loyalty, Transparency, Open-mindedness, Inclusivity, Diversity, Innovation, Creativity, Adaptability, Flexibility, Courage, Perseverance, Ambition, Drive, Self-discipline, Independence, Teamwork, Collaboration, Empowerment.

Integrity is a word that will vary in definition to each individual. For me, it is consistently choosing honesty and moral principles in all situations, doing what you say you will do. You will add your perspective to your beliefs. Honesty, one's moral compass, implores each of us to choose how we will communicate, hopefully without deceit or manipulation.

Take the time and research the different values and go through them, one by one; circle the ones that you most identify with. Eventually, you will narrow them down to about 5. These will become YOUR Core Values. Implement them into your lifestyle, in your personal and business life. They are your compass that allows you to stay in alignment with those core values.

Being in alignment is a dynamic and evolving process. It requires self-awareness, regular reflection, and a willingness to adapt as circumstances change. It's a conscious effort to ensure that your actions are in harmony with your deepest values and sense of purpose. Review the list of Core Values and choose your top 5—some are similar in definition and may be combined, others are stand-alone values. Choose those that resonate with you and complement your desired purpose in life.

Since the title of this chapter speaks to Authentic Living, let me be clear here: YOU get to decide what this means to you. The word Authentic will differ to each one of us depending on our core values and our purpose in our lives.

For me, and I'm sure many readers will agree, to be authentic is being true to oneself, embracing individuality, and expressing one's beliefs openly. Simply, just be yourself! As long as you are steadfast in knowing who you are, identifying YOUR core values and living in alignment with them, you cannot help but be able to be an influential individual.

Remember, when you are in alignment, you are better equipped to face challenges and setbacks. Your sense of purpose provides motivation and resilience. You can inspire and positively influence those around you.

So, now that we know that your core values, aligned with your actions and choices, reflect the fundamental beliefs and principles that matter most to you, how does one determine what they truly are, what are the next steps? I am a firm believer in actionable steps to achieve a goal.
Here is what I would do, if I wanted to really understand how to transform my life through Authentic Living, known as **The Alignment Effect:**

Create your list of your core values by asking yourself the following in any situation:

1. What Is Important to Me That Will Guide My Actions and Decisions?

Reflect back on past situations, recall what has shown up at that time and why you made the decisions you made—what were the common threads?

2. What Qualities or Traits Do I See in Others that I Admire and Why?

Think about those that you admire, whether they are friends, family members, public figures, or historical figures. Identify the qualities and traits in them that resonate with you. These qualities can serve as a starting point for defining your own core values.

3. What Aspects of Life Bring Me the Most Fulfillment and Satisfaction?

Consider the activities, experiences, and moments in your life that have brought you the greatest sense of fulfillment and satisfaction. Explore the common themes or values that underlie these moments, as they can offer insights into what truly matters to you.

By asking yourself these questions, you can gain a deeper understanding of the principles and values that are most important to you, ultimately helping you choose your core values with greater clarity and intention. Then, aligning them with your true purpose in life will lead to a greater life of fulfillment and leads to a true transformational Journey!

Now, live these values to their fullest. When you find yourself falter, and you will, simply do self-reflection and notice where you are, how you are feeling about the choice you just made and compare it to your core values.

I'm always asking myself these questions, too: "Am I living at my fullest potential? Do I attract that which I truly value in my life? Is my purpose being fulfilled every day of my life? What can I do more of to create the life I Desire?" And my most important question of all is, "Why do I do what I do?"

When you can answer these and many more you will come up with, I believe you are truly in alignment with authentic living and your true purpose.

EILEEN GALBRAITH

About Eileen E. Galbraith: As a Financial Architect for Business, entrepreneurs hire Eileen to build their influence and scale their profits because most lack essential methods and channels to create success, lack funding opportunities, and may face continuous struggles resulting in business disarray. So, Eileen helps them define, align, and design a visible, credible, and sustaining business. Financial disarray is a precursor to failure—do not let that happen to your business!

Eileen is a Compassionate Kick-ass Coach. She can kick your butt in financial shape and make things happen, but she's also very compassionate. She knows what people need, what they want, and how to deliver it.

Eileen is a Certified FICO Pro, an International Best-Selling Author and Speaker, a sought-after Business Success Coach, and the Founder of Renewed Abundance and Credit Knowhow. She has run multi-million-dollar businesses throughout her career and increased cash flow and profitability throughout her markets. Recognized as a professional Business Coach, Eileen positions her clients toward optimal possibilities, such as optimizing their personal credit to position themselves to build credit in the name of their business. This all-important step opens the doors to Financial Creditability, Fundability, and Business Growth.

Eileen has a high-energy, no-nonsense approach and loves supporting people with their goals. Just look for the Dancing Queen, and you will find Eileen!

Author's Website: *www.CreditKnowhow.biz*

Book Series Website: *www.TheBookofInfluence.com*

ELIZABETH ANNE WALKER

ALIGNING YOUR TRUE NORTH

I realized this as I pondered the flickering candlelight on a quiet evening. It wasn't just about liking myself or seeking approval from others. It was about aligning with my true purpose, echoing Dale Carnegie's legacy in my journey. Much like the stories I've shared and learned from, this alignment journey begins with an introspective quest and leads to creating impactful connections rooted in authenticity and shared values.

In my earlier days, I was akin to a chameleon, adapting and molding myself to be the person I believed everyone wanted me to be. I was the beacon of success, the one whose words were gospel and whose presence symbolized achievement. But as the tide of public opinion shifted, I found myself adrift, a 'has been' in the eyes of the world.

Dale Carnegie once illuminated the path of influence through genuine interest in others, empathy, and the power of appreciation. Reflecting upon his teachings, I realized that my journey was not merely about likability but about creating alignment—within myself and with those around me.

The essence of creating alignment lies not in the outward exhibition of likability but in the inward journey of understanding one's values, principles, and the immutable truth of one's purpose. It's about the courage to stand firm in your beliefs, even when the winds of change threaten to sway you.

Consider the story of an inventor who was secluded and immersed in his work, initially unnoticed and unliked. Yet, his contributions revolutionized lives, aligning his inner purpose with the needs of humanity. His story wasn't about seeking likability but steadfast dedication to his mission, aligning his work with the greater good.

The narrative of the prom king and queen basking in the glow of their popularity reminds us that external validation is fleeting. Proper alignment comes from building a legacy, not on the fragile foundation of societal approval, but on the solid ground of contributing to a cause greater than oneself.

In the world of business and beyond, likability has its place. However, the deeper, more enduring connection comes from alignment. When leaders and individuals align their actions with their core values and the collective vision of their teams or communities, they create an environment where trust, respect, and genuine collaboration flourish.

As I embark on this journey of realignment, I am reminded of the crucial questions that guide our paths: Who do I choose to be? How do I choose to act? With whom do I align my efforts? What version of myself brings me joy and fulfillment?

In this pursuit of alignment, likability becomes a byproduct, not the goal. It's about being authentic, moral, and true to your values. It's about leading with empathy, listening deeply, and recognizing the importance of others. Dale Carnegie wisely taught us these are the cornerstones of creating lasting impact and influence.

To those who feel like 'has beens,' remember: this is merely a sign to realign, to turn up the volume on your true self. Choose your path with intention, act authentically, and align with those who share your vision and values.

In the quiet moments of self-reflection, I hear the echoes of my grandfather, Angus George Suthers: "Blow your own trumpet, girly—no one else will!" But now, I understand it's not just about being heard; it's about playing a tune that resonates with your true north, creating a symphony of aligned actions and purposeful living.

In this book, "The Book of Influence," I invite you on a journey of alignment inspired by Dale Carnegie's timeless principles and infused with personal insights and stories. Let's discover the power of aligning with our true selves and creating a legacy of genuine influence and connection.

ELIZABETH ANNE WALKER

About Elizabeth Walker: Elizabeth is Australia's leading Female Integrated NLP Trainer, an international speaker with Real Success, and the host of Success Resources' (Australia's largest and most successful events promoter, including speakers such as Tony Robbins and Sir Richard Branson) inaugural Australian Women's Program, "The Seed."

Elizabeth has guided many people to achieve complete personal breakthroughs and phenomenal personal and business growth. With over 25 years of experience transforming the lives of hundreds of thousands of people, Elizabeth's goal is to assist leaders in creating the reality they choose to live, impacting millions on a global scale.

A thought leader who has worked alongside people like Gary Vaynerchuck, Kerwin Rae, Jeffery Slayter, and Kate Gray, Elizabeth has an outstanding method of delivering heart with business.

As a former lecturer in medicine at the University of Sydney and lecturer in nursing at Western Sydney University, Elizabeth was instrumental in the research and development of the stillbirth and neonatal death pathways, ensuring each family in Australia went home knowing what happened to their child, and felt understood, heard, and seen.

A former Australian Champion in Trampolining and Australian Dance sport, Elizabeth has always been passionate about the mindset and skills required to create the results you are seeking.

Author's Website: *www.ElizabethAnneWalker.com*

Book Series Website: *www.TheBookOfInfluence.com*

ERIN LEY

HOW TO WIN THE GAME OF LIFE

In *How To Win Friends And Influence People*, Dale Carnegie brilliantly states, *"The two highest levels of influence are achieved when:*

1. *People follow you because of what you've done for them.*
2. *People follow you because of who you are.*

In other words, the highest levels of influence are reached when generosity and trustworthiness surround your behavior."

We are the sum of the five people we're surrounded by, and I believe that our character dictates who those five people are. I've been fortunate in life to be surrounded by the most amazing family and friends. With that said, I didn't always feel like I was fully aligned with who I truly am.

In my early twenties I was working on Wall Street, fully licensed, in the late eighties and early nineties. After a few years I felt completely unaligned with who I am. I began conforming and capitulating when it came to my boundaries, and I began tolerating way more than I would have. It was a free-for-all at that time where I witnessed and was on the receiving end of complete insanity. Feeling trapped is an understatement because of my financial commitments such as a new car, a payment for a rented Hampton house with friends, and a certain financial income I was used to when I was making more money than most of my friends.

Then I was diagnosed with non-Hodgkins lymphoblastic lymphoma, a rare and extremely lethal form of cancer in 1991 with a two-and-a-half-year protocol. It was at that time where I began to create alignment with myself and those around me. It was nerve-wracking and yet an exciting time as well.

I began reading personal and professional development books which introduced me to a whole inner world I never knew existed. Quite honestly, I was incredibly superficial before finding out about the hidden power we have within us. I was outer-world based and looked to the outer-world for validation for everything, how smart I was, how pretty I was, how successful I would become. Everyone outside of me was going to tell me. I took my personal power and handed it over to those around me on a silver platter daily. I believe that most of us are programmed and conditioned to do that without realizing it.

Once I began tapping into this hidden power through meditation, visualization, and affirmations, I became stronger and more aligned with myself than I ever was. There were guys I worked with who drove to my house to apologize for how they treated me at work. They knew I was strong and withstood a lot in the workplace all the while never compromising my values and morals. Then they witnessed me in the fight for my life and I was winning. After creating alignment within, I created alignment in the outer world with the people, places, and things I experienced.

The cancer brought me deep within, to the core of my being, where I found myself. The courage and confidence I experienced shaped me into the woman I am today.

At the time, I called everyone I felt like I had resentment towards and cleared the air. I practiced a lot of forgiveness, and I let go of what I couldn't control regarding others. The energy around my relationships with others became pure.

Fairly recently, in 2016 I became officially divorced from my ex-husband. Once again, my identity was thrown in the air, my future became questionable, and it was very similar to the cancer diagnosis. I temporarily lost my feeling of alignment with myself and with others. I was so confused as to who I was once again.

When I was experiencing low-vibration feelings such as guilt, shame, anger, resentment, fear, all disempowering feelings, so many negative circumstances began to happen. My hot water heater flooded my basement, my car was hit from behind which required six surgeries on my lower back, and when I was in the supermarket with my daughter who was only thirteen years old at the time, I had five dollars and prayed it would be enough for the milk and bread for my three children. My ex-husband stopped paying child support and I had to take him back to court.

As I walked out of the supermarket, I thought to myself that I must change my mindset. These are exactly the steps I did with the cancer, divorce, and now daily:

1. Meditate within the first seventeen seconds of waking up on abundance and well-being.
2. Write out what I am grateful for.
3. Write out a crystal-clear vision of exactly what I want to create over the next twelve months.
4. Write and read aloud my affirmations three times in the morning, six times in the afternoon, and nine times in the evening (Nikola Tesla's 3 6 9 Method for manifesting).
5. Play my list of empowering songs.
6. Dance around the bathroom as I get ready for the day–movement is medicine.
7. Set my state by saying Thank you God for me waking up. There's sixteen hours of pure potential, sixteen hours of endless opportunity ahead of me today. I can't wait to see the people, places, and things you have in store for me today.

As I began to get my mindset under control by only entertaining the thoughts that were empowering and rejecting the negative disempowering thoughts, my whole life changed. I went from caring way too much about what the neighbors thought like I did when I was much younger, to not personalizing anything at all. That alone was incredibly freeing and freedom on every level was my goal.

Our results in life are a direct reflection of the thoughts we think, the actions we take, and our self-image. If you're not getting the results in life that you want, become aware of the thoughts you're thinking. Awareness is key. In order to create alignment, you need to become self-aware.

During the divorce, family and friends insisted I get a job. I knew I could grow my business in a magnificent way, and I didn't allow self-doubt to enter my mind. Self-doubt is a dream crusher. I stopped everything during the divorce because I was shocked and heartbroken by the situation. My sister was diagnosed with cancer at the same time, and I became the point of contact based on my past. I had to stop everything I did in my business to focus on the family. How could I empower anyone if I felt disempowered?

During that time my ex-husband began playing games with child support which motivated me to snap out of the illusion of fear I was in, and I began to grow my business in the most miraculous ways. I was completely transparent and authentic in my communication as I was building my business once again.

While networking again in 2016 I said, "I have no idea how to say what I do in my business in thirty seconds. I'm newly divorced with three young kids. I haven't networked since the eighties. I've been a Life Coach and Business Strategist for decades, I have written a bunch of books on personal development, speak on stages to inspire people, and have a radio show called *Onward And Upward With Erin Ley* on *Blog Talk Radio*."

Everyone I encountered was incredibly kind, compassionate, and helpful. Some of my best friends I have today came from the networking I did back then.

My life and business grew in the most miraculous ways. My children who are now twenty-one, twenty-two, and twenty-six years old and I are doing so well and I keep saying that I've never been happier, healthier, and wealthier in my life than I am these days. I say on a daily basis, "Thank you Ronnie Ley for inspiring me to live my best life."

Things that seem to be traumatic at the time turn out to be our biggest blessings. I know this is the case for me regarding cancer and divorce. These days, I teach, preach, and live by creating and maintaining alignment, with myself and others. And not just alignment, I'm talking about the most powerful authentic alignment.

Never give in to fear and self-doubt. Love, forgiveness, and confidence are the keys to life. What someone says or does to us is meaningless compared to our reaction to their words or actions. A tree has everything it's going to become in the acorn. When it's fully grown, it doesn't wonder if it has too many branches. It becomes the full expression of exactly what it was designed to become. I want that for you as well.

I'll leave you with a quote I made up in 1991 in the hospital bed in Memorial Sloan Kettering Cancer Center, "Celebrate life and you'll have a life worth celebrating."

Always remember to live onward and upward. Feel free to reach out to me at *www.ErinLey.com* if you need help doing exactly that.

ERIN LEY

About Erin Ley: As Founder and CEO of Onward Productions, Inc., Erin Ley has spent the last 30 years as an Author, Professional Speaker, Personal and Professional Empowerment and Success Coach predominantly around mindset, vision and decision. Founder of many influential summits, including "Life On Track," Erin is also the host of the upcoming online streaming T.V. show, "Life On Track with Erin Ley," which is all about helping you get into the driver's seat of your own life.

They call Erin "The Miracle Maker!" As a cancer survivor at age 25, single mom of 3 at age 47, successful Entrepreneur at age 50, Erin has shown thousands upon thousands across the globe how to become victorious by being focused, fearless, and excited about life and your future! Erin says, "Celebrate life and you'll have a life worth celebrating!"

To see more about Erin and the release of her 4th book, "WorkLuv: A Love Story," along with her "Life On Track" Course & Coaching Programs, please visit her website.

Author's Website: *www.ErinLey.com*

Book Series Website & Author's Bio: *www.TheBookOfInfluence.com*

FATIMA HURD

CLARITY & YOUR INNER COMPASS

Dale Carnegie mentions the three Cs as the first principle: "Don't criticize, condemn, or complain."

When I think about this, I often take into consideration referring to others. I find that oftentimes, the main person we direct these three Cs towards is more towards ourselves. We are the hardest on ourselves. We are quick to criticize, condemn, and or complain about ourselves quicker than we do to others.

I am 100% guilty of doing this. I spent many years looking for the answers to success outside of me; I thought success came from the exterior surroundings and never thought to look inward to understand the lack of success in certain areas of my life. I read many books, often hoping to find answers that mentioned looking inward, but it never dawned on me to ponder what that meant. Recently, I went through a journey of awakening.

Again, oftentimes times I was seeking to find the answer to the magic of success through books.

I discovered that my lack of success came from the lack of understanding of who I was and what I wanted in life. What I thought I wanted was influenced by the outside world—and the expectations I placed on myself.

Alignment is creating boundaries that help us live our lives with integrity of who we are. The reason I was so quick to condemn and criticize myself was because the choices I made were never in alignment with who I am and what I want. The negative thoughts and feelings came from the internal conflict of not being comfortable with self-expression and going against my truth. As a child, I was not allowed to speak my truth: I was always told how to feel, and what to do—but as an adult, I had no excuse. Yet something was still holding me back from expressing myself freely and allowing myself to create healthy boundaries that at the time seemed to me to be selfish.

I used to cringe when I would think about the word selfish; with time, I've come to embrace it. As a child, all I ever heard was a negative tone attached to the selfish. I remember always being told I shouldn't be selfish and that I needed to share, but why? That set the tone for the habits and the negative effect it had on my adult life. All my life, I felt burdened with always playing nice, or thinking about the person's feelings first before mine. And where did that get me, allowing others to advantage of me? I would find myself constantly struggling emotionally, mentally, physically, and financially. Who paid the price? My family and I did.

There was such a repetitive pattern in my life; I made myself an easy target. My sympathy and compassion for others made me vulnerable to others who saw it as an opportunity to take advantage. There were many times I felt it all through my body that something wasn't right, but I chose to ignore it. At any point, I could have spoken up and expressed how I felt, but I never did. I always stayed quiet, at the cost of my peace of mind.

Whenever I would deny myself the opportunity to express how I felt, I'd pay the price later. This came in the form of anger and frustration, depression. This of course would take its toll on my mental, and physical health which would manifest for days or weeks as depression. After beating myself up, I would come out of it, until I would go through the same process. I didn't know this obviously at that time, this I had to figure out like I have everything else in my life.

When I finally decided to stop sweeping it under the rug and sit with this, it hit me. One day, I was sitting at my desk contemplating how the heck things get so bad. In December of 2023, I found myself in bad place mentally. Things at work had gotten to be too much. I remember waking up and thinking to myself every day, "Do I have PTO?" Every day all I did was criticize, complain, and condemn everything I've done wrong in my life. Gratitude was always the center of my being, but in that very moment, I just couldn't feel anything.

One day, I was listening to an audiobook. In the book, they made mention of a young lady who loved animals and all her life all she ever heard was that she was going to be a vet when she grew up. She went to college to get her degree as a veterinarian, and towards the end, she ended up going on a trip where she discovered she didn't want to be a vet. She wanted to be a speaker and work with the youth. And she did. I was inspired.

That is when it dawned on me, how many times do we tell ourselves we are good at something and stay prisoners of that belief even though in our being, we are entirely misaligned with that idea? I loved working with kids, and I can't tell you how many times I was told to go back to school to get my credentials for teaching because I was good at working with kids. I knew that was not my calling, or at least not in that environment.

However, being told that gave me a state of importance, thinking I was really good at something—but I was not really enjoying it. I wanted to believe I did, and I stayed. But all I did was complain, condemn, and criticize because I was unhappy. I felt stuck. I was comfortable, and being there gave me a sense of importance. This became clear to me when I chose to take the leap and move on to another job.

Things got tight, and my car broke down. At this point, I needed a new car. My wonderful husband started looking into purchasing me a new car that we could afford. I remember him showing me different vehicles and me thinking, "Why can't I just buy the car I want?" Well, we can't afford the car I wanted; why did I ask? I knew why, the logical answer was I didn't make enough money.

Well, I was done at the point where I decided that I was going to buy the car I wanted and it was an Audi, we didn't have the money, but my husband had fantastic credit. I got my car, the one I wanted, because that's what I wanted! I felt immense gratitude that I got to choose the car I wanted, and I enjoyed driving it even though, at the time, I did not how I was going to pay for the car; I knew I would figure it out. And that meant getting another job.

I realized that I was comfortable at my job, but staying was not an option. I prayed for God to lead me as he always has done. Then it hit me: a friend of mine worked a AT&T. She had a base pay and worked off commission. I was nervous because the truth is I never worked a commission job before, but I was good with people. And I know she was making good money. I took the leap of faith and called her. I started my job in less than a week.

Going back to knowing that it was ego keeping stuck, I realized this when I put in my resignation to my position. Everyone kept asking why I was quitting. I remember a teacher asking me and telling me how much she was going to miss me, and how good I was at helping the students. She saw a significant improvement in some of the students I worked with and she was proud of them. I remember pausing or a moment and thinking, "Do I really want to tell her?" My own opinion about the job was that it was under me, but why? So, I owned it and told her I was going to work at AT&T selling phone service plans.

She looked at me and said, "Well, I know you will excel there too." I thought for a minute why I felt so nervous telling her and realized why it had taken me so long to leave. One, they loved me, and saw so much potential in me, and two, I was humbled by this experience because it made me realize that most of the time, we get in our own way to keep us safe. My ego wants to feel important, and it did at the school district. Because we all want to feel important, it's human nature, and I was making a difference, or was I?

I moved on and started my job, the money was great, and I learned so much about myself. I felt that my new job played a vital role in discovering who I was. I realized that I had to own it, and I did.

My new job was very different from what I was used to. But I know now why I am here. I realized that being nice would get me in a lot of trouble. See, when I first started, I didn't realize the elephant in the room when it comes to sales. I learned quickly that in sales, you can't always be nice, because, at the end of the day, that could potentially take money away from your pocket. I experienced the different side, staying in integrity and learning to maximize your talents to sell with integrity.

So, my choice to work there came with the price of not seeing my family, so being nice and giving away my sales to my coworkers who were not meeting their sales quotas was a disservice to myself, my family, and them. The first two months I learned quickly that as much as I wanted to help, I learned to say no, whenever asked if they could help them with giving up my sales.

However, I'm all about teamwork—I helped in other ways. I helped them by suggesting ways that would help them sell more. I think that helping them that way is a lot more valuable than giving them something I worked for, and that was in alignment with me, not giving them my sales because they were not meeting theirs. In the end, working here also awakened my competitive side, how to take in the good with the bad and keep the balance. When I don't have a great day, I give myself grace and know that the next day is mine, which keeps the moment going. Staying in alignment with what truly makes you happy is essential to winning in life.

I know now that when I am not aligned, I have to look inward and see what boundaries are sacrificing are keeping me misaligned with my true purpose because, remember, it's not just about the destination it's about the journey. I know there is more to come, and my advice is that when things are not looking out how you want them to first look at what you are settling for, that is not aligned with your purpose because that is when we get stuck. I understand now what all the self-help books mean when you don't have clarity that interferes with your inner compass.

FATIMA HURD

About Fatima Hurd: Fatima is the Owner and Photographer of Fatima Hurd Photography. Fatima enjoys working with entrepreneurs because it allows her to create images that truly capture the essence of who people are by being intentional with their content, so it aligns with their target audience.

She is a partner with *City Lifestyle* magazine and captures the photos of their business partners through Branding and event photography.

With over ten years of photography experience under her belt, Fatima's photography career has evolved into supporting her clients by coaching them to be confident and authentic in front of her camera.

Fatima has an extensive background in energy and self-development work. She is a 10X Best-Selling Author in *The 13 Steps to Riches* book series. She has leveled up her photography business by adding coaching to her services. She coaches her clients to feel safe and inspired to create change in their lives and see life through a new lens filled with endless possibilities!

Author's Website: *www.FatimaHurd.com*

Book Series Website: *www.TheBookOfInfluence.com*

FRED MOSKOWITZ

CREATING A WIN-WIN THROUGH STRATEGIC PARTNERSHIPS

Strategic partnerships provide an opportunity for people to come together, to scale and grow a business, and to be a part of something larger than themselves. Partnerships work best when each of the individual member partners bring to the table differing and complementary strengths and skill sets. When it comes to strategic partnerships, it is vitally important for everyone involved to have a shared understanding of the business strategy and objectives, and to agree on an aligned strategy. And, in having created this aligned strategy, one of the major benefits is that it creates value for all parties involved. When embarking on a strategic partnership, consider that there are clear benefits for each party.

Before starting out, partners must ask themselves some hard introspective questions about the partnership. Can we work well together? Is there compatibility between us? Are our goals complimentary? Are the skillsets and strengths that we bring to the table complimentary? Below are four primary elements that help to develop a success-oriented partnership:

Mission & Vision

It is essential to have an alignment of core values, vision, mission, and purpose. This is accompanied by a sharing of mutual goals. There is an agreed buy-in and commitment from everyone involved. Consider that the objectives do not need to match exactly, however they should be in line and largely congruent with each other.

Equitable Sharing of Responsibilities & Work

To ensure enduring success, roles and responsibilities should be divided in an equitable manner. Partnerships often fail when one or more of the partners begin to get the sense that they are shouldering a disproportionate share of the workload and responsibilities.

Open Communication & Transparency

Fostering an environment of open communication and transparency helps to bring alignment into a business setting. The open and consistent sharing of information and updates with everyone in the partnership helps to keep all members engaged and involved. With this information, each individual contributor is able to better understand the big picture along with how their work and individual contributions align with the overall business objectives.

Engagement & Involvement of Each Individual

Alignment is also created through the active involvement and empowerment of each individual contributor. Everyone becomes more engaged when they have an opportunity to contribute ideas and to know that their voice is heard.

When a partnership is successful and has come to a conclusion, there will not be a question in anyone's mind if success has been achieved. At the end of the project, everyone comes away with a feeling of accomplishment and celebration. The flow of conversation then shifts to an energy of, "That was great, and now what's next?"

What are the ingredients for creating alignment?

- Well-defined goals and objectives. It is imperative that these are memorialized in writing when the partnership is formed.
- Honest and open channels of communication at all times.

- All parties are interested and fully invested (financially, energetically, and emotionally) in the ongoing success of the enterprise. Everyone feels that they are working independently while at the same time sharing equally in both the risks and rewards.
- A high level of trust and depth of interpersonal relationships among the partners.

Have you ever been in a canoe or other boat with two or more people paddling? If you have, you can relate to the idea that all the paddlers must work in coordination and in harmony in order for the canoe to move swiftly and accurately towards its destination. If not, the canoe will begin to rotate or spiral in the water, and even though it may be moving, it makes no progress towards reaching its destination.

How Not to Form a Partnership

Sometimes, partnerships or "joint ventures" do not go well. It is easy for people to be misled or experience disappointments from not understanding the rules of the game, which must be clearly defined and spelled out in advance by all parties involved.

While many people enter into a partnership with good intentions and a fair amount of innocence, without proper planning and due diligence it can quickly turn into a failing business complete with fallout stemming from financial, emotional, and relational losses. As soon as someone begins to feel that they are being taken advantage of, or that one or more people are not pulling their weight in the partnership, it becomes a very slippery slope.

I'd like to share a personal story from my own experience. About a decade ago I was invited to join a partnership opportunity with seven other people to form a business. The idea was that all of us would put in our capital which was used to jumpstart the business, and then we would divide the work among the eight of us and split the profits in the end. The time period for this partnership was to be for 2 years, and at the end each of us would take our capital and then go our separate ways. Things got started out on the right track; however, after about 9 months, a pattern began to emerge in that only three of us were actually doing the work. What happened was that the other five individuals contributed their capital and then did not participate very much except for showing up to our monthly meetings.

Our mistake was that we did not have clear systems and oversight in place to delegate the tasks and work items. The second mistake was that we did not get buy-in and a clear commitment of effort from all involved. Unfortunately, we left too many tasks to get done, with the mistaken idea that each of the partners would take initiative to handle the work that was needed.

In the end, the three of us pushed through and got everything done, and I was extremely relieved the day that we wrapped up the partnership. We did not make as much profit as we had hoped, however what we did gain were the learning lessons from the experience and I certainly walked away significantly wiser. What we learned were numerous lessons about how not to form a partnership, and in hindsight it would have been wise to have one of us assigned to the role of project manager (or to perhaps hire someone from the outside to fill this role who would assign tasks to the members and keep everyone accountable).

Apple Inc. – The Story of a Highly Successful Partnership

Everyone is familiar with the iconic brand of Apple Inc. Apple was co-founded by Steve Jobs and Steve Wozniak in 1976, in a garage located in the Silicon Valley region of Northern California. Steve Jobs handled the marketing and sales, while Steve Wozniak handled the technical and engineering areas. The computers and products brought to market by Apple went on to completely revolutionize the personal computer industry and built up a massive following by users and consumers. In their partnership, the combination of the founder's different but complementary skill sets resulted in a highly successful venture.

Final Thoughts

In this chapter, I have shared actionable strategies for creating alignment when it comes to business partnerships. Partnerships that are formed with strong alignment among the members will be well set up for success. Investing the time and effort up front to do strategic planning so that there is buy-in on the mission, the sharing of responsibilities and workload, open communication, and strong engagement will result in a robust partnership that has the ability to bring tremendous value to the marketplace.

FRED MOSKOWITZ

About Fred Moskowitz: Fred Moskowitz is a best-selling author, investment fund manager, and speaker who is on a personal mission to teach people about the power of investing in alternative asset classes, such as real estate and mortgage notes, showing them the way to diversify their capital into investments that are uncorrelated from Wall Street and the stock markets.

Through his body of work, he is teaching investors the strategies to build passive income and cash flow streams designed to flow into their bank accounts. He's a frequent event speaker and contributor to investment podcasts.

Fred is the author of *The Little Green Book of Note Investing: A Practical Guide for Getting Started with Investing in Mortgage Notes* and contributing author in *1Habit To Thrive in a Post-Covid World.*

Author's Website: *www.FredMoskowitz.com*

Book Series Website: *www.TheBookOfInfluence.com*

GENESIS GOMEZ

SYNCING SOULS: RESILIENCES, LEADERSHIP, & ALIGNING FOR SUCCESS

"I've learned that people will forget what you said, people will forget what you did, but people will never forget how you made them feel."
~ Maya Angelou

Being a visionary leader is both glorified and heavily criticized, sometimes in the same breath. It can be fulfilling, fun, and inspirational to many, as well as produce much-needed products and services for the masses. However, a lack of focus, funding, and support can cause the visionary leader to have too many unrealistic ideas and no follow-through, ultimately leading to self-sabotage and loss in the "game" they are playing. How can they overcome the negatives and make sure that their vision comes to fruition? It is not by changing or "fixing" what makes them "special," it is by creating alignment with those who complement their unique ways. Let me explain.

Merriam-Webster describes alignment as: the act of aligning or the state of being aligned, especially the proper positioning or state of adjustment of parts (as of a mechanical or electronic device) in relation to each other. What does this mean for the people in your life you are creating alignment with? Does this mean that you need to completely share the exact same ideals and thoughts? No, not necessarily. You don't even have to be on the same page at the same time, but you do need to be in the same book to have conversations that lead you down the path of understanding.

Once you are on the path of understanding, you can start putting together building blocks to lift each other up to get where you want to go. The people you align with must have common ground, for example: once you are happy, you attract people who are also happy, creating an alignment based on happiness. But it doesn't stop there.

As a visionary leader building a business, when you are dedicated to making your vision work, you start to attract people who also see your vision and want to help bring it to fruition. These people are in your same book because they have read the story, maybe even wanted to do something similar to what you are starting but are on different pages, bringing different experiences and expertise to the table.

You were blessed with the vision and the know-how to get there, but they were blessed with the tools of organization, discipline, and execution. By creating alignment, you allow them into your vision and your world, not hiding your talents or snuffing theirs, but harnessing the blessings each of you bring to the table to bring the vision to life and provide a solution to a glaring problem.

A business is usually started to solve a problem, for which a visionary was given the solution in a dream, thoroughly thought out, or a random thought that popped into their head one day. They then need to find an executor to help them strategize, structure, and put systems into place to start building this vision from the ground up. In cases where the visionary also has to be the executor for a bit, the alignment starts with themselves. Having real talks, studying, writing, strategizing, and figuring out who they want to align with for their vision to come to fruition. It is by being the best version of themselves and allowing people who complement them well to come in and do what they are good at.

This can be hard for some people. I am one of those people who has been a "I will do it myself" and "Jack of all trades" type. Has this served me well up to this point in my life? Certainly, but I also know that in order to go to the next level and grow my international business, I need to be better at creating alignment. Once I grasped this concept, things started to shift and change for me.

Recently, I opened a business called Reigning Resilient Queens. It started as an anthology book, gathering women from all walks of life to tell their stories of grit and resilience amid anything from a "papercut" to a "gash wound" and everything in between. I wanted to create something that showed our brains don't process them much differently. I was tired of being told, "I haven't gone through anything near as bad as you; I cannot complain, you poor dear." "You poor dear?" How can my story make you feel anything less than empowered?

But in that same breath, why was I thinking, "Why are you complaining; what you went through was nothing?" One day I realized I was doing the same thing they were doing, so I went to work. Once I understood how our brain processes trauma, I wanted to provide something to the world so they could better understand this concept. I wanted a place where women could empower each other through their stories and feel seen, heard, and supported with no judgment, only a place of understanding.

As I gathered the author queens, I began to realize that this was more than just an anthology book; it was truly a movement. The women I had brought onto the team, the people around me I told about the project with my passion, and the way I started to show up was more. I kept hearing how needed this is in this world and how many people will benefit. I kept hearing what a difference I am making in my words, my videos, who I am, and what a Queen I am for what I am doing.

And so this grew. I knew that I needed help and I needed to let go of the notion that I have to "do it all," so I reached out and started creating alignment within the author queens. We now have structure, defined roles, and are working on programs, retreats, other book volumes, and resources to help the whole person. Men (Kings) are jumping on board and seeing the movement as something they have been needing as well.

My journey for creating alignment has been a long and tiresome one. I did not start off with the best upbringing; I did not always have "my people" around me, and for much of my life, I had to depend on myself while two babies (now all grown up) depended on me. I fought for our lives in multiple ways; I fought to survive, so thinking about finding alignment was the last thing on my mind, or so it seemed.

As I moved through education, jobs, corporate America, and eventually found my love for being an entrepreneur, I didn't realize what I was doing was creating that alignment within myself. I was learning to find the best ways of managing my emotions, communicating with myself and others, finding the skills that best fit my personality and skill set, failing, winning, persevering, never giving up, and always moving forward. I was preparing myself for this moment, this calling, this mission. I had to get myself into alignment with myself, my kids, the universe, God, and how I interacted with other humans before I could ever start to align with the people who could help me move this movement forward.

Since making the choice to create alignment, I wouldn't say it has been easy, but it feels less like I am swimming upstream and more like I am in alignment with the Universe. I have met people and been put into situations that I wouldn't have otherwise and experienced things that have opened my mind to more possibilities, less judgment, more forgiveness, and less friction. Things just are what they are in a sense.

I have a different perspective on the world and can truly listen for understanding instead of wanting to be understood. I know now that the people who do not understand me are not in alignment with me, and by trying to force them to understand, I am fighting the alignment within myself and expelling energy that could go to better use. I know that I am attracting my people, my audience, my life's work by simply being in alignment with myself and my people who are around me.

This doesn't mean that the people who are out of alignment need to leave my life altogether, but it means they get less of my time and energy; they get moved to a different bucket, per se, because again, I want to ensure that my time and efforts go toward those that will create the magic I am looking for in my life and my business so I can bring my vision to life and help those who are in alignment.

We need alignment in our cars for them to drive well. We need alignment within our bodies and minds to operate properly. We need alignment in our organizations to grow. We need alignment in most things in this world for them to do well. Creating that alignment starts with us and the work we are willing to put in to have whatever work properly or to get where we want to go.

Creating alignment:

- Don't be afraid to look deep inward and have the hard talks with yourself.
  - If you cannot be real with yourself, then you will not create alignment within or around you.

- Let be what is.
  - Give yourself grace and understand "to err is human, to forgive is divine." ~ Alexander Pope

- You are going to make mistakes and cannot avoid them; judging yourself and others will only hurt you in the long run and ruin your chances for true alignment.

- Change is inevitable.
  - Go with the flow as much as you possibly can. You cannot control every aspect of every minute of every day. All you can do is ensure you are a good human and do no harm to others in a malicious way, but be prepared to protect yourself.

- Understand your strengths and weaknesses.
  - Find people to align with that can pick up your shortcomings as you can theirs. Finding those symbiotic relationships will ensure you go further in life than the "I got it" concepts.

- Be clear with your boundaries and intentions.
  - No one can read your mind; you must communicate.

  - Do not discount your worth or your feelings; remember you matter.

- Be honest always.
  - Lying will only cause a low vibration in your body. You don't have to share everything with everyone but don't lie, especially to yourself.

We will always have to grow and adjust. Just like a car needs to be realigned every few years or our bodies need the doctor or chiropractor to be in alignment, so do our organizations and ourselves. Measure where you are and tinker as needed, as one of my old mentors always used to say.

You got this!

GENESIS GOMEZ

About Genesis Gomez: Genesis Gomez is an accomplished supermodel, entrepreneur, Best-Selling Author, and inspiring public speaker, who is dedicated to empowering individuals to pursue their wildest dreams. With her expertise in coaching, Genesis specializes in cultivating a Model Mindset that helps people break into the modeling industry or attain the self-belief and confidence to accomplish their ambitions. Genesis is the founder and CEO of Model Mindset Mastery Services, a coaching program that focuses on the whole person—from their outward appearance to their mental health, financial success, and business growth. With her wealth of experience in the modeling industry and as a successful businesswoman and entrepreneur, Genesis provides her clients with the tools, guidance, and support they need to succeed in all areas of their lives.

But Genesis' coaching goes beyond just helping people look and feel their best—she is also passionate about helping her clients find their purpose and meaning in life. Through her coaching, she has helped hundreds of people discover their true potential, manage their finances more effectively, finance their dream homes, and grow their businesses.

With Genesis as your coach, you can be confident that you are working with someone who truly understands the challenges and opportunities that life can present. Her experience, expertise, and passion for helping others will inspire and motivate you to take action, overcome obstacles, and achieve your wildest dreams. So, if you are ready to transform your life and create a better future for yourself, look no further than Genesis Gomez—the coach who can help you master your mindset and achieve success in all areas of your life.

Author's Website: *www.GenesisAshleyGomez.com*

Book Series Website: *www.TheBookOfInfluence.com*

IAN STERMER

THE FOUR P'S OF ALIGNMENT

I recently noticed my car pulling to the left when I was driving. This wasn't a big deal, as it took only a little effort to keep turning the steering wheel a bit to the right, to compensate. In reality, this tiny tire misalignment was affecting my fuel efficiency, my tire wear, and the safety of my driving.

In life, as in driving, a small misalignment can have consequences ranging from a minor inconvenience to a catastrophic accident. Just as a car has myriad pieces that must all be in alignment to function properly, our lives also have pieces that need to be aligned to allow us to reach our goal of a fulfilling life.

Dale Carnegie's seminal work, *How to Win Friends and Influence People*, is full of excellent examples of how to interact with people to create positive interactions and genuine relationships. At the core of these is the idea that we must be genuine if we are to create genuine relationships. Our thoughts, actions, and interactions must be in alignment.

I break down alignment into 4 P's: Purpose, Principles, Processes, and People. If any of these parts are out of alignment, the result will be inefficient at best, and catastrophic at worst. Once again, an automobile provides an excellent example.

Before the first car was invented, someone sat down and set a purpose or a goal. They wanted to allow people to go from point A to point B in a mechanical device. To do this, they needed to understand the principles of mechanics and physics. Next, they needed to design a process that would fulfill the purpose while adhering to the laws of physics and engineering. Finally, they need to find the right people. They needed people to build the car, sell the car, buy the car, and drive the car. These 4 P's needed to be in alignment for automotive transportation to be successful.

Arguably, the most important person in making the automobile successful was Henry Ford. He understood these 4 P's. He knew his purpose: to make the automobile the dominant form of transportation. He understood the principles of mechanics, as well as business. Of course, he is most famous for his understanding of processes, from the assembly line to interchangeable parts and mass production. Last, but certainly not least, he understood people. He recruited the best engineers, motivated and enabled his workforce, and gave the world a product that they wanted and needed.

Our own lives follow the same path. We must start with Purpose, and then move through principles and processes before reaching the people stage. While each stage needs to be continually reassessed and refined, the order is crucial.

The first stage is Purpose. In Lewis Carroll's work, "Alice's Adventures in Wonderland," Alice reaches a crossroads and asks the Cheshire Cat which path she should take, not caring much where she should end up. The Cat replies, "Then it doesn't much matter which way you go."

If we don't have a purpose in life, a goal we want to reach, then it doesn't matter much which way we go. Alice did have a purpose but was so confounded by the strangeness of Wonderland that she could only think to try to go somewhere, anywhere.

Often in life, we also get so wrapped up in the minutia of our lives that we don't take the time to ask where we really want to go. How often have we climbed the metaphorical ladder only to realize it was leaning against the wrong wall?

Each of us has a purpose that is unique to us. We may share many commonalities, but our true purpose is as unique as each of us. Finding this purpose takes time, effort, and soul-searching. Even in the rare cases that our purpose is placed in front of us, gift-wrapped with a bow, we still need to unwrap it and examine it to see what it is.

This purpose not only shows us what we want to do, but also why. The why is our motivation. Ford's why may well have been to get rich, but it was a sufficient Why to create something that literally changed the world. Without that purpose, the what and why, even the best automobile would be just a bunch of metal pieces stuck together.

Once we have our purpose, our What and Why, we can move on to principles. I have chosen the word Principles because it is a homonym. It means the underlying laws by which something works, such as the principles of physics, but also means our own underlying laws of ethics.

Both of these definitions are important. Once we find our purpose, we need to understand how to achieve it. If our purpose is to build a better automobile, we need to understand the principles of mechanical engineering. The word "better" relies more on our personal principles. Is better faster, because we desire fame or thrills, or does better mean safer so that human suffering can be lessened? Maybe better is more economical so that more people can take advantage of it, or that profit margins can be increased to either pay workers more or just make yourself richer. Your personal principles will also determine what sacrifices you are willing to make to achieve this goal. Will you give up time to study and learn? Money to research and experiment? Family time or even your health?

These first 2 steps are mostly internal. They are things we individually decide and work on. The third step, Processes, begins to take us outside of our own mind and into the physical world. It takes ideas to reality.

Processes can range from our methods of doing things to assembly lines and computer programs. It is putting thoughts and ideas into practice. In automotive terms, it is where the rubber meets the road.

Leonardo da Vinci drew his design for an "aerial screw," what we often refer to as a helicopter, in the late 1480s. While we don't know how strong his purpose was, and its adherence to the principles of aerodynamics is debatable, it seems to have never reached the process stage. It was never built. As such it is now only a minor, if interesting, footnote in history. Likewise, if we find a purpose and align it with the correct principle, but never create the processes to give it life, it will also be only a minor footnote to our lives.

The final step is people. While all of these steps overlap to some degree, people are especially important at every stage. In his book, "Good to Great," Jim Collins teaches us we must first "get the right people on the bus." As we find our purpose, we need to align ourselves with people who share that purpose. As we learn the principles to follow, we need to align ourselves with people who know and believe in those principles. As we develop processes, we need to align ourselves with people that understand how those processes work.

While People is the final step, it is also interwoven throughout the first three. Indeed, if we are seeking to align ourselves with the right people at each step, and we are seeking the right people for the right reasons, we will find those people attracted to us, and us to them.

We need to put in the work, and we may need to step away from some relationships. These spaces opened will be filled with the "right people," as Jim Collins calls them. We win friends and influence people by having a clear and strong purpose, understanding and adhering to correct principles, and creating productive processes.

Dale Carnegie does not teach us how to fool people into being friends, or how to fake friendship. Likewise, he doesn't teach us how to exert influence over people. He teaches how to have real friends and real influence by being genuine and caring. As we do this, we will find that we are aligning with the right people, and more importantly, the right people are aligning with us.

IAN STERMER

About Ian Stermer: Ian is a serial entrepreneur, international speaker, corporate trainer, and business coach. He cut his teeth in the hospitality industry, where he gained a love of helping people smile a little more. Ian has spoken before thousands from New York to San Francisco to Hong Kong. His decades of real-world experience and his unique perspective on life have made him a popular speaker with businesses, civic groups, and professional organizations. He has created training programs on customer service for some of the top hotels in the world, including the Mandarin Oriental and Marriott Hotels. Solopreneurs, salespeople, and small businesses have sought his expertise in training themselves and their staff on customer service, sales, and creating collaborative partnerships. He is currently teaching courses on financial literacy and how to use humor to reduce stress and improve sales.

Ian has facilitated small business and entrepreneurship workshops ranging from improving skills and mastering new techniques to mindset shifts and leadership training. His unique coaching method has helped numerous business owners improve sales and customer satisfaction. Ian has successfully started and ran businesses in the Customer Service, Human Resources, Business Coaching, and Finance Industries. He has turned around failing businesses and created new growth markets for existing businesses. He currently runs Stermer Financial, a financial services company. In addition, he is on the Executive Team for Champion Circle. Aside from business, Ian is most passionate about his family. Nothing is more important than building a happy and healthy family.

Author's website: *www.IanStermer.com*

Book Series Website: *www.TheBookOfInfluence.com*

JESSA CARTER

UNCOMFORTABLE ALIGNED ACTION

To create alignment and leverage it as a form of influence you must recognize that you are already a leader and you are already influencing yourself and others every moment of every day.

You may not yet identify yourself as a leader or someone with influence. If this is you, I invite you to make that shift right now. Or, you may already identify yourself as a leader who is out in the world with known influence and impact. Either way, stay with me!

You matter. You are a leader. You have influence. And you have an impact. But is it meaningful? Is it aligned?

You are consistently leading, influencing, and impacting yourself and everyone around you.

Did you make your bed this morning? No judgment. I simply invite you to recognize that whether you did or didn't, you were leading. You made a choice that either had a supportive influence and positive impact on your day, or a choice that had an unsupportive influence and negative or neutral impact on your day.

Did you kiss your dogs, your kids, or your husband and tell them, "I love you, have an amazing day" before you left the house? Again, no judgment. I simply invite you to recognize that whether you did or didn't, you were leading. You made a choice that either had a supportive influence and positive impact on your life and someone else's life, or a choice that had an unsupportive influence and negative or neutral impact on your life and someone else's life.

Take full ownership of your role as a leader in your life and recognize the ripple effect that has not only on yourself but on the life of every single person you encounter. As well as the ripple effect it has on your results. Know that you have the power to create a supportive influence and meaningful, positive impact in your life that radiates out to the rest of the world.

How? How can you create a ripple effect of supportive influence and meaningful, positive impact? Before you can create alignment with others, you first have to create alignment within yourself. To do this, your actions must be aligned with your core values and you must be willing to take uncomfortable action.

That said, I am not suggesting you take any ole' action, the goal is to take ***Uncomfortable Aligned Action.*** If you get to know me, (I encourage and invite you to connect with me!) you'll learn there's always meaning behind my madness, so please allow me to explain.

Uncomfortable Aligned Action is the key to bridging the gap from where you are to where you'd like to be. It is the one shift that will have the most profound positive impact in the ideal direction, in the least amount of time.

You appreciate speed right? I know I do! That said, I don't want to put the cart in front of the horse. I'm going to give you the key for speed, but you need a solid runway for lift-off!

For starters, what is the difference between uncomfortable action, aligned action, and uncomfortable aligned action?

Uncomfortable action is any action that requires you to step out of your comfort zone, even if it's just a tiny bit outside of your comfort zone.

Know that uncomfortable action itself is powerful. Your next level of greatness, your next level of success: personally, professionally, romantically, or financially lies only inches outside of your comfort zone.

That's great news! Right? It certainly was for me!

Aligned actions are actions that are congruent with your desired outcome. I recommend you start by being clear on your desired outcome. Get clear about the desired outcome you choose to create personally, professionally, romantically, and financially. Why? Because if you aren't clear on where you're going, how can you get there? If you aren't clear on where you're going you're almost sure to get something you didn't want in the first place.

So I invite you to get clear! Grab a sheet of paper and a pen and step into action right now! Take a moment to get clear on what it is you truly desire. No guilt, nothing is too big.

1. What do you desire? Are you in a profession or business you love? If, yes, what's beyond it? If not, where do you choose to be?
2. Have you reached the financial success you truly desire? If yes, what's beyond it? Maybe you make great money but don't have as much time freedom as you'd like? If not, what is your desired financial outcome?
3. Are you in a 10/10 extraordinary divine romantic partnership? If yes, how can you make it even more extraordinary? If not, do you choose to be? What do you believe is possible in a romantic partnership?
4. Now, for each of these categories, ask yourself, who is the person I get to become to allow, receive, and have my desired outcome? What actions am I willing to take that are congruent aka aligned with my desired outcome? What uncomfortable actions am I willing to take that are congruent aka aligned with my desired outcome?

Please be honest with yourself about the quality of your actions. You might be taking action, but if those actions aren't congruent or don't align with your desired outcome, you'll end up with an undesired outcome. Take full responsibility and recognize that inaction is a choice, that guarantees you are not moving closer to your desired outcome. I know from personal experience how much that sucks which is why I encourage you to be honest with yourself about the quality of your actions or lack thereof.

Last but not least, now that you've gained some clarity around your desired outcomes know that reaching your desired outcomes as quickly as possible will require you to take *Uncomfortable Aligned Action.* Taking *Uncomfortable Aligned Action* means that you are choosing quality actions that are aligned and congruent with your desired outcome ***including*** actions that require you to step outside of your comfort zone.

Growth, change, and transformation do not occur in your comfort zone.

Remember, you don't have to leap outside of your comfort zone. Your next level of greatness or success is only inches outside of your comfort zone. That means you can move forward inch by inch, and each inch takes you to another level.

What happens once you step out of your comfort zone? Think of it as rungs of a ladder. When you move up the ladder to the next rung that is currently uncomfortable, with a little time and consistency what was uncomfortable becomes comfortable. You've expanded your comfort zone and you've leveled up! Which is awesome!

Every day you are presented with new opportunities to climb the ladder and make what was once uncomfortable your new comfortable. Even baby steps outside of your comfort zone are still steps in a forward direction. #winning

You've been doing this your whole life without even realizing it! The first time you got on a bicycle, it was uncomfortable, riddled with uncertainty, and scary as hell! But you did it!! And even if you fell (aka 'failed') you got up and you did it again. This is life!

Anything new to you will have some degree of uncertainty or discomfort. And it might be scary. But if you are willing to *Fall* aka *Fail* forward enough times, the only possible outcome is success.

Consider the bicycle. If the first time you fell off you allowed the fear of it happening again to prevent you from ever attempting to ride again, you'd never learn to ride. If you were a stubborn kid like me, you fell off the bike and you were determined to get it right! You did it again, and again, until poof! You could ride with ease, without fear of falling off, and it was fun as hell! Again, this is life...personally, professionally, romantically, and financially!

This is why *Uncomfortable Aligned Action* is the key to moving the needle forward in your life, business, or relationships the fastest.

Get on the bike, be hell-bent and determined to make your dreams your reality no matter what it takes, how long it takes, or how many times you have to fall off the bike to get it right. If you are willing to consistently fail forward, the only possible outcome is success.

If at first you don't succeed, correct and continue. Take responsibility for becoming the YOU that co-creates the life, the business, the wealth, and the romance you desire. Continue to take Uncomfortable Aligned Action to get the results and the desired outcome you choose. Make a committed decision to grow in your leadership and your influence. And be willing to do whatever it takes, for as long as it takes.

You are always 3 feet from gold, don't ever give up, don't ever quit. Where you are now is closer than you've ever been, keep going!!

Cheers to You! Cheers to a life of growth and Uncomfortable Aligned Action! And Cheers to your continued success!

Love, Blessings, & Prosperity,
Jessa

JESSA CARTER

About Jessa Carter: Jessa Carter, The Peaceful Billionaire, is a top 1% Neuroscience Expert and the go-to Life and Wealth Strategist for many of the biggest CEOs, Entrepreneurs, and Leaders in the conscious business industry. Jessa's challenges and struggles on her journey to optimal health, divine romance, and financial excellence changed the trajectory of her own life from a rewarding yet exhausting 10-year career in Neurosurgery into a purpose-driven mission to bring the pinnacle of Neuroscience and Innovation into the lives of heart-centered professionals and entrepreneurs. She applies her gift of attuning the mind for maximum peace, passion, and profits with simple cutting-edge, science-based tools and strategies so that your next-level successes are attainable without stress, overwhelm, or burnout.

Jessa is the founder of the The Peaceful Billionaire Institute for Wealth Creation, award-winning author of the Best-Selling Book *The Peaceful Millionaire* and author of the upcoming books *The Peaceful Multi-Millionaire* and *The Peaceful Billionaire*. She is also a passionate acclaimed international speaker and has shared the stage with Sharon Lecter, Les Brown, and many other transformational leaders at the Think and Grow Rich Legacy World Tour, Uprise Business Amplifier, Money Forum Live, Ultimate Wealth Camp, and has contributed her expertise to the Los Angeles Tribune newspaper and many more.

"It is the plunge deep within the ocean of self that expands one's capacity to experience the vast depths of others and the world around us." ~ Jessa Carter

Author's Website: *www.ThePeacefulBillionaire.com*

Book Series Website: *www.TheBookOfInfluence.com*

JILL LUBLIN

EMBRACING CHANGE IN YOUR PUBLICITY

The one constant in the media and all forms of publicity is **change.**

Over time, every aspect of your message and your business consistently evolves and improves. You discover more about your audience and what they're seeking. You understand what helps generate more leads or drive more sales in your business.

Everything you learn must then circle back around and get integrated into your publicity. Just like anything else in your business, publicity is a system that needs attention.

While this seems like a simple concept, so many businesses forget to complete this cycle or loop these changes back into their overall marketing strategy.

This might be as simple as forgetting to update your new headshot or biography, or it can go as far as missing new products or service offerings that would entice future sales.

Instead of reading this chapter passively, be sure to either take notes on areas where you need to make updates or even take a few moments to stop and update your material directly.

If you want to go a step further, you can even use this chapter to create a checklist or calendar appointment that you use to ask these important questions before you submit your next pitch or take on your next publicity opportunity.

Question One: How are You Presenting Yourself?

You're the face of your publicity for your business, so are you presenting the most up to date version of you in your pitches?

This means that everything is completely up to date. Here's just a few of the areas you need to consider:

- **Update Your Headshot Every Year:** Maybe you've changed your hairstyle. Maybe you've gained or lost a little weight. Everyone looks a bit different with time. Ditch the old headshots, videos, or promotional materials to make sure that "what they see is what they get" and there's no big surprises when you're ready to make your appearance.

- **Refresh Your Biography Every 90 Days:** Just as the press is looking for what's "newsworthy," your bio needs to stay current with your most recent appearances, events, promotions, and opportunities. You never know which credential or accolade is going to catch the eye of a booker or producer.

- **Keep Your Taglines or Introductory Statements Current:** With each appearance or opportunity, or simply with the passage of time, you're going to get better at delivering your message in short and succinct ways. As you discover these, you need to make sure that you're taking time to refresh your media kit and websites with these improvements. These are the things that will help you stand out and look unique compared to the hundreds or thousands of other pitches that the media sees each day.

- **Write More Than You Need and Edit Down:** Understanding how to best edit and refine your material is a skill set that everyone must develop over time. It's okay to start with a lot of additional information, down to the little details, and then edit everything down into a cleaner and sharper format. Having these details handy will help you notice the highlights and put the extra information in other places (such as your website) that won't be cluttering up your media kit or pitch letter.

- **Update Your Appearances, Events, and Media as they Happen:** Too often, great opportunities go to waste because they never make it through to your biography, press kit, or media page. This means that as often as possible, you want to update your appearances and credentials. I also recommend that you *create or store your own copy of appearances* in addition to linking out to the media site. You don't want to be caught off guard if a media link changes or your appearance temporarily goes down and this happens often. This is especially true as your appearances become months or years old.

There are certainly more areas like these that will require your consistent attention, but these fundamental areas get passed over far too often. You want to look your best from the very beginning, which means everything about YOU needs to be on point.

Your publicity system needs as much attention as any other system in your business!

Question Two: How are You Relating to the Changes in Your Industry?

While you're changing and evolving, both your future customer and your industry are evolving right along with you.

New technologies are introduced. New strategies are developed. Your audience has different needs based on these changes or how their needs change.

This doesn't mean that you necessarily need to reinvent your business every time the "next big thing" comes along, but you certainly need to have knowledge and awareness of your industry as a whole.

You don't want to come across as dated or behind the times if and when these subjects are brought up during an appearance *even if you're not necessarily integrating or focusing on these new areas in your business.*

In short, you don't have to live on the cutting edge, but you do need to know that it exists and will impact your industry in some way, shape, or form.

Question Three: How are You Staying "Newsworthy?"

In a 24-hour media world, there are almost endless opportunities to stay newsworthy.

When it comes to being newsworthy, you have the opportunity to **both create and react to the media cycle.**

As you have big events, launches, appearances, or events, you want to make sure that the media is aware. This may mean press releases or even a consistent publicity campaign based on your launches. This is also what most people think of when they think of newsworthy events in their business.

However, you have just as much opportunity to react to what's happening in the world when it makes sense. There may be social causes or specific pieces of news that merit your reaction. Don't let these important opportunities pass!

These subjects don't have to be industry specific. They may simply reflect or represent the values of your business and how you want to be seen by your audience.

Question Four: What's Next?

One of the most fundamental rules in publicity is having a **clear next step for your audience to take.**

There must ALWAYS be a next step.

As you've seen in the previous questions, this certainly applies to you and your business. Knowing what should be happening and *when* it needs to happen is important. Where and when do you put up your appearances? How often are you updating your information?

But since we've already addressed you, let's talk about creating effective next steps for your audience.

Most importantly, your next step during any appearance must be clear, simple, obvious, and easy to take. It should feel like something that makes perfect sense based on the information or subject matter that you're presenting during your appearance.

This next step can be a resource, an additional connection point, or an opportunity for them to start a conversation based on what they've heard. Each of these tried-and-true approaches is still effective right now and they're unlikely to change in the future.

As your strategy improves over time, you'll understand that creating an effective customer experience normally begins with the *end in mind.* Early on, you may not have the puzzle completely assembled and you're adding new products, programs, or services on the fly based on what customers need.

Over time, as your offers get dialed in, this changes and it becomes easier to work backwards. You know that you offer a solution for your audience and it's just a matter of helping them get from "Point A" to "Point B."

From a publicity standpoint, these next steps must be **simple.** Here are just a few tips that will keep things clean:

- Don't overwhelm with too many specific details. If your audience wants more detail, they'll get it when they take the next step.
- Focus on the "why" more than the "how." Your customer wants to know why this matters and won't care about the "how" until they're convinced that what you offer matters.

- Use simple web addresses whenever possible, especially those that are easy to spell. You want any next step to be memorable and easy to access. There are many people that purchase specific domain names just for this reason such as "ask(yourname).com" or "connectwith(you).com." These are easy to research and pick up as needed for various next step offers.

These are just a few considerations and you'll discover what works best for you as you put them into practice.

How are You Stepping Out of Your Comfort Zone?

Once all of the details are in order, it's important to look at your publicity strategy as a whole.

It's too easy to get stuck in a routine or opportunities that only take you to a certain level. You may need to expand your reach to larger platforms or take risks that may feel a little uncomfortable at the moment.

Consistency should be a habit, *but adapting to change is where the exponential growth and success begins.*

As you level up, the opportunities you approach should level up alongside you. Embrace this growth curve and jump on it whenever you can.

If this is your first step, your challenge is to **go for it!** If you're well into your publicity journey, **now is your time to level up!**

You always have the opportunity to change and take on the challenge of being the star that you are. Don't wait for it to happen to you, but instead become the agent of change that makes amazing things happen in all areas of your life.

I know that you have something great in you that the world needs. Now it's up to you to show it off!

JILL LUBLIN

About Jill Lublin: Jill Lublin is a 25+ year Media Magnet. She is a world-renowned publicity expert, international speaker and 4x Best Selling author. Jill has made thousands of stage appearances alongside celebrities such as Tony Robbins, Jack Canfield and Barbara Corcoran to name a few. She has worked with over 100,000 clients implementing her signature formula for getting media attention, creating next-level visibility in the marketplace that results in boosted sales. These lead and profit generating formulas are included in her signature program, the *Publicity Breakthrough Bootcamp* and her monthly *Kindness Circles*.

LinkedIn: *Linkedin.com/in/jilllublin*
Twitter: *twitter.com/JillLublin*
Instagram: *instagram.com/jilllublin*
Facebook: *facebook.com/jilllublin*
Facebook business page: *facebook.com/publicitycrashcourse*
Free Gift - Jill's Publicity Action Guide:
PublicityCrashCourse.com/freegift

Author's Website: *www.JillLublin.com*

Book Series Website: *www.TheBookOfInfluence.com*

JOANNA JAMES

YOUR INTERNAL DIRECTION, NATURAL PATHWAY

There is an old fable about the day God decided to give humans the 'power to create' anything they wanted. However, God didn't want humans to find this power until they had become spiritually conscious.

So, he gathered all the wise creatures to seek their advice. The eagle said, "Give it to me and I will take it to the highest mountain," but God said, "No, soon humans will conquer the mountain and find it." The salmon said, "Leave it with me and I will hide it at the very bottom of the ocean," but God said, "No, humans are explorers and soon they will go there too." The cow said, "Give it to me and I will bury it deep in the Great Plains," but God said, "No, soon humans will rip open the skins of the earth and they will find it there."

All the creatures were stumped, but then an old turtle spoke up. "Why don't you put it deep inside their heart, as that's the very last place they will look?"

God said, "Done!"

When thinking about how to write this chapter, I asked an important question: Why do we need to create alignment at all? The topic presupposes that we are out of alignment or somehow need fundamentally corrected.

The subsequent line of questioning would then be: If we are already innately aligned and connected with life, then how did it come to be that we are out of alignment in the first place?

This leads me to consider whether alignment is perhaps less about what we need to do in order to create congruence and more about the things that prevent us from living our true nature?

Everywhere we look there are souls seeking their true purpose, as if this discovery is the golden ticket everyone needs. There's so much anxiety that's created by the pressure of getting this right, and it is the expectations of what, where and who, that then creates the bulk of our distress internally. How ironic we apply this rationale to something so fundamental as our birthright as if it even needs examination. And yet for millennia, the plight of humanity remains the same: a lifelong journey of discovery to know who I am and what is life.

What if beyond all these expectations there was an alignment that was so pure, so unquestionable in its integrity that denial of its existence is what drives most of humanity into confusion and disconnection? And if it really is that simple, why is life on earth so difficult?

Just as the fable indicates, if the truth we seek is hidden so obviously within our reach, why is it that it is so challenging to glean? Can you imagine living life with no necessity to ask any of these questions at all; particularly when this is fundamentally the life every person is destined to live?

Over the ages, humanity has sought the counsel of sages to share their wisdom on enlightenment, when we already had all the answers to everything we seek. If this is in fact the case, then it is not about creating alignment but more essential to identify the things in life that detract from our natural state of being.

Life is not predetermined; we are, in fact, always in constant motion with a multiplicity of possibilities at any one moment. As everything and everyone is in a constant state of flux, to subscribe to a finite answer is to deny the very nature of life itself! The revelation that there is nothing in fact to discover, that life is more about the ability to focus on our sense of self while life spins around us.

Strangely, this thought brings me comfort, when you consider the infinite range of possibilities, there is simply no good reason to create stress around controlling things. The only thing we can in fact control is how we think, feel and act in any given moment. It is in the surrender to this that we are liberated to create anything we believe. In this moment, we are aligned; this is when our hearts and minds are synchronized.

For most of my life, I desperately sought to understand what enlightenment was. There had to be something significant to discover in all of it. However, this relentless pursuit beyond myself often left me feeling desperately out of sorts and even more confused. This was intertwined with brief sparks of insights so profound that everything fell into clear view, only to fall back again into a disorientated point of view. It seems the very purpose of being human is this dance of distortion, where life lessons continually fall in and out of view.

Far be it for me to preach that I have the clarity to be definitive on how reality really works, but here are a few things that I have experienced in my lifetime to be true. Take them with a grain of salt because life is an experiential thing not based on theory.

We exist on many levels and in many forms concurrently. While we are in a physical body, we are also made of pure energy. The external world we experience with our senses is not the only reality and in fact we create everything we experience with our thoughts and feelings internally. Whilst we like to believe that we are in control of this process mentally, we are in fact prisoners to our mind which is writing our reality. Every line of script is coded with the perception of associated meanings that we attach while we are daydreaming, often not aware of the program we are creating.

Creating alignment is mastering the experience of being conscious of what we are creating.

The joke of all time is that we are not given any instructions on how this process works. We are distracted by the day to day, and the latest Instagram post, not realizing that most of the life we live is in fact a hoax. With a constant dialogue happening internally created by the past, we are typically not aware of the instructions we are listening to. We strive to be free in the future, yet instead recreate more of the past. The more our unconscious feeds the beast, the more focused it becomes, until it pervades all areas of our being with the stories that are unsung.

What a sobering depiction it is to be a human being, if we understood what we were signing up for we probably wouldn't come. Fortunately, we are given one essential thing to assist us on the journey, and that is free will. Only trick is that it is held deep within the maze of our life stories and hidden from our view. This is the key that has been hidden within our hearts.

You see, the fundamentals of creating alignment is the ability to freely choose what you believe at any moment. (A belief is a repetitive thought infused with emotion.) It is in each moment that life truly shifts and we can live like magicians, casting spells of our choosing. Hence why the potential outcomes are so many: we create our life's moment by moment.

So, if it really is this simple, then why is life’s design so darn difficult you ask. I honestly don't have the answer to that one, and am not sure I ever will for the scope of that understanding is well beyond me. I do know that we worry about a lot of things that are irrelevant in the scheme of things and often miss the most important of simple things.

Creating alignment is about finding your internal direction, a natural pathway hidden deep within. No one can tell you what’s wrong or right way to discover; that is up to you to decide. Just know that it does exist, so keep seeking until you find it.

JOANNA JAMES

About Joanna James: Joanna James - is known as a revolutionary difference maker in the Design, Construction and Banking sectors and is featured in publications such as Entrepreneur, USA Today, The Advisor, MPA, Australian Broker, Flaunt, CIO and Insights Success.

As Australia's youngest registered female architect & builder she is known as creator of the world's first 'Bio' home, featured on TV series 'I Own Australia's Best Home.'

Joanna created the Shambhala@byron retreat which welcomed celebrity singer Sting as her first guest. Her book Mind Body Spaces raises awareness around our health and the spaces that we live in.

A pioneering entrepreneur for the Mortgage Ezy Group of companies, her contribution shines through the 32 Industry awards including 3 times BRW fastest company.

A passionate advocate for women in business, Joanna has also been recognized as Principal of Year (WIFA), Top 100 Female Entrepreneurs and Top 100 Female Mentors.

Contributing to the FBAA Artemis Forum, she works to raise opportunities for Education, Advocacy and Awareness for women within the Australian Finance Industry.

Author's Website: *www.JoannaJames.com*

Book Series Website: *www.TheBookOfInfluence.com*

JON KOVACH JR.

THE SPIRIT OF HARMONY

"The only way to influence people is to talk in terms of what the other person wants."
~Dale Carnegie

Alignment encompasses harmonizing our thoughts, actions, and values, creating a powerful synergy within us. Everything flows effortlessly when our decisions become more intuitive, our relationships more fulfilling, and our goals more achievable. It is the key that unlocks our true potential and propels us towards success and fulfillment.

Practicing mindfulness, self-reflection, and staying true to our authentic selves can cultivate a more profound sense of alignment. By aligning our thoughts with our beliefs, our words with our actions, and our dreams with our efforts, we can create a life that is not only meaningful but also profoundly satisfying.

Creative Alignment: A Law of Magnetism

As I've discussed in previous works, the Law of Magnetism governs the attraction between individuals, transcending physical and emotional draw. It is the essence of human connection, drawing us towards those with whom we share common interests, values, and beliefs.

Think of alignment as a magnetic force that guides us towards like-minded souls, forging bonds that transcend superficial differences. Just as opposites attract in physics, complementary qualities and shared aspirations draw us towards one another in human relationships.

Emphasizing alignment's role in human attraction and relationship building, the creative alignment process stretches the mind beyond norms and societal expectations. For example, finding attraction in people one dislikes and admires can help expand acceptance and appreciation for someone already admired. Creating alignment is all about magnetism—the same natural laws attract humans to humans.

The Power of Imagination

Creative alignment is not merely about finding common ground; it is about stretching the boundaries of our imagination and daring to see beyond surface-level differences.

What brings likeness to somebody? In the previous book in this series, we talked about the Likability Factor. But when it comes down to creating alignment, a huge opportunity awaits us: alignment is not only a creative process but a creation process.

The creative process of alignment is all about stretching the mind and getting resourceful. When it comes to building a connection or a relationship and creating alignment, the creative way is going outside the norms and the bonds of typical and societal relationship conversations.

Exploring creative and deeper alignment in human connections opens the door to possibilities and growth. By stretching our minds beyond conventional boundaries, we allow ourselves to see people in a new light, perhaps even those we never thought we could find common ground with. It's about recognizing that each individual holds unique qualities that can resonate with our values and beliefs if we are willing to look closely. This introspective journey deepens our understanding of others and enriches our self-awareness.

The key to creative alignment lies in our ability to transcend preconceived notions and embrace the full spectrum of human complexity. By opening our minds to new possibilities, we unlock the transformative power of alignment in its purest form.

Manifesting Alignment in Action

Having explored the creative realm of alignment, let us focus on the creation process—the tangible manifestation of alignment in action. As I've come to understand, creation is not merely a passive endeavor but an active expression of our deepest desires and intentions.

Physically creating alignment involves deliberate gestures and actions that signal our willingness to connect with others. Something as simple as maintaining eye contact or positioning ourselves to face someone directly can signal our openness and receptivity to alignment. Therefore, physical creation is primitively in our blood.

Having an awareness of your physical activity can set the bar high for creating alignment with others where you can build and enhance a relationship.

The Inter-Intellectual Alignment Process

Mind to mind—this could be done through electronic mail, social media, or any other virtual aspect of creation and communication that requires an intellect of response, receiving, and communication channels. This means you can use tools and resources to enhance relationships with people. Let's go with the electronic mail, an email example.

Email is an excellent example of a communication platform you can use to reach people. And in the world of sales and marketing the email marketing strategy is still alive, but it is still an effective means and tool for reaching people today. Many thought that millennials would be the generation to kill email, but I don't think so. As they've integrated into the workforce and started making their mark. They have adapted and adopted the electronic mail system to communicate effectively as a generation.

Also, intellectual alignment is all about information. When you want to create alignment, you know you want to use a vocabulary that is not only equal to but exciting for the individual; creating alignment is about deciding what to say and how to say it to make that influence or magnetism with another person.

The intellect serves as a bridge to establish a common ground of understanding and connection among individuals, enabling them to harmonize with the purpose and bonds they share and their heartfelt aspirations. Through our intellectual capacities, we can create a language of empathy and mutual comprehension that enriches our interactions and fosters more profound relationships.

But alignment transcends the physical realm and permeates our intellectual and emotional spheres. In intellect, alignment is forged through exchanging ideas, sharing knowledge, and mutual pursuit of understanding. Considering the influence of language on perceptions and alignment, how we use language plays a crucial role in shaping how we perceive things and fostering unity. By carefully selecting our words and communicating with clarity and empathy, we can bridge gaps between individuals, creating a sense of resonance and connection beyond surface-level differences.

Expressing genuine care for others, both as individuals and professionals, can have a significant impact. For instance, instead of engaging in superficial conversations, you can initiate the alignment process by acknowledging a person's dedication and work ethic. Focus on acknowledging their intangible skills and talents rather than superficial compliments. By recognizing their capabilities, abilities, and the rationale behind their actions, you can demonstrate appreciation for their intellect and ability to convey messages that uplift others.

It also helps to recognize and let people know that you recognize their influence on others through their work, whether you like them or you don't. It doesn't matter. Similarly, alignment at the emotional level is rooted in empathy, compassion, and genuine care for others. As the saying goes, "People don't care how much you know until they know how much you care." By acknowledging and honoring the emotional dimensions of alignment, we cultivate trust and intimacy, laying the foundation for meaningful relationships.

In all its forms, alignment is a dynamic and multifaceted process, requiring intention, effort, and a willingness to bridge the gaps that separate us. Through conscious creation and cultivation, we harness the transformative power of alignment to shape our relationships and influence the world around us.

The Creation Process

Unfortunately, because of the world of entertainment, we have become a generation of consumers, but some of our God-given rights and talents are what make the creative processes divine:

- Creators are builders.
- Creators are developers.
- Creators are storytellers.
- Creators are lifebuilders.
- Creators are self-sufficient.
- Creators are idea generators.
- Creators are problem solvers.
- Creators care about a mission.
- Creators can disseminate information.
- Creators care about processes, outcomes, results, and solutions.
- Creators are caregivers of the world, we all have creative power.
- Creators are not just creating— they're providing incredible information through a creative process.

I recall a keynote speaker who came to my college to speak on the topic of the September 11th terrorist attacks. He was one of the lead engineers who helped clean up the fallen towers and helped design the famous memorial site that now stands in place of the buildings.

His speech was a poignant reminder of the resilience of the human spirit in the face of tragedy. As he shared his experiences and insights, he completely blew my mind. He shared that although creating boundless opportunities on a blank canvas can be exciting and common ground for starting an excess of ideas and choices can hinder decision-making early on. Remember, creators are problem solvers. When planning the memorial site for the fallen towers, they faced many constraints from the New York City government, construction firms, real estate owners in the area, neighboring companies, and numerous city regulations. These limitations, although burdensome, ultimately pushed them to build something truly remarkable.

He highlighted how definite limitations and boundaries may seem restrictive but can serve as valuable guidelines for sparking true problem-solving creativity. By embracing these constraints as creation enablers, unleash creativity in new profound ways. This insight was genuinely mind-blowing and unforgettable.

Building Bridges, Breaking Barriers

As we reflect on the profound implications of alignment in our personal lives, let us not overlook its broader significance in society. Alignment is the foundation of social cohesion, which binds communities together and fosters collective progress.

In a world marked by division and discord, the need for alignment has never been greater. Whether bridging cultural divides, fostering political consensus, or promoting social justice, alignment constructs positive change, uniting contrasting voices in pursuit of common goals.

Consider the potential transformation brought by mastermind groups, where individuals unite with harmony and purpose to achieve common goals. We witness the strength of alignment in action by drawing inspiration from influential figures like C.S. Lewis and J.R.R. Tolkien, whose renowned Inklings group ignited literary masterpieces. The Inklings were a celebrated writing group originating from Oxford University. This diverse gathering of prominent writers, including C.S. Lewis and J.R.R. Tolkien, shared their ideas, creating timeless classics like the *Lord of the Rings* series. These literary works have impacted our lives and emerged from the collaborative process of a mastermind group.

The mastermind methodology is a robust process that produces accelerated results and outcomes. When individuals come together with unity and a common goal, magic unfolds. This magic is harnessed through the collective strength of individuals tackling challenges.

The mastermind process relies on a structured approach rather than total freedom, hinging on various aspects of alignment. The mastermind techniques outlined in *Think and Grow Rich* by Napoleon Hill represent contemporary society's most refined and authentic alignment methods. Currently, the mastermind approach fosters alignment by integrating creative and creator processes.

A mastermind isn't just a method of communication; it's a practice that encourages pure accountability and delivers results. A mastermind involves gathering two or more individuals who come together in an environment that fosters harmony and unity to achieve a specific goal or solve a problem. This goal could involve overcoming challenges, acquiring resources, sharing knowledge, generating ideas, and accessing tools. Regardless of the objective, it is considered a powerful form of creation. As a creator, you are more than just a builder; you are a visionary.

As explained by Napoleon Hill, the mastermind process exemplifies the creative and collaborative aspects of alignment, unleashing the collective genius of individuals united in purpose. Mastermind groups harness the full force of alignment through synergy and solidarity to manifest their visions and aspirations.

In the words of Hill himself, "When a group of individual minds are coordinated and function in harmony, the increased energy created through that alliance becomes available to every individual in the group." Thus, alignment emerges as a personal endeavor and a collective force for positive change and transformation.

Embracing Alignment as a Catalyst for Change

For me, alignment encompasses tolerance, agreement, openness, acceptance, and consent. These traits and attributes collectively influence others through the power of alignment.

As a business owner, entrepreneur, motivational speaker, and salesperson, my community and followers must resonate with the principles I advocate. By implementing the strategies I offer, they can achieve their desired outcomes. Nevertheless, I understand that I cannot cater to everyone, nor is it necessary.

My Creative Process: Instead of trying to appeal to everyone, I focus on connecting with individuals with specific interests and mindsets. This alignment draws them towards taking the actions required to reach their objectives and see results.

Alignment revolves around relationships. Negative perceptions often arise regarding sales and conversations because individuals do not want to feel pressured to purchase. To improve this, there is a need for skilled trainers to teach effective sales techniques, leading to a more favorable sales experience worldwide. It's crucial to avoid being perceived as pushy in the eyes of potential customers.

Focusing on alignment as an attractive and visible aspect can be crucial and beneficial, rather than assuming that you lack interest or connection. Alignment is all about love. Here's a positive example of alignment as we thoroughly focus on providing results.

When an author agrees to contribute to our books and book series, they embrace our vision and mission of spreading positivity to the desired audience. Each author embeds their names, philosophies, and identities into our image, aligning themselves with our business. Aligning with like-minded individuals who share your values is vital.

Individuals don't have to share the same beliefs. For instance, Christians and Buddhists don't need to have identical faiths to be in harmony. They can share alignment through their devotion to God, care for humanity, and desire for peace on earth. Instead of focusing on differences, it's about finding common ground.

Alignment is a critical factor that can bring various groups together or create divisions among them. It plays a crucial role in establishing influence and followership. Recognizing the importance of alignment in community building is essential, as it is a fundamental aspect of societies and human nature, reflecting the innate desire for companionship. Few individuals can genuinely thrive in isolation without longing for human connections, highlighting our inherent need for relationships.

Our blood creates connections that can save lives. The bond of companionship drives us daily. Humanity thrives on these connections. In essence, alignment serves as a valuable resource for many. It revolves around shared interests, where love and alignment are vital for growth and success in personal or business spheres. Quality is attracted through alignment, and it is through alignment that you establish influence over others.

I highly recommend that those who are reading this book and this chapter should keep on reading and absorb the insights shared by others about the significance of alignment in today's world. Dale Carnegie discussed this concept in his book, *How to Win Friends and Influence People*, emphasizing that anyone can establish alignment if they are open to it. Refusing to align can lead to quick exclusion from many communities and societies. Social outcasts often struggle because humans seek companionship, even if isolating oneself from society seems appealing. Building connections is essential.

Establishing alignment for me involved forming connections with a community of individuals I didn't fully comprehend and didn't fully comprehend me.

I resided in Makati, a city within Metro Manila, Philippines. During my time there, I was responsible for organizing and promoting a tranquil yet enjoyable music event for the community within a local church. We aimed to advertise a public event and encourage individuals to attend and witness diverse performers who could inspire others.

A variety of musical performances was arranged by volunteers, including a well-known individual named John Schmidt, internationally known on YouTube as the Piano Guy, who would be the last performer. In this scenario, Filipino culture found it challenging to grasp Western culture, and white American culture was somewhat excluded from the dialogue. Despite this, American culture saw this person flying to the Philippines to perform for free as a gesture of goodwill. His fame came from uplifting and inspiring the Filipino people, particularly after the recent tragic typhoons that affected their city.

Creating interest took a lot of work as individuals preferred to steer clear of American music at the event. They were seeking something more relatable and aligned with their interests. In that culture, only a few people are inclined to play the piano, which differs from the mainstream instruments in the Philippines. We only grasped the Filipino culture after conducting thorough research to uncover the reasons behind the lack of attendance at the event.

Once we realized that a thriving free entertainment event requires a shared interest, inviting people to a Church set an expectation that they might encounter preaching or that our aim as a religious group was to inspire. Could we have promptly reached this objective? Did we grasp the concept of establishing alignment?

The process of establishing alignment commenced. Instead of framing the events as a spiritual church gathering, we highlighted them as a chance to listen to songs that have resonated with and been downloaded by millions worldwide. Live performances drew attention to something significant in the surroundings, bringing together a full chapel and cultural hall with nearby attendees. However, our aspirations were shattered upon learning that political rallies were scheduled to march through downtown Manila streets on the same day, resulting in the shutdown of public transportation and limiting access for people to join the event.

When the doors opened, we were astonished to find hundreds of people waiting in line to enter the church and enjoy the music. This achievement was only possible by acknowledging the importance of alignment and drawing in individuals to attend, sit through long hours, and appreciate the music.

In conclusion, the power of alignment is undeniable, permeating every facet of our lives and shaping the world in which we live. From the creative realms of imagination to the tangible manifestations of action, alignment guides us toward greater connection, understanding, and influence.

As we continue our journey through *The Book of Influence* series, I implore you to embrace alignment as a catalyst for change—a tool for building bridges, breaking barriers, and forging a more harmonious and interconnected world. Through conscious intention and purposeful action, we harness the transformative power of alignment to shape our destinies and impact the world around us.

Remember, alignment is not merely a passive state but an active choice—a commitment to seek out common ground, foster genuine connections, and build a world guided by empathy, understanding, and mutual respect. Therefore, alignment can be created if you understand who you're creating alignment with. That's why it's creative and powerful.

So, I encourage you to focus on alignment merely as a tool and something you can use daily as you use your resources and God-given talents to build relationships and create a world of influence.

JON KOVACH JR.

About Jon Kovach Jr.: Jon is an award-winning international motivational speaker and global mastermind leader. Jon has helped multi-billion-dollar corporations exceed their annual sales goals, including Coldwell Banker Commercial, Outdoor Retailer Cotopaxi, and the Public Relations Student Society of America. In addition, in his work as an accountability coach and mastermind facilitator, Jon has helped thousands of professionals overcome their challenges and achieve their goals by implementing his accountability strategies and Irrefutable Laws of High Performance. Jon is the Founder and Chairman of Champion Circle, a networking association that combines high-performance-based networking activities and recreational fun to create connection capital and increase prosperity for professionals. Jon is the Mastermind Facilitator and Team Lead of the Habitude Warrior Mastermind and the Global Speakers Mastermind & Masterclass founded by Speaker Erik "Mr. Awesome" Swanson.

Jon speaks on topics including accountability, The Irrefutable Laws of High Performance, and The Power of Mastermind Methodologies. He is a #1 Best-Selling Author and a featured keynote on SpeakUp TV, an Amazon Prime TV series, with his keynote speech titled, Getting Unstuck. In addition, he stars in over 100 speaking stages, podcasts, and live international summits each year. Jon's motivational messages have been viewed by over 500,000 people online. His positive messages have trended and been used by global brands on TikTok and Instagram, such as: Red Bull, Michael Bublé, NHL, Powell Books, GoDaddy Studio, Canada's Wonderland Amusement Park, and the LSU Cheer Team.

Author's website: *www.JonKovachJr.com*

Book Series Website: *www.TheBookOfInfluence.com*

JUSTIN MORRIS

JOY = ALIGNMENT WITH YOUR HIGHEST SELF

Lessons Learned from Dumpster Diving & Mouth Appliances

Every High Schooler that has ever had to wear a retainer has a recurring nightmare. If you know…you know. The nightmare goes something like this.

You sit down to eat your lunch, excited to chat it up with your homies (don't worry, you'll never have to hear me say that again). You pop out your retainer giving it a little slurpy slurp before you pull it completely out of your mouth just to make sure there aren't any surprises left on the appliance for your "crush" to see.

A mental reminder is seared into your brain, "Don't forget to put your retainer back in before you dump your tray or you will be DEAD when you get home!" You discreetly place a napkin over the retainer because that is the polite thing to do. Next thing you know, you are solving the world's problems of teenage acne, who's asking who to the next dance, and "Oh my word, I'm SO done with Pre-Calculus!" The bell rings and your entire table stands up, still talking and laughing as you proceed to the massive, larger-than-life garbage cans to dump your trays and head to class.

Does this nightmare ring a bell to any of you? I totally resonate with this story because, well—I lived it! I'm assuming you know what happens next?

Trust me, you probably won't guess the ending to this story.

As I sat in my next class period, I ran my tongue across the roof of my mouth and realized that something was different. In an instant, I'm pretty sure my heart sank to the basement level of the school and I literally saw my life flash before my eyes! No, my life didn't flash before my eyes because I was worried about what would happen when I got home, but rather because I knew what I had to do. I had to put on the long yellow gloves and dumpster dive through the massive garbage bins full of half-eaten cake, mashed potatoes, gravy, chocolate milk, and mystery meat in search of a transparent piece of plastic wrapped in a white napkin. Yeah, it was like looking for a needle in a haystack…only a lot messier, a whole lot stinkier, and in front of the next group of students eating lunch.

My life was over.

The beauty of this predicament is that I had a choice to make and for some reason that no human who has never had to wear a retainer can understand, I chose to risk social ruin for a piece of plastic.

For the next hour, I sifted through every piece of gooey rubbish, one by one, piece by piece. I drowned out my surroundings, the looks of pity from the "nerdy table" (my peeps) and the sneers from the cool table (the peeps I wished were my peeps, but #nohopeofeverfittinginwiththatcrowdnow).

Why on earth did I risk so much?

Let's take a look at this through the lens of creating alignment.

I have found that TRUE JOY = ALIGNMENT WITH MY HIGHEST SELF. During our lives, we are met with many experiences that can threaten to rob of us of that joy, but if we can understand the concept of what it looks like, sounds like, and feels like to align each experience we have (yes even the painful, hard, and challenging ones) with our highest self, we can find joy in even the most confusing and trying of times.

Raise your hand if you think I'm "blowing smoke." I know. I know. It sounds impossible to experience joy and fulfillment during times you feel like you can't even scrape yourself out of bed.

Stay with me here for a little bit longer, especially if you would like to explore what this looks like for you.

If we really look at what alignment is, it boils down to the concept that Alignment consists of three components:

1. **Alignment with God:** To truly find alignment in this area requires that you seek for someone or something higher than you. Because let's face it—there are A LOT of experiences in this life that require supernatural help from unseen hands.

2. **Alignment with ourselves:** This area requires a deep level of **SELF INTEGRITY** which requires us to be very honest about the things that are within our control and the things that are not. It also requires us to allow ourselves "grace" that we are doing our best when we feel we are failing. Alignment with ourselves also requires us to have profound **SELF AWARENESS**—which happens to be an amazing gift we can all seek to acquire in our lives. It is the ability to intuitively understand what our physiological, emotional, psychological, and spiritual needs are. When we can use these two ingredients (Self Integrity and Self Awareness), we will find it is much easier to live in an aligned and authentic way.

3. **Alignment with our Stewardships:** Oh boy. Yes. This one is HUGE. The "Stewardship Principle" is fascinating in that it requires us to have a deep sense of ownership for what is ours and let go of everything that is not. Our gifts, talents, homes, cars, employment, responsibilities as a mother/father, husband/wife. You get the drift. But, it also pertains to our health issues, bad habits, weaknesses, poor choices, addictions, and the list can go on and on. Being aligned in our stewardships requires us to take ownership of EVERYTHING

> that is ours. To release the blame game and just seek to find gratitude in every situation and experience and challenge in our lives that are within our control—and let go of the rest.

Let me let you in on a little secret. When you are intentionally seeking to create alignment, it doesn't necessarily matter which one of these three areas you focus on, because if you are TRULY and HONESTLY aligned with just one of these three areas, you will find that you are aligned with all of them.

So, what does this all have to do with dumping my retainer in the trash? Well, let me just finish the story for you.

After spending about an hour inspecting every particle of biological goo in the massive garbage can, I had to step away. Not only did I not find my retainer, but I was also covered in a layer of slime that I would rather just forget. I won't mention the smell.

I walked back to my locker with my head down, shoulders slumped. I had one more class before I had to go home and break the news that I had thrown away something that was in my stewardship…a very expensive something that would result in financial pressure to purchase again.

I absent-mindedly turned the combination knob on my locker and opened it up to gather my books. I bet you'll never guess what was sitting on the top shelf of my locker.

Yep. My retainer.

It was equal parts laughing at me and equal parts glittering with all things angelic. I was both happy and mad. I wanted to kiss that retainer. I knew that would be weird, so I stuck it in my mouth instead.

You see, that experience taught me some very important lessons. But, the most important one being the joy that I felt as I aligned myself to God, myself and my stewardship. It's funny how everything else around you can just melt away when you focus on what really matters. And what

DOES REALLY MATTER? Well, now you have three things to help you determine what that looks like in your own life.

Now, go do amazing things, and in the words of Beethoven, "Don't only practice your art, but force your way into its secrets. For it and knowledge can raise men to the divine."

JUSTIN MORRIS

About Justin Morris: Justin Morris is the creator of The Color Alignment Protocol, and brand new, ground-breaking energy alignment modality which utilizes the energetic power of color. He has used color to create physical spaces of healing for the last 20 years in his career as a professional interior designer in spaces like corporate offices, homes, resorts, and temples for the Church of Jesus Christ of Latter-day Saints.

Justin has taken his life-long study of color, psychology, and an incredible intuitive gift for seeing the colors inherently attached to a person's soul and use them as a guide to get to the core issues people are facing. As a Life Coach, and International award-winning keynote presenter, he now teaches people to be the designer of their own life and use color to bring out the highest version of themselves.

Justin has been married to his wife, Nancy, for 23 years and together they have 6 amazing and talented children. They currently reside in Ogden, Utah.

Author's Website: *www.JMSpectrum.com*

Book Series Website: *www.TheBookOfInfluence.com*

LAUREN COBB

CREATING ALIGNMENT WITH YOUR PERSONAL BELIEFS

At this point in life, I understand the complexities and demands of a busy life. Yet, I've come to realize the incredible importance of creating a life that aligns with my personal beliefs. It took me a while to learn and at times I am STILL learning how to harmonize the various aspects of my life with my core values, allowing me to live a more meaningful, authentic, and fulfilling existence.

The most hectic times in my life are when I am trying to pack on responsibilities and obligations for myself to others when it doesn't truly align with my life. Life becomes MESSY and STRESSFUL and NOT FUN.

There are a few things you can do to help align and balance your life. It requires you to dig deep and be honest with yourself!

The first step in creating alignment is to identify your personal beliefs. What are the principles and values that are non-negotiable for you? This can take some time to sort out. These also can grow as you grow! One of mine is when I am scheduling things out. My kids always come first. I know my kids need a mom who is present and there for them. A second one is that it must align with my personal belief in God. If it is something that will hinder relationships and closeness to God, I won't partake in it. These things that are non-negotiable are your do's or die's. You will stand unmovable in these things.

As mentioned above, one of my roles is a Mother. I am a M om to 3 beautiful daughters who I am SO thankful for in my life! As a mother, your beliefs and values may revolve around providing a loving and nurturing environment for your children. Explore how you can align your parenting style with your beliefs, ensuring that you're fostering the values you hold dear while nurturing a strong and supportive relationship with your children. This is something my husband and I work on together. We each have things that are important to us, and we discuss them and work out how we implement them to have a cohesive parenting front.

Another role of mine is a business owner. This one is TRICKY. As most of us know, when you're the one behind the scenes it takes a lot of your time, brain power, and more to keep things going. Being a business owner means making decisions that impact not only your financial success but also the world around you. Create a business that aligns with your personal beliefs by integrating ethical practices and a mission that resonates with your values.

There are many more roles that I hold and they change from time to time. But if I will be true to myself with what I can take on in life and what I need to let someone else do, then my life is a lot more peaceful and aligned with my talents and what I can reasonably accomplish.

Balancing these roles requires effective time management and prioritization. Identify which aspects of your life are most closely tied to your core beliefs, and allocate your time accordingly. This will ensure that you invest your energy and effort where it matters most.

Don't be afraid to ask for help or delegate tasks when necessary. Surround yourself with individuals and or a village who understand and support your vision for a life that aligns with your personal beliefs. Building a team that shares your values can be instrumental in achieving alignment.

In the midst of these roles, don't forget to care for yourself. Practicing self-care is essential to maintaining the physical, emotional, and mental strength needed to pursue a life in alignment with your beliefs. Make time for activities that rejuvenate and nourish your well-being. For me, that is making the time to be with my girls after a full day of school, dance, and sports, to spend the evenings together to wind down and help them process their day as well. It brings my soul peace to know my girls are safe, happy and in a good head space to get rest and start the next day on the best foot they can.

Another one is prioritizing my exercise time! This one took me a LONG time to implement. My health got to a bad place last year before I really took it seriously. At that point, I still needed my village to help me get there! But it is one of my TOP priorities.

The journey toward alignment is always there. Knowing my personal beliefs and bandwidth helps with making decisions on the spot, but I also do a weekly check in with myself. I pull out my calendar and journal and I see what I have done the last week and how I was responding to life. Was I stressed? Was I not prioritizing myself, my health, my sleep? Then I see what I have coming up in the next week and if I need to make changes so I can stay true to myself. Regularly reflect on your personal beliefs and how they manifest in your life. Be open to adjusting and refining your path as you grow and evolve.

We each have a unique set of roles and responsibilities, but these roles can be aligned with your deepest values and beliefs. It's not about striving for perfection but about consciously making choices that reflect who you are and what you stand for.

Aspects of life to consider if you feel out of alignment: Are your CORE beliefs firm? Do you fully understand and resonate with these beliefs? Write down what are your desires in life? Is there an area you feel you need to focus on more than another at the time?

Identify what roles you currently have in life. Spouse, Parent, Teacher, Church Leader, Business owner… list them all!

Write down what demands each role has on you. Is there a specific time for a role that you are to show up for? Write down the times of meetings for each one, get into the nitty gritty!

Are there roles that you are currently doing that do not align with your values and time commitments?

Are there any roles that you can ask for help with?

IMPLEMENT THE CHANGES YOU KNOW YOU NEED TO MAKE.

Life really does become more fulfilling and peaceful when you are living true to your beliefs and in harmony with the values and desires you have.

LAUREN COBB

About Lauren Cobb: Lauren Cobb is a wife to her amazing and supportive husband Tyler. A mother to 3 beautiful daughters who've taught her more in the last 12 years than she has learned in the first 23 years of her life.

At a young age Lauren knew she had a lot of ambition and drive. As she became an adult, she knew that entrepreneurship was her passion and thankfully married someone who supported that! Together with Ty they own a graphic and media design company that they've built from the ground up. Growing and seeing the successes from their own efforts has been one of the most rewarding experiences!

Self-development and leadership have been a big part of Lauren's life since she was 14. She traveled and taught leadership to youth across the country throughout her high school years. She knows first-hand how self-development is crucial to success in life. Knowing who you are and finding your purpose and passion is important.

As Lauren and her husband Ty are building their businesses and seeking a network and friends who are aligned with their values, they've found in Champion Circle and learned how to properly mastermind. Lauren is a member of the corporate executive team at Champion Circle Networking Association, founded and led by Jon Kovach Jr. Masterminds have changed her life and their business for the better.

Author's Website: *www.TyCobb.MyPortfolio.com*

Book Series Website: *www.TheBookOfInfluence.com*

MALEAH BLISS

UNWAVERING IN YOUR BELIEFS

"What if we could buy?"

This question popped out of my husband's mouth as we were looking for a new place to rent on the evening of July 18, 2021.

"That would be cool," I said, "but I don't know how we could do that."

"Yeah, but what if we can? Wouldn't it be worth it to at least find out?"

This conversation started a whirlwind of activity and change in our lives. That Sunday night, we called a mortgage broker friend and got pre-approved by Tuesday, talked with a realtor friend on Wednesday, and then looked at houses and made an offer on Thursday the 22nd, which coincidentally was my birthday. Twelve days after that, we closed. In 16 days, we went from not even believing it was possible to purchase a home, to being homeowners.

How? We created alignment.

Before I dive deeper into the story, I think it is important to define alignment. The Miriam-Webster dictionary defines it as:

1. the act of aligning or state of being aligned, especially: the proper positioning or state of adjustment of parts (as of a mechanical or electronic device) in relation to each other.
2. a: a forming in line.

b: the line thus formed.

3. the ground plan (as of a railroad or highway) in distinction from the profile.
4. an arrangement of groups or forces in relation to one another.

I define it as knowing what you want so that you can take big action toward it. If we are to create alignment in our lives, we need to know what we want so that we can properly position ourselves to get what we want. In very simple terms, we have to KNOW and GO.

But since we humans like things to be more complicated than they need to be, here are six steps that will help you create alignment in your life:

1. Have an idea.
2. Be open to exploring and be vulnerable.
3. Gather the right people and resources.
4. Decide.
5. KNOW.
6. Take big action.

Then watch as everything you decide you want happens.

Let's go back to that Sunday night, two years ago.

When my husband first put forth the idea that we at least explore the option of buying a home, I initially dismissed it. I knew that we did not have any kind of down payment saved and even though we had decent credit, I wasn't sure if it was "good enough" to purchase a home. It felt like a pipe dream, but he wouldn't let me just dismiss it. His gentle insistence of, "But what if we could?" opened me up to be willing to **explore** the idea and be **vulnerable** enough to gather the right **people and resources** to at least see if we could qualify.

As we talked to our lender, they were able to pre-approve us easily, not only for a (much larger than we even wanted) mortgage, but also for a loan for our down payment. I was stunned, because I did not know that getting a loan for the down payment was even in the realm of possibilities of things that are available.

It's so easy to forget that we don't know what we don't know and that when we act (or don't act) from a space of not knowing that we don't know something, we are often met with failure and disappointment. And, unfortunately, we often blame ourselves for that failure and disappointment, instead of recognizing our lack of knowledge. (Because we STILL don't know that we don't know!)

If my husband had not convinced me to be vulnerable enough to ask the people in our life that DID know, and we would have remained in the dark and I would've continued to believe that purchasing a home was out of our reach.

Because we sought counsel from people that knew more than we did, and they showed us what was possible, at that point, I **decided** that I wanted to go for it.

Once we had our preapproval in place, we talked with another friend. After we had shared the type of loan we had, our timeframe that we hoped to purchase in, the price we hoped to stay under, and the things we wanted in our home, he asked us what would happen if we didn't find a house in the timeframe we needed. We told him that it would not be an issue for us to rent an Airbnb for a short period of time, if it was needed to finish closing, but that we didn't foresee that as being a problem because we were manifesting this house.

He asked was because we were buying at the height of the 2021 housing market. One of our realtor's clients had literally put in 32 offers before having their offer accepted. He was skeptical of this "manifesting" but said, "OK, we'll see how this goes."

We picked out five houses to go look at the next day and I asked the spirit for a sign that we would know the house when we got there.

My **decision** to go for it had turned into **knowledge** that it would happen.

We had already looked at the first four houses and were on our way to the fifth and last house, having not gotten a clear sign and we were feeling fairly confused.

We pulled up to the fifth house, and we all got out to go in, but my children got distracted by the homeowner's cats, and stayed outside while my husband, the realtor, and I went inside.

We had barely walked into the kitchen when my kids came running inside, and said, "MOM!!! It's raining on your birthday!"

We put in a full price offer that afternoon. At the suggestion of our realtor, and in our commitment to **big action**, we included a letter to the sellers. It was as follows and explains how we knew it was "the one."

7/22/2021

> *Hi there,*
>
> *We are Maleah and Eric and we LOVE your home. We are hopeful homesteaders and were so excited by your property. We love the mature trees, chicken run, backyard space (we have 3 kids, so the playground is an AMAZING and unexpected addition) and we love the way you have re-done everything. Thank you for opening up the space between the kitchen and the living room. It makes it so homey, comfortable and open feeling.*
>
> *We would really love to purchase your home so that we can love it as much as you have. My hubby (this is Maleah writing the letter) can hardly wait to get a garden in and is hopeful that we will be able to put in some cold frames before the cold weather hits so that we can hopefully have some greens into the winter and then is SO looking forward to having the space to have a LARGE garden next year.*
>
> *Fun story, I grew up in the Seattle area and I LOVE rain. It just feels like home to me. On Sunday, when I reminded my kids that Thursday (today) was my birthday, they asked if it was going to rain (because I always say that it's my present from the earth when it does. LOL).*

I looked at my weather app and it showed that it was going to be sunny with no rain in sight for the next 10 days. So, I told them that we would have to manifest it. I also told God and the Universe to show us the right house when we saw it because we are on a tight schedule for finding a house because we have to move by the 1st of September. Well, we were inside your home and heard my son call out, "MOM! It's raining for your birthday!" And we went outside into the backyard and got drenched.

To me, this was our sign to put in an offer. I hope and pray that you accept it so that we can continue loving and caring for the property as much as you have. 🩶

With thanks and hopefulness,

Maleah and Eric

PS: I'm so glad the trees all got really good drinks no matter who you choose.

After putting in our offer, I went outside and sat on our balcony. I did a guided meditation, letting go of my doubts and my fears, and then dreamt about and seeing us in that house. OUR house. After I finished the meditation, I let go of the outcome and knew that whatever happened would be perfect for us and would be perfectly in alignment.

We were one of 23 other offers. We were absolutely not the best offer. The sellers, however, liked me, and my letter ended up being worth $15,000.

They came back to us and told us that if we would match the top offer in price, they would accept our offer, even though the top offer had promised to pay $15,000 in cash over the appraisal, if it did not appraise for the amount they had offered.

We matched the top offer and they accepted. Our realtor kept saying, "I can't believe you got it! I just can't believe it!" He then offered me a job writing letters to sellers. (Ha!) He had never seen a letter make a $15,000 difference in the bottom line of a deal, especially in the crazy seller's market that we were in.

The next 12 days were a whirlwind of inspections and deadlines, but we got them all done in record time and closed early.

It was almost surreal how quickly and easily the process went for us. When you decide what you want, and then you take big, HUGE action, everything works in your favor.

It has been the perfect space for us.

Last week, I was at an event and had the opportunity to ask academy award nominee Janeshia Adams-Ginyard what she would tell the average person to get into alignment. (She had talked about alignment over and over again while she told us about her journey to being cast in Black Panther and the many other marvel movies she has now been in.)

She said, "You have to be so unwavering in your belief in your thought process that it WILL happen."

Now go out, and be so unwavering in your outcome that the people and the resources that you need will be brought to you.

MALEAH BLISS

About Maleah Bliss: Maleah Bliss loves to share her passions and journey with others. As the owner of Salt City Payments, Maleah has a wealth of experience in business and finance, but what truly ignites her passion is personal development, mycology, and connecting with people.

Maleah loves learning and she is currently in school to become a Doctor of Medical Qigong. She is an author and speaker teaching about business, personal development, and how to achieve your full potential. She also loves to paint.

Maleah believes in the power of connection, and she is always looking for ways to positively impact the lives of those around her. Whether through her writing, speaking engagements, or business dealings, Maleah is driven by a desire to help others reach their full potential.

Author's Website: *www.MaleahBliss.com*

Book Series Website: *www.TheBookOfInfluence.com*

MARIS SEGAL & KEN ASHBY

SYNCHRONIZATION: UNLOCKING THE POWER OF ALIGNMENTS & AGREEMENTS

Experiences in our lives most often begin with a want, a desire, a deep longing, and then a human connection which leads to a relationship to support us in fulfilling that desire. It could be the desire for a romantic attachment, which is likely where your mind already had gone as you read this passage, or it could be the desire to have a new job.

Including first our relationship with ourselves, we are all in a relationship with someone or something from the time we wake up in the morning. In each of these relationships there are "alignments" and "agreements," and it is in the synchronization of the two that vibrant, deep, and lasting relationships are possible. In this intricate dance of relationships, there exists a profound and transformative power in synchronizing alignments and agreements.

We've been living, loving, working side by side for nearly twenty years, choosing each other every day as partners in every aspect of our lives and we've learned a thing or two along the way. "We have one life to live, one body and one planet, and relationships cannot be avoided! How we show up in our relationships is our choice and our daily choices determine our future."

In both professional and personal spheres of our lives, “alignment” plays a pivotal role in fostering strong relationships and achieving collective objectives. Whether it's with your family, with your team at work, friends and/or community, harmonizing individuals' values, attitudes, and actions are essential to creating alignment. Let’s clarify that alignment and agreement are not the same. We can be aligned with someone (or a group) and respect where they stand. We can agree in principle as to the “purpose” and/or the “why” and still not be in full agreement as to the approach. Think about it, from our earliest days as kids, we were taught alignment.

Maris: As the youngest of three sisters, we were close and playful and, yes, fought like siblings do. This is often how a conversation would go. One sister would ask, “Who wants ice cream?” and, of course, I would be the first to jump up with a “Me, Me, Me, Me,” then there would be a declaration from both elder sisters that because I said it first, and I was the youngest, that it would be my turn to go to the freezer and serve up ice cream for all.

Wouldn’t you know it, somehow it was always my turn. While we were all in agreement that our purpose was to eat ice cream, I was not in agreement that it was my job as the youngest sibling to always serve. My alignment came easier, knowing that I loved bringing the joy of chocolate, coffee, and hot fudge to my sisters, just to see their smiling faces. However, as I got a bit older and wiser, we did realign that we would begin to take turns serving each other so we could all experience generosity and gratitude!

As simple as this childhood example is, it offers a perspective that when we are clear on the vision (in this case, eating ice cream), there is more room for varied approaches, and it does not always have to be “our” way. In fact, we benefit from collaborating and weaving varied views for a win-win for all.

We are fortunate to have spent many decades in the global relationship and event marketing space. Durning our work with heads of households and Heads of State, and from boardrooms and big brands to classrooms and the world class kids, we identified four Universal Relationship

Rhythms! These rhythms have become known as "The RFactor." These relationship rhythms are Respect, Responsibility, Reframing, and Resilience. When working in-sync, these rhythms offer a powerful framework for cultivating alignment within teams, families, and ourselves. The following paragraphs outline the significance of these rhythms and how they can be effectively employed to create a harmonious and thriving lifestyle.

Respect: The Foundation of Alignment

Respect forms the bedrock of any successful relationship, be it in a professional team or within a family. In the context of teams, respecting each member's unique perspectives and contributions is crucial. When individuals feel valued and acknowledged, they are more likely to engage fully and invest in the collective project. Practicing presence, active listening, encouraging open dialogue, and promoting diversity of thought are all ways to foster heightened respect within teams.

Within families, respect is equally vital. Each member's feelings, opinions, and boundaries "get to" be honored and valued. What if children were taught first to respect themselves, and then their elders and others? In return, adults "get to" respect the autonomy and individuality of the younger generation. Notice the language here, "get to" versus "should," which leaves the door open as a conversation versus a demand. By creating an environment of mutual respect, family members will feel safe expressing themselves, leading to improved communication and stronger emotional bonds.

Responsibility: Empowering Ownership & Accountability

Being Responsible is not about accepting blame when things go wrong; it is even more so about clear communication and empowering individuals to stand in ownership of their actions and choices. In teams, fostering a sense of responsibility involves entrusting individual members with autonomy and encouraging them to take initiative and collaborate. By instilling a culture of openness, curiosity and accountability, teams can move forward collectively and learn from their stumbles and strides.

In families, clear messages and shared responsibilities can promote a sense of belonging and cooperation. Parents who engage children in age-appropriate tasks teach them the value and feelings of connection when contributing to the family unit. When each member feels responsible for their actions and the well-being of others, it strengthens the family and team bond and encourages a supportive environment.

Reframing: Embracing Change & Adversity

Life is full of challenges and uncertainties. The rhythm of reframing involves adopting a positive mindset and seeking opportunities for growth, even in difficult situations. In our Relational Leadership work as coaches, trainers' authors, and speakers, we've seen teams, leaders encourage a culture of adaptability and innovation. When challenges arise, reframing allows teams to see setbacks as steppingstones to improvement, promoting a growth-oriented mentality.

Similarly, in families, the ability to reframe situations enables them to weather storms together. Rather than succumbing to despair during tough times, families can use reframing to find silver linings, build resilience, and support one another through thick and thin.

Resilience: Bouncing Back Stronger

Resilience is the capacity to bounce back after facing adversity or stress. Both teams and families encounter challenges, and resilience is what enables them to withstand those tests. In teams, cultivating resilience requires leaders to support team members in developing coping strategies and fostering a culture that values mental and emotional well-being. Resilient teams are better equipped to manage pressure, maintain focus, and emerge from challenges stronger than before.

Within families, resilience strengthens the bonds between members, allowing them to endure hardships together. Encouraging open communication and providing emotional support during challenging times promotes resilience within the family unit. This resilience, in turn, nurtures a sense of security, belonging, and trust, which are foundational elements of a harmonious family dynamic.

Creating alignment within teams and families is an ongoing process that offers daily opportunities to choose how we are showing up. Ask yourself, "Am I choosing the Universal Relationship Rhythms of Respect, Responsibility, Reframing, and Resilience to build trusting individuals and teams that are prospering and thriving in every relationship in their lives?"

By promoting respect, encouraging responsibility, embracing reframing, and cultivating resilience, both teams and families will forge deeper connections, achieve collective goals, and navigate challenges with greater belonging and ease. Embracing these rhythms not only enhances productivity and performance but also contributes to overall well-being and fulfillment in both professional and personal spheres. As we implement the RFactor in our daily lives, we create a more aligned harmonious world, both at work and at home.

Like the harmonious orchestration of instruments in a symphony, aligning our values, goals, and aspirations with all our relationships creates a sublime symphony of unity. This synchronized "score" is the invisible thread that weaves hearts together, fostering a deep connection and understanding. Alignments lay the groundwork for shared visions, while agreements function as the roadmap to traverse the journey together. This synergy empowers us to weather the storms that inevitably cross our paths, providing us with the resilience and support to face challenges head-on.

Reflections:

1. Can you recall when you identified and addressed a misalignment in a relationship by focusing on the "respect" ratio?
2. How can the willingness to "compromise" play a role in striking a balance between an individual need and shared goals?
3. Do you have a relational misalignment or disagreement which you can open to new possibilities by "reframing" the situation?

Maris Segal & Ken Ashby

About Ken Ashby & Maris Segal: From Mindset to Marketing, Ken Ashby & Maris Segal, a husband and wife dynamic duo, have spent the last thirty-plus years bringing an innovative, collaborative voice to issues, causes, and brands.

As entrepreneurs, activists, business strategists, executive producers, coaches, authors, speakers, and trainers, Ken & Maris work with the public and private sectors from boardrooms and classrooms to the world stage. They are known for creating high-touch experiences that unite diverse populations across a broad spectrum of business, policy, and social issues.

Their leadership expertise in Business Relationship Marketing, Organizational Change & Cultural Inclusion, Personal Growth, Project Management, Public Affairs, and Philanthropy Strategies has been called upon by companies and their agencies. Their experience includes: consumer and financial brands, Olympic organizers, Super Bowls, America's 400th Anniversary, Harvard Kennedy School, Archdiocese of LA and NY Papal visit planners, the White House and celebrities across the arts, entertainment, sports, and culinary genres.

With Ken's expertise as an award-winning singer-songwriter, they launched ONE SONG, a songwriting workshop series designed to unleash creativity in individuals and teams.

Their **DRIVE** method: **D**esire, **R**elationships, **I**ntention, **V**ision and **E**mpowerment sits at the core of their companies Prosody Creative Services, ONE SONG, and Segal Leadership Global to set a path for every client to Build High Performing Businesses & Elevate Personal &

Professional Leadership for Maximum Impact & a 360-degree Thriving Life!

Author's Website: *www.SegalLeadershipGlobal.com*

Book Series Website: *www.TheBookOfInfluence.com*

MICHELLE MRAS

COMMUNICATION DISCONNECT

When I was a junior in high school, I had a teacher who was also the debate club coach. At the time, I had no idea what debate entailed, but I became quite aware of it as my teacher began to prompt me to join the club. He told me I had an innate talent for debate. When I looked at him perplexed, he explained that my personality made me ideal: my vocal tone was even, my demeanor was calm, and I was quite gifted at approaching subjects from multiple points of view. I didn't understand the gift that I had developed throughout my youth: I have always been the "peace maker."

I am the fourth child of six. Our father is from Southern Louisiana and our mother is from the Philippines. I spent my formative years living in the Philippines constantly maneuvering through language and cultural hurdles not only from the country, but from within my home. My father maintained his Louisiana dialect and my mother spoke at least four Philippine dialects in addition to English.

I learned early that not everyone had my experiences or perspective. Not everyone expressed their thoughts the same, and not all loud tones or fast spoken phrases are meant to be aggressive. My father and mother had completely different tonalities and speech patterns. When my father was loud, he was happy. When my mother was loud, she was angry. Naturally, when they were quiet in tone, it meant quite the opposite. I learned to listen to understand and not to respond just to tone. I became a watcher of body language because my father moved less when upset and my mother moved more.

What communication habits have you developed from your childhood? How do they serve you? It's important to examine how you naturally listen and respond. Only from that introspection can you understand how you communicate, listen, and, in turn, determine where you need to develop your skills as a communicator.

Communication is how we connect with others regardless of whether we do it verbally or non-verbally. As an Executive Speaking Coach, I pay close attention to how people communicate and how they can best improve those skills. We must learn to listen, understand it is not "about us" and when we are communicating, the other person is always responding from their perspective. These three factors (listening, perspective and what's it for them) in all communication whether from the stage or face-to-face are foundational to effective communication and most importantly, creating alignment. We will break the three factors down from how I learned these skills living in another country where English was not the primary language.

Listening

What you hear and what the other person is saying is not necessarily what is intended. You must combine what you know with what is happening around you to interpret the meaning. A great example of an innocent misunderstanding is when my fiancé, Michael, first met my mother's side of the family.

He and I drove to Georgia where many of my uncles and aunties had relocated when they left the Philippines. They were gathered at my grandmother's house to meet us. When we arrived, we found my uncle mowing the grass. It was a sweltering, humid afternoon in Atlanta, Georgia. We made introductions between my uncle and my fiancé. He pointed us to the front door as he went back to his tedious yard work. Michael said as we walked away, "Do you need help?" My uncle replied with an exasperated, "Yes, please!"

I introduced Michael to the aunties and my grandmother who were in the house cooking for the festivities that were later that evening. Once he made his rounds of chit-chat, he went out to help my uncle. I joined with the cooking preparation and once we were done, we sat, shared stories, and laughed. Several hours had passed when Michael and my uncle came back into the house. Michael plopped down on the floor next to me while my uncle went to the kitchen to grab them both a glass of lemonade. My uncle returned with Michael's frosty cold glass and Michael eagerly accepted. My uncle raved to the family how Michael was such a strong worker and volunteered to work outside on such a horribly humid day. He went on about all the work they did together in the blistering heat.

Then, he looked at Michael with a huge smile and inquired, "So, do you feel like fainting?" Michael responded, "I'm tired, but feel fine." My uncle looked perplexed and repeated his question, "No, do you feel like fainting?" Michael replied the same as before. Finally, he tried one more time with exaggerated hand gestures, "Not fainting. Fain-Ting, like Fain-ting the pence." One of the aunties corrected him in their native tongue of Tagalog, "You are using the wrong pronunciation." Then, my uncle understood but they still had to explain it to Michael.

To this day, we still laugh about this miscommunication. In the Philippine language, the sounds of the English letters "F' and "P" are identical.

Perspective

In this scenario, Michael couldn't understand why he kept getting asked if he felt like fainting. It was a sweltering day in Georgia, but he had not complained or shown any signs of heat exhaustion. On the other hand, Michael's response did not make sense to my uncle. My uncle was asking about "painting the fence" but was getting answered about how Michael felt.

If we didn't have a room full of aunties who understood the accent and clarified my uncle's meaning, the request could have become heated with the insistence of fainting rather than painting. My fiancé later admitted that he was getting slightly annoyed that my uncle thought he couldn't handle the hard work. He was glad that it was a mispronunciation.

What's in it for Them

What we all failed to recognize in the interaction between my uncle and fiancé was that my uncle had a big smile on his face when he asked Michael if he felt like fainting. The facial expression didn't fit the wording. Therefore, there must be another meaning. Creating alignment is that subtle. What my uncle was after was to have more help. The conversation from the initiation of volunteering assistance to the lemonade and asking if, "You feel like painting" was about what he needed.

It is human nature to think of ourselves first. That is why so many people admire the works of people like Ghandi and Mother Theresa. They went against the natural tendency and put others before themselves.

Bottom line, in creating alignment with others, you must communicate clearly. Seek to understand before you respond with haste, anger, or judgement. I train within my coaching and speaking engagements that body language speaks louder than words. If my fiancé had watched the body language of my uncle, he would have noticed the inquiry about his physical health was not attached with a look of concern, rather a face full of glee and anticipation. His body language stated, "I am a little embarrassed to ask more from you," not "Are you okay?"

Listen to understand, not to respond.

Listen to understand the circumstances and perspective.

Everyone you interact with is wondering, "What's it for me?" That is, with the exception of you, of course, because you have studied and now have read this chapter about creating alignment.

"To effectively communicate, we must realize that we are all different in the way we perceive the world and use this understanding as a guide to our communication with others."
~ Tony Robbins

CREATING ALIGNMENT

To make friends and influence people, you must learn to step back and allow others to speak. My experience in debate helped me understand subjects and fight for views that did not match my own. I learned that every argument, even those I don't agree with, is founded in the other person's perception of reality and experience. Listening to understand is fundamental for effective communication. I have made it a practice to allow others to have their space to speak freely without judgment or retaliation.

Having others feel good around you is a powerful tool to create alignment. My childhood and family life have provided me with a lifelong practice at creating alignment. I was watching body language and matching tonality because of the multiple languages and accents within my family and extended family both in the Philippines and in Louisiana.

You have the same opportunity to learn from those around you—pay attention. Practice these skills on your family, both young and old, strangers you meet, and friends. You'll find as you practice outside of your circle, you will never meet a stranger. The ability to create alignment is a sure way to create relationships that last.

MICHELLE MRAS

About Dr. Michelle Mras: Dr. Michelle Mras is an award-winning, internationally recognized inspirational speaker, published #1 Best Selling Author, intuitive leader, wife, and mother who has been stirring audiences and individuals to action through her compelling message of self-leadership, resilience and living a life of intention. Michelle's infectious presentations and coaching inspire her clients to rise above negative self-talk to reclaim their inner grit.

Michelle encourages you to be your best version every day and live unapologetically. Her fiery spirit and passion drive her to candidly share the key moments that transformed her into the irresistible force she is today. Learn more about Michelle and her writing at www.MichelleMras.com

Author's Website: *www.MichelleMras.com*

Book Series Website: *www.TheBookOfInfluence.com*

MORGAN TAYLOR RUDNICK

ALIGNMENT BEGINS WITH MIND, BODY, & SOUL

Creating alignment can be unique to each individual, but in my opinion, creating alignment begins with the mind, body, and soul. I believe you cannot have true alignment without all three.

Being an aligned being does take work, but aren't we all seeking to be in full alignment with ourselves so we can pursue our greatest dreams? When we are aligned, we're able to honor our natural gifts, skills, abilities, and talents. We can really tap into our hearts desires and create from a place of love and flow.

Of course, we can't always stay in alignment; it's near impossible, as people, places, things, and situations can throw us off and this okay. The key to calling your energy back and getting back in flow, alignment, is being aware.

Let me share a story about my client, Luna. Luna is a single mother who was going through a horrible divorce with a violent individual and felt like she had no sense of who she truly was. She did not know how to move forward; she was living in survival mode. She could not see past the fear and anxiety and had trouble feeling safe in her body and environment. She was exhausted from constantly looking over her shoulder and thinking something bad was going to happen to her and her family.

We discussed societal conditioning and working on the deconditioning process. Society conditions all of us, creates these deep-seated fears, these should and should nots. These beliefs become deeply engrained in us and it becomes a part of story.

Luna's mental landscape and inner dialogue was like a swamp—negative thoughts were running amuck. It was hard for Luna to move forward when her thoughts were keeping her trapped. Luna became fed up one day and wanted to explore other options that can help her move forward.

We did some mediation techniques together and started to focus on what her body was trying to say instead of living in the mind. Living in the mind can cause all this fear, anxiety, and ultimately keep us stuck. Once we listen to what our body wants, we can quiet the mind "chatter in our head" and honor these desires.

As we were conducting our therapy sessions, we started to explore spirituality and what it means to be an aligned being. We started to focus on practices such as Human Design, energetic road mapping, astrology, etc.

We explored what made Luna happy. What did her envisioned life look like? This got her to thinking about spiritual practices, things she has always had a passion for but was told it would make no money or "it was stupid."

After Luna was able to break free from these thoughts, she was able to connect to her spirituality (a part of her that never left, but was lying dormant), and she was able to implement daily practices that helped her stay in the present moment.
Some of these practices included:

1. Journaling
2. Intention setting
3. Positive affirmations
4. Meditation
5. Breathwork
6. Cupping

7. Acupuncture
8. Walking in nature
9. Play

We worked on connecting to her inner-child and identified ways she could play, which allowed her creativity to shine through. After 30 days of these practices, Luna was able to explore her desires from a heart centered space.

After a few months of being on this healing journey, she was able to start feeling safer in her body and was able to gain insight into what some of her desires were. She wanted to be an energetic guide for others. She wanted to guide people through their own journeys. Her healing journey came with its own set of challenges but as she was more aware she was able to lean into the resistance and take small action steps to move through it. Luna felt like her fire was lit and she now needed to move forward with her deepest desires.

Today, take a moment to sit with yourself and clear your mind. Start to feel your breath and your feet firmly planted on the ground, then ask yourself, "If I had a magic wand, what would my most envisioned life look like? What would I create? What are my truest desires? What does alignment mean to me?"

Morgan Taylor Rudnick

About Morgan Taylor Rudnick: Morgan graduated with her Master's in Psychology, with an emphasis in Marriage and Family Therapy. She felt a special calling to focus on helping those with past traumas overcome them while lessening the trauma's impact in the development of mental illness and addictions.

Prior to earning her Master's in Psychology, Morgan studied Kinesiology and Nutrition and earned a certification as a Health and Wellness Coach. She believes that the mind, body, and soul are interconnected, and we cannot treat one without addressing the others.

Morgan is the Co-founder and Chief Executive Officer of a substance abuse and mental health facility that strives to create a customized approach to recovery. Her goal is to bridge the gap between Western and Eastern practices to create a holistic-based approach to treatment.

Additionally, Morgan and her business partner serve as Energetic Branding Consultants, helping business owners align with their unique energetic type and build a brand that honors that.

Morgan and her business partner also service clients looking for a more spiritual approach that includes services such as: human design, astrology, numerology, tarot and oracle cards, and other spiritual practices to help map out a unique blueprint for each individual.

Author's Website: *www.CustomizedConsultingServices.com*

Book Series Website: *www.TheBookofInfluence.com*

NADIA FRANCOIS

THE INFLUENCE OF ALIGNMENT ON THE CULTURE OF AN ORGANIZATION

Alignment is defined as a state of agreement between individuals within a system or organization. In the business world, alignment refers to the coordination of goals, actions, and strategies ensuring individual harmony with the mission of the organization. Effective alignment promotes clarity, cohesion, and unity leading to optimal outcomes and productivity which are all positive traits that most companies strive for.

Alignment plays a very important role in shaping the culture of an organization. It influences values, behaviors, and the overall environment and allows team members to feed off the positive synergy.

As leaders, we are responsible for upholding the mission of our organization by first, being the example and secondly, by clearly articulating the mission, vision, and goals to the team. When team members understand their roles, confusion and duplication of efforts are avoided and the overall culture of the business is influenced positively. To achieve this level of influence we must consider the actions required to obtain alignment:

Cultivating Positive Relationships

Cultivating positive relationships is essential to achieving personal and professional success. When we are working towards common goals, values, and objectives a connection is made and trust is built, fostering a long-term relationship. Nurturing these relationships, moving with integrity and compassion sets a tone and emphasizes to each party that they can rely on each other. Reliability and honesty are essential in building a solid foundation. All parties are clear on their contributions and expectations fostering a lasting connection. These positive relationships fuels alignment and empowers team members to bond and collaborate.

Effective Communication

Communicating effectively is a huge component of achieving alignment and influencing the culture of an organization. Effective communication involves being open, honest, and respectful. Expressing ourselves clearly and receiving the perspective of others helps us to understand their thoughts and experiences. We are then able to show compassion and empathy and genuinely show interest in their well-being and when people feel that someone is listening and values their opinion they will communicate even more openly and effectively.

Recognition & Reward

Showing appreciation for the efforts and accomplishments of team members goes a long way. It shows them that their contributions and skills are valued, and they are being noticed. When team members align with the goals, values, and mission of the organization, they have a sense of pride and fulfillment in their actions. They will continue to strive for excellence and to execute the objectives of the organization and obtain optimal results.

Lead by Example

As leaders, we must lead example because people do what they see and not what you say. Being the change we wish to see promotes ownership and accountability. We are allowing team members to witness alignment through our actions, decisions, and communication. Displaying the core values throughout our daily walk and talk is how to lead by example. When the team members observe this consistently and authentically, it shapes the attitudes, behaviors, and productivity within the organization, positively influencing its culture.

Promote Innovation & Creativity

Encouraging team members to be innovative sparks creativity and brings about a willingness to adapt to change and new ideas. Team members that are allowed to have creative input are more invested in the success of the organization and are better equipped to align with the company culture. This also fosters collaboration, trust, and the need for continuous improvement. Innovation and creativity drive alignment towards common goals and initiatives highlighting inclusive decision making and diverse perspectives.

Provide Support

A major component of alignment is support. When a team is properly supported, they make confident decisions, are more accountable, and are better equipped to overcome obstacles. Knowing that the company leadership has their back and will be fair in all situations boosts morale and confidence. Support functions in a number of capacities including financial and emotional. This means that all necessary supplies and equipment are in good repair and available for use, compensation is competitive and above market rate, and a positive working environment is provided. Leaders that are supportive empower individuals to easily adapt to change, openly express themselves, and share ideas.

The power of influence in forging alignment can transform the culture of an organization using these foundational principles. Alignment influences the culture of an organization when leaders cultivate positive relationships, communicate effectively, recognize and reward individuals, lead by example, promote innovation and creativity, and provide support.

Of course, there are other principles that can be attributed to alignment, but these stand out the most to me. The response to these actions directly affects the growth and development of an organization's leadership team and those they serve. Alignment creates a harmonious synergy that attracts like-minds and enhances the performance of individuals working toward a common goal while upholding integral values and objectives.

Trust, credibility, respect, and purpose are aligned creating an environment of inclusivity, confidence, and open communication. The organization's culture is positively impacted along with the mindset and development of its team members.

NADIA FRANCOIS

About Nadia Francois: Nadia Francois is a serial entrepreneur with a heart for people. A hairstylist by trade, Nadia holds current licenses in Cosmetology and Barbering, a B.S. in Business Administration, and a certificate in Women's Entrepreneurship. The Louisiana native began her entrepreneurial journey at the age of 19 and has used her experiences and knowledge to help other business owners start and grow their ventures. In 2018, Nadia served as the inaugural Ms. Black Louisiana Empowerment representing her state by serving at several community projects and by hosting outreach activities.

The Beautypreneur and non-profit founder became a first-time author in August of 2018. In 2019, she was nominated for Business Woman of the Year by the Greater Southwest Louisiana Black Chamber of Commerce. In July 2020, the What's Your Super Power Empire began with an anthology and expanded into the digital TV world. In 2021, Nadia continued to enhance her digital footprint with the addition of *Power Conversations Magazine & Podcast* which are additional extensions of her WYSP Digital Media which caters to minority entrepreneurs and their advancement.

In 2022, Nadia was awarded the "Game Changer" award by the Beauty Industry Community Awards Organization, has spoken on various global platforms and is launching her newest #1 Best-Selling Book, *A Mother's Prayer* anthology. This goal-getter contributes her success to grace and mercy. Her number one assignment is being the mother and sole provider for her four sons, the driving force behind her persistent hustle and diligent pursuit of greatness.

Author's Website: *www.NadiaFrancois.com*

Book Series Website: *www.TheBookOfInfluence.com*

NANCY DEBRA BARROWS

THE POWER OF ALIGNMENT: UNLEASHING THE EXTRAORDINARY

"If you want to go fast, go alone. If you want to go far, go together." This profound African proverb beautifully captures the essence of alignment and its significance in both personal and professional realms. Understanding the factors that impede people and teams from aligning is of paramount importance as it enables us to overcome obstacles and forge powerful, productive communication channels.

In my role as a communication coach specializing in "Power-Filled Communication," I have the privilege of collaborating with executives, companies, and individuals to demystify the common barriers that hinder effective communication. With over two decades of experience as a speech-language pathologist focused on social cognition, I deeply appreciate the value of aligning ourselves with others and within ourselves.

Reflect on those instances when you encountered communication breakdowns or sought to mend such situations. Instinctively, you comprehend the challenges that arise during those moments, and your expertise lies in successfully navigating through them.

CREATING ALIGNMENT

As you embark on the journey of becoming a Power-Filled communicator and a catalyst for alignment, the initial step is to recognize the initial subtle signs that things have veered off course. Once you master this awareness, it is time to peel away the superficial layers of discourse reaching below the surface, to the root of the problem.

In creating my business, "The Chick With The Toolbelt," and developing The Power-Filled Communicator coaching method, I focused on the underlying disharmony that often arises from unfulfilled basic human needs. Those obstacles that most frequently contribute to communication breakdown.

- The need to feel that you and your ideas and perspective matter.
- The need to feel valued as a team member, even within a small team of two.
- The need for respect and an acknowledgment of equal importance among fellow team members.
- The need to be genuinely heard and understood.
- The need to have a voice and contribute to decision-making processes.

Alignment plays an indispensable role in meeting these fundamental needs. However, the creation of alignment goes beyond the sole pursuit of achieving results or goals.

Aligned communication recognizes and cherishes the significance of both the process and the relationships involved. It necessitates the employment of authentic encouragement, valuing the relationship(s) and effective communication strategies, all underpinned by a genuine display of respect and empathy.

Dale Carnegie, renowned for his timeless teachings, shines a spotlight on the power of alignment in personal growth and interpersonal relationships, in his book, *How to Win Friends and Influence People*. His wisdom illustrates how alignment can transform lives, foster genuine connections, and unlock the extraordinary potential residing within each of us.

Alignment transcends being a mere buzzword; it stands as a fundamental principle at the very core of human interaction.

At its essence, alignment entails discovering common ground, cultivating harmony, and collaborating towards shared goals. In this pursuit, empathetic understanding, active listening, and an open-minded embrace of diverse perspectives are essential. By aligning our actions, intentions, and values with those of others, we set the stage for remarkable outcomes and accomplishments.

The art of active listening lies at the heart of alignment. I cannot overemphasize the transformative power and urge you to genuinely and wholeheartedly listen to others. Active listening demands our full presence, a genuine desire to understand, and the willingness to suspend judgment. We must remain curious.

When working with clients, I refer back to the "But, why?" phase that occurs while growing up. Children repeatedly ask, "Why?" and continue to probe, without judgment, to seek understanding. Through this deep immersion into the thoughts and experiences of others, we forge profound connections and gain invaluable insights into their motivations and aspirations. Active listening fosters mutual understanding, embraces diverse opinions, and serves as the bedrock upon which alignment is built. It connects us human to human.

Empathy acts as the bridge that connects us to one another. It grants us the ability to understand and share the feelings of others. By nurturing empathy within ourselves, we can align our actions and choices with the needs and desires of those around us. Empathy cultivates trust, kindles compassion, and creates an environment that nurtures alignment. By genuinely displaying interest in the thoughts and emotions of others, we establish positive connections and foster a sense of trust.

The potency of alignment reaches its pinnacle when individuals unite around shared goals. As we rally together with a common purpose, our collective efforts synergize, propelling us towards unparalleled success. When working with clients we focus on the power of praise. Recognizing and celebrating the contributions of each team member becomes imperative, ensuring that everyone feels valued and deeply connected to the shared mission, because when this is not the case, you are left with chaos and destruction.

Cultivating a positive and enthusiastic atmosphere by authentically expressing your own excitement and letting individuals know, and feel, like valued contributors, augments the spirit of cooperation and collaboration, increasing the likelihood of garnering support and winning people over. In other words, success!

The impact of alignment extends far beyond individual interactions, permeating the fabric of our surroundings. When we align our actions with our values, we inspire and encourage those around us to do the same. Alignment becomes an infectious force, transforming relationships, teams, and entire organizations. This transformation manifests in heightened productivity, enhanced collaboration, and the creation of a harmonious work environment.

Alignment is not limited to professional settings alone; its principles are equally applicable within personal relationships. Employing active listening, using empathy, creating respectful space for different perceptions and suspending judgment—creating alignment—we reduce misunderstandings, hurt feelings and abandoned, unfinished interactions that may lead to resentment and silencing voices.

By creating alignment in our actions, thoughts, and values with people in our lives, we cultivate deeper connections and foster a profound sense of understanding. To promote alignment in personal relationships, empathy, active communication, and a genuine willingness to see the world through others' eyes are essential. By aligning our lives with the people we deeply care about and those new to our lives, we forge enduring bonds that withstand the tests of time.

Alignment serves as a guiding light, illuminating the path towards extraordinary relationships and personal growth. Power-Filled Communication coaching imparts the wisdom that true success lies not solely in individual achievements but in our ability to connect, empathize, and align with others. As we wholeheartedly embrace the transformative power of alignment, we unlock the boundless potential to create lasting impact, foster meaningful connections, and contribute to building a better world.

Let us harness the extraordinary possibilities that lie within alignment and embark on this transformative journey together. Sign up for a free, one-on-one, 15-minute consultation to discover how Power-Filled Communication can transform YOUR life, relationships and business! *Calendly.com/nancybarrows*

Nancy Debra Barrows

About Nancy Debra Barrows: 2X #1 Best-Selling Author, known as the Queen of Engagement, Co-Founder of peakAboo analytics, named a 'LinkedIn Top Voice' and one of the 'Top 50 Most Impactful People on Linkedln', Nancy Barrows is a 20+ year Entrepreneur of a thriving private practice, Keynote Speaker and Coach who, using her 20 years of experience and expertise in Social Cognition, developed her program, The Chick with the Toolbelt. She partners with clients on showing up, finding their voice, and fully engaging their community across platforms and media, guiding them to reach their personal and business growth goals and build robust revenue streams, while sharing tools to maintain these changes independently.

Highlighted on ROKU TV, LinkedInLIVE, Apple Podcasts, Spotify, YouTube, Twitter, Anchor, GooglePodcasts, Stitcher, AmazonMusic, Audible, Voice Your Vibe.com and more, Nancy's LIVE every Wednesday and Saturday, co-hosting the Global Award-Winning Live Shows #WhatsGoodWednesday and #ShoutOutSaturday, which have been featured on NASDAQ, Forbes, Thrive Global, Yahoo Finance, ROKUTV, AmazonFire, The CW, multiple #1 best-selling books and syndicated on a SmartTV Network. Nancy has thrived through adversity and employs her experience to help others find their voice.

By telling her story and creating the #RadiatingReal movement, she is making a positive impact, encouraging and inspiring others to do the same. Book your FREE 15-minute consultation with Nancy: *calendly.com/nancybarrows*

Author's Website: *www.linktr.ee/VoiceYourVibe*

Book Series Website: *www.TheBookOfInfluence.com*

DR. ONIKA SHIRLEY

JOURNEYING TOGETHER TODAY FOR FUTURE SUCCESS

"The task of leadership is to create an alignment of strengths so strong that it makes the system's weaknesses irrelevant."
~ Peter Drucker

In today's fast-paced and seemingly ever-changing environment, it is vital that leaders master essential competencies and build trust to keep everything aligned during periods of transformation. During these periods, it is important to create alignment and to have others with direct impact involved early on. As a business owner, I have discovered that there is a core set of actions to ensure this is even possible from the very beginning. In many coaching conversations over the last few years, I have implemented the following three core actions and adopted them as foundational pillars to contribute to my success.

1. Set and regularly communicate clear expectations. Give those involved a purpose, confirm everything, and follow up.
2. Secure commitments from others that's dedicated to meeting those expectations. Don't assume anything.
3. Hold people accountable for not fulfilling their commitments. Hold regular one-on-ones.

When things move rapidly, it's easy to fall in the trap of failure if everything is not aligned. I have found that when a person is not personally responsible for doing the work themselves it's vital to communicate clear expectations, secure dedicated commitments from others and hold them accountable to their yes. This simple three step process creates alignment with others and this process can make or break a business. This approach has been said by many and probably done by even more, but we have also heard the cliché that its easier said than done.

Whether you're managing a two-person household or a team of ten, it's nearly impossible for your home or your business to grow and move on to the next level of success if your whole team isn't on the same page and reading out of the same book. When there's a common goal, those that are fully invested will work cohesively and bring forth their greatest efforts. I think creating alignment is important and it's certainly a contributing factor to helping the household, the team and/or the business move forward together. I want to lean more toward alignment in the marketplace during our time here and I like to refer to as marketplace alignment.

What is marketplace alignment?

I am defining marketplace alignment as when those that are called to serve have a clear understanding of their audiences' goals and objectives and have a clear vision for collaborative and individual long-term success. When we as individuals truly come together, we tend to accomplish so much more much faster, and I have found it to be true that we are better together.

As a person that serves in ministry, in the marketplace, and in manufacturing, essentially the idea is to identify critical priorities and to align goals, specific roles, and procedures to ensure that everyone is on the same page and working toward the same outcomes. As I walk in a role of leadership in all three areas identified, it's important that we start off by identifying issues, concerns, and opportunities. Then it's equally important to develop an action plan to deal with the critical priorities. This includes explicit accountabilities for each action item.

I have learned through experience to ONLY assign specific actions to those that are in the room and are invested in the achievement of the desired outcome. I feel like it can be a waste of time to get outsiders that didn't attend to have a vested interest, and therefore they have no ownership for any action.

Creating alignment has changed previous outcomes from "Problematic" or "Cautionary" to "Good." This is a great start towards the success in which we desire. When things aren't aligned, breakdowns in the system are uneven, the business becomes difficult to control and outcomes start drifting off course. Misalignment makes it harder to hit your targets and it can make it feel like failure even when success is possible.

In all, when being intentional on important and complex issues involving a diverse set of people, it is essential to ensure that everyone understands the outcomes expected, why these are important, the role that each individual plays, and how they will interact as a team to accomplish those objectives. Some critical lessons I have learned over the years have been:

1. Be clear about the desired outcomes from the beginning.
2. Understand the challenges you're aiming to overcome.
3. Only include key stakeholders in any of your meetings: those who can impact results and those who have a vested interest in the results.
4. Determine what resources will be needed to accomplish these results.
5. Follow up follow up follow up! Without adequate follow-up things will essentially fall through the cracks and remain unchanged.

Failure to focus on creating alignment will inevitably affect performance, productivity, and your peace. It's not enough to just have the right processes in place, but there need to be shared culture as well as vision to thrive in the process and grow beyond the last place of success. If your people aren't eating, breathing, and living your values everyday, achieving and maintaining success will be hard at best, and at worse simply impossible to sustain and maintain.

As I have worked as a consultant and as an employer, I had to set clear expectations from the beginning. People need to know what's expected of them and they also need to know what they can expect from the people that's leading and guiding them. It can't be one sided. It's vital that this process allow space of input at every stage and on every level.

When being a part of something, people want to feel included. This alignment of energy and emotions is a powerful agent of change, and it can be replicable. It guides people through the different stages and processes and keeps them on the path to future success. Alignment is not easy, but it is possible. Alignment can be thought of as the bridge that fills the gap. The gap could cover fulfilled expectations, motivating individuals involved, and hitting the set targets.

Les Brown said, "Align yourself with people that you can learn from, people who want more out of life, people who are stretching and searching and seeking some higher ground in life." Les Brown is right. The people we surround ourselves with matters. These people can be partners, employees, friends, and/or family. It doesn't matter how good a strategy may be—if we fail to get the right people behind it, we will not be able to execute it.

The constraint becomes more acute as the nature of how we work changes. As a team player and a team builder, an increasingly fluid process requires greater exercise of judgement, applied in context of the agreed upon outcomes. Post Covid-19 businesses can't depend on merely telling people what to do; instead, business owners must help our people see things in the same light as we see them and assist them in understanding why it is vital that they make choices consistent with the strategy to experience overall success. As we develop an environment and start to shift mindsets, we will begin to experience success and expect change.

Why the focus on influencing others and creating alignment? As my pastor would always say, leaders are not leading if no one is following—he is just a man taking a walk. Influence is about changing how others think; alignment is about bringing individuals together around some shared perspective or plan and has a lot to do with what is they do.

If we are to "do better," and win at what we call success, we must stand toe to toe with the challenges of differing views and build alignment around something other than the "lowest common denominator." We must be willing to work together sufficiently to move forward.

Carnegie's lessons have withstood the test of time and his advice on how to communicate, lead and work effectively and efficiently remains timeless yet today. Dale Carnegie said, "People rarely succeed unless they have fun in what they are doing." Can I challenge you to create alignment with those you have been called to serve and have fun while doing it?

DR. ONIKA SHIRLEY

About Dr. Onika L. Shirley: Dr. Onika L. Shirley is from West Helena, Arkansas. She is the Founder and CEO of Action Speaks Volume, Inc. She is a Procrastination Strategist and Behavior Change Expert and is known for building unshakable confidence, stopping procrastination, and getting your dreams out of your head into your life. She is a Master Storyteller and International Speaker and serves in Global Ministry. Dr. Onika has worked in manufacturing for the last sixteen and half year where she has held several leadership positions including production operations manager. During her time as production operations manager, she actively worked on creating an environment of unity and a place to work on one accord working towards the same mission and vision. She worked to be more productive while having key members hold themselves accountable for their area of responsibility.

Dr. Onika International Best-Selling Author, International Award Recipient, Serial Entrepreneur, and Global Philanthropist impacting lives in the USA, Africa, India, and Pakistan. Dr. O is a Motivational Speaker and Christian Counselor. Dr. Onika is the Founder and Director of Action Speaks Volume Orphanage Home and Sewing School in Telangana State, India, Founder and Director of Action Speaks Volume Sewing School in Khanewal and Shankot, Pakistan. She founded, operated, and visited an Orphanage home in Tuni, India for four years and she supported widows in Tuni, India. She is the founder of Empowering Eight Inner Circle, ASV C.A.R.E.S, ASV Next Level Living Program, and P6 Solutions and Consulting. She has served for 13 years as a therapeutic foster parent for the State of Arkansas, but Dr. O does is most proud of her profound faith in Christ and her opportunity to serve the body of Christ globally.

Author's Website: *www.ActionSpeaksVolumes.com*
Book Series Website: *www.TheBookOfInfluence.com*

ROBYN KAYE SCOTT

FROM THE TOP OF YOUR MOUNTAIN

Consider creating an experience and presenting yourself with the unique opportunity to pursue your passion. You get to witness the genuine connection unfolding right before your eyes. This comes naturally to us because we are Connection Catalysts. To us, it makes sense. I want you to recognize and understand that this is only natural for some.

We thrive on fostering connections between people, igniting sparks of inspiration, and cultivating a sense of community. As Connection Catalysts, we believe in the power of bringing individuals together to share their passions, dreams, and aspirations. By creating a space where authenticity reigns supreme, we pave the way for meaningful interactions and collaborations to flourish.

Imagine a world where each person is encouraged to pursue their unique interests and talents, supported by a network of like-minded individuals who cheer them on every step of the way. This is the world we envision, where pursuing passion is not just a solitary journey but a collective celebration of individuality and creativity.

So, embrace the opportunity to be a part of this transformative experience. Let yourself be swept away by the magic of genuine connections and the endless possibilities that arise when we come together with open hearts and minds. As you embark on this journey, remember that being a Connection Catalyst is not just a role—it's a way of life that celebrates the beauty of human connection in all its forms.

You possess a unique gift and talent! You need to comprehend how exceptional you are just the way you are. Celebrate yourself as much as you celebrate the realization of your plans!

Embrace your individuality and cherish the qualities that make you stand out from the crowd. Your talents and abilities are what set you apart and make you shine. Remember to credit yourself for all you have achieved and the person you are becoming. Keep nurturing your gifts and continue to pursue your dreams with passion and determination. You are a remarkable individual, and the world is waiting to witness your greatness.

As you journey through life, remember to always stay true to yourself and embrace the unique qualities that make you who you are. Your individuality is a gift that should be celebrated and treasured. Take pride in your strengths and continue to work on areas where you wish to grow.

Believe in your potential and never underestimate your impact on the world around you. Your uniqueness makes you unique, so don't be afraid to let your light shine bright. Keep pushing boundaries, challenging yourself, and striving for excellence. The world is full of possibilities, and you have the power to make a difference with your distinctive talents. Keep being your unique self, and always remember the incredible value you bring.

You are someone who can unite people. You create an immersion where individuals can detach from the external world and enter your space to be present. They can be themselves and connect with other authentic beings. This opportunity allows you to leave a lasting impression, create enthusiastic supporters, generate lifelong friends, and initiate a ripple effect that changes everything!

You have a remarkable ability to bring people together and foster genuine connections. By providing a space where individuals can truly be themselves and interact with others authentically, you have the power to leave a profound impact. Through this unique immersion experience, you not only cultivate enthusiastic supporters and lifelong friendships but also set in motion a ripple effect that has the potential to transform lives and shape the world around you. Keep embracing your gift of unity and authenticity, for it holds the key to creating a positive and lasting influence on those around you.

That is the essence of authentic connection. It is how we touch, move, and inspire people. Recognizing, celebrating, and acknowledging that you are forever changing lives with what you have created is crucial. Together, we have made a significant difference and impact.

Together, we have woven a tapestry of shared experiences, each thread representing a moment of connection and understanding. As we navigate the complexities of life, our interactions become the bridges that unite us in a shared journey. The beauty of authentic connection lies in its ability to transcend barriers and bring hearts together in harmony. Every word spoken and every gesture made resonates in the hearts of others, shaping their perspective and leaving an indelible mark.

In a world that often feels fragmented and chaotic, genuine connection is a beacon of hope, guiding us toward empathy, compassion, and unity. As we continue to touch lives and inspire change, let us carry forward the legacy of kindness and understanding, knowing that our collective impact has the potential to transform the world one connection at a time.

As you well know, this is not merely a one-time event. This marks the beginning of your evolution into the fully realized expression of a Connection Catalyst!

As you might anticipate, the growth continues! Each new event will foster further development. You may refer to this book often and take advantage of working with me beyond these pages! I have dedicated my career to supporting Connection Catalysts and am always here for you.

I am thrilled to witness the ongoing expansion that lies ahead! With every new opportunity that comes your way, you will undoubtedly experience even more growth and progress. Feel free to revisit the wisdom shared within these pages as often as needed, and remember that my guidance extends far beyond this book. I am wholeheartedly committed to empowering individuals like you who are passionate about fostering connections and making a positive impact. Please know that I am here to support you every step of the way.

This is about being able to replicate your event or swiftly create a new one! The clarity, skills, and tools gained from reading this book will empower you to create any event, anywhere. You make a significant difference in this world, and honing your skills is crucial when you aim to make a difference!

What you do with this knowledge and integrating it into your unique approach is your contribution to humankind. I want to acknowledge you in every possible way for taking the time to read this book, investing in your growth, and committing to bringing people together.

Your commitment to learning and personal growth is truly commendable. By embracing knowledge and incorporating it into your methods, you are not only enhancing yourself but also making a positive impact on the world around you. Your dedication to unity and connection is a decisive contribution to humanity. Thank you for investing in personal development and your willingness to unite and uplift others. Your efforts do not go unnoticed, and your actions inspire others to do the same. Keep shining bright and spreading your light to those around you.

ROBYN KAYE SCOTT

About Robyn Kaye Scott: Robyn Scott is a coach, speaker, Best-Selling Author, entrepreneur, female empowerment leader, and a networking queen. Robyn helps manage a prospecting program for Divinely Driven Results. She is a Habit Finder Coach and has worked closely with the president, Paul Blanchard, at the Og Mandino Group. She is also a certified Master Your Emotions Coach through Inscape World. Robyn is commonly known in professional communities as the Queen of Connection and Princess of Play. She has been working hard for the past nine years to hone her skills as a mentor and coach.

Robyn strives to teach people to annihilate judgments, embrace their own stories, and empower themselves to rediscover who they truly are. She is an international speaker and also teaches how to present yourself on stage.

Her first book, *Bringing People Together: Rediscovering the Lost Art of Face-to-Face Connecting, Collaborating, and Creating* was released in August 2019 and was a bestseller in seven categories. She is also a national multi-number one Best-Selling Co-author in the historic hit series *The 13 Steps To Riches* based on Napoleon Hill's work in *Think and Grow Rich.*

Author's Website: *www.RobynKayeScott.com*

Book Series Website: *www.TheBookofInfluence.com*

RYAN FRITZSCHE

ALIGNING INFLUENCE WITH AUTHENTIC CONNECTION

In my journey through the complex and ever-evolving world of merchant processing, the foundational principles of influence, as articulated by Dale Carnegie, have been a guiding light. Reflecting on my career, I see a path marked by learning, adaptation, and a relentless pursuit of understanding—not just the mechanics of my industry but, more crucially, the people within it.

Success in this field is not solely about mastering the technical aspects of merchant processing but also about mastering the art of human connection. Every transaction, deal, and negotiation is ultimately about building relationships, understanding needs, and creating value for all parties involved.

Dale Carnegie's principles of influence, such as showing genuine interest in others, listening actively, and empathizing with their perspectives, have proven to be invaluable tools in my interactions with clients, partners, and colleagues. By focusing on building trust, fostering open communication, and seeking mutual benefit, I have been able to navigate the challenges and seize the opportunities that come my way.

As I continue on this journey, I am committed to honing my skills as a merchant processor, relationship builder, and trusted advisor. By staying true to these fundamental principles of influence, I can forge stronger connections, achieve greater success, and make a positive impact in the ever-changing landscape of the merchant processing industry.

Starting in 2005, I found myself navigating the merchant services landscape, initially driven by necessity. My entry into this field was not born out of a passion for finance or technology but out of a need to address my financial over-leverage. This period of my life was characterized by a certain naivety and a brute-force approach to sales that, in hindsight, was less about providing value and more about survival. I sold merchant accounts that needed to be more suboptimal for my clients. This was a pivotal moment, a realization that sparked a significant shift in my professional ethos.

From that moment on, I felt a newfound sense of purpose and clarity in my work. It was like a light had been switched on, illuminating the path ahead with fresh ideas and perspectives. This pivotal moment ignited my passion to strive for excellence and push beyond my boundaries. It began a transformative journey toward growth, innovation, and fulfillment in my professional endeavors.

Understanding & Addressing Real Needs

Dale Carnegie emphasized the importance of genuinely understanding others' needs and perspectives. In the early days, I saw my role through a narrow lens: sell at all costs. However, this approach felt increasingly discordant with my values. I began to invest time in truly understanding the challenges and aspirations of my clients, transitioning from a transactional mindset to one rooted in empathy and support.

This shift wasn't just moral; it was strategic. By deeply engaging with my clients, I became more than a vendor; I became an advisor, a confidant, and, in many cases, a friend. This alignment with Carnegie's principles transformed my business. It was no longer about selling a product but solving a problem, a far more fulfilling and effective mode of operation.

As I focused on building genuine relationships and providing valuable guidance, my clients began to trust me more deeply. This trust led to increased loyalty and referrals, as they saw me not just as someone selling a service but as a reliable partner in their success. Embracing this approach not only improved the satisfaction of my clients but also brought me a sense of purpose and fulfillment in my work. As I continued to prioritize understanding and addressing the needs of those I served, the success of my business naturally followed.

Building Trust Through Authentic Connections

Trust is the cornerstone of influence. Carnegie knew this, advocating for sincerity and genuine interest in others. My journey underscored this truth. I noticed a dramatic relationship change as I transitioned from selling to serving. Once wary, clients became collaborative partners. We shared successes, tackled challenges together, and, through these experiences, built a robust network of mutual support and respect.

Trust forms the foundation of any meaningful connection. As humans, we gravitate towards sincerity and authenticity, which Andrew Carnegie recognized as vital in building influence. Throughout my journey, I came to appreciate the power of genuine interest in others. It was a transformative shift when I embraced the mindset of serving rather than just selling.

This change deepened relationships and allowed for a more collaborative dynamic to flourish. Clients who were once guarded and cautious gradually evolved into trusted partners. Together, we celebrated victories, faced obstacles head-on, and, in doing so, cultivated a strong and resilient network founded on mutual support and admiration. This experience underscored the profound impact of trust and genuine care in fostering meaningful connections and building lasting relationships.

One of the most profound lessons I learned was the power of admitting mistakes and learning from them. Missteps were inevitable in an industry as dynamic and sometimes opaque as merchant processing. However, I fostered a culture of transparency and continuous improvement by embracing these as learning opportunities and sharing these experiences openly with my clients and peers.

Navigating Change & Complexity Together

The merchant services industry is fraught with complexity. Regulations change, technologies evolve, and businesses' needs grow increasingly sophisticated. Carnegie's advocacy for becoming genuinely interested in others' interests guided me through these changes. By staying curious and committed to my client's success, I could navigate this complexity, not as a solitary expert but as part of a collaborative community seeking mutual growth and success.

In facing the challenges of high-risk accounts or navigating the intricacies of e-commerce, the principle of alignment—genuinely understanding and working within the unique contexts of my client's businesses—proved invaluable. This alignment allowed us to anticipate and embrace changes as opportunities for innovation and growth.

By maintaining this alignment, we were able to foster a culture of adaptability and creativity within our team. Instead of fearing change, we learned to see it as a chance to explore new possibilities and push the boundaries of what we thought was achievable. As a result, we were able to not only navigate through challenges but also thrive in the face of uncertainty. Our ability to adapt and innovate became our greatest strength, propelling us toward new heights of success and fulfillment.

Influence Through Giving

Finally, Dale Carnegie spoke of the influence that comes from making others feel important and appreciated. This principle found expression in every aspect of my work. From personalized advice to recognizing and celebrating the successes of those I worked with, I found that the most potent influence was wielded not through authority or expertise alone but through genuine appreciation and support for others' aspirations and challenges.

Reflecting on my journey within the merchant services industry, I am struck by the enduring relevance of Carnegie's principles. Influence, I've learned, is not about persuasion or manipulation. It's about alignment, understanding, and, above all, genuine connections. In navigating the complexities of modern business, these timeless principles have guided me to success and enriched the lives of those I've had the privilege to work with. It's a testament to the idea that, even in our fast-paced and ever-changing world, the fundamentals of human connection remain our most powerful tools for creating alignment and achieving influence.

RYAN FRITZSCHE

About Ryan Fritzsche: Ryan Fritzsche is the Founder and CEO of MSS Pay, a full-service merchant service company, helping thousands of businesses accept payments from their customers. Specializing in meeting the needs of the business with the software, hardware and payment types, Ryan uses this expertise to continue to consult and serve businesses nationwide.

Prior to founding MSS Pay, Ryan consulted with and co-owned many Chargeback Management companies and was responsible for helping businesses manage their risk and analyze data to improve business practices and customer satisfaction.

Ryan also spent 8 years working in different facets of the payment industry from sales, customer support, technical support, management and served in executive positions. This experience truly allows Ryan to run and operate a successful company today.

Ryan is an entrepreneur, professional in the payments industry, adventurer, philanthropist, father of four, husband, and an active person in his community.

Author's Website: *www.MSSPay.com*

Book Series Website: *www.TheBookofInfluence.com*

SALLY WURR

CAN'T WE ALL WIN?

"If your path demands you walk through Hell, walk like you own the place."
~ Unknown Author

There are many times in life where we need to pause and see things from someone else's point of view. Instead, we put blinders on and do not realize how our actions can impact others. Do your actions create a hell or misery for those around you?

The term "Walking Through Hell" could mean you found yourself in a bad place or the actions of others have put you in that situation. There is no point in just staying there. You need to keep moving to get out. Move with confidence and own the situation you have found yourself in, until you are past it.

It is up to you whether you give into the misery or walk through it like you planned it and owned it. Just because someone else put you in a situation does not mean that you have to accept it. Even when that "someone" is you.

During our life journey, things happen to us that we do not plan. Sometimes, someone else has the control and they are only looking out for their interest and not ours. This can create quite a bit of havoc. If only they would take the time to have conversations with the people that are being impacted and understand how they see it, they might have any possibility of both sides winning.

One of my earliest recollections of walking through what I considered "Hell" was when I was in my early 20s. I was a hairstylist in an upscale salon in Santa Barbara, California. The salon had beautiful large glass windows so we could watch people walking along the outdoor mall. At the time, we were paid a commission based on how much money we personally brought into the salon. Even though it was commissioned work, the owners took out the required taxes and paid us as W2 employees.

This type of set up worked well for everyone as we all worked as a team to keep the salon running smoothly. We took turns answering the phones and booking appointments for each other. We dusted, swept, and kept the salon looking pristine as all times.

One day, the manager of the salon had a meeting with everyone. The owners had decided that effective immediately we were all independent contractors, 1099 employees. We were no longer employees of the firm.

Going forward, it would be our responsibility to book our own appointments, collect the money and purchase all our own supplies. We would also be responsible for our own taxes. Keep in mind, this was before cell phones existed. Our clients only knew the salon number to book appointments.

There was no warning and thus no time to prepare. Many of my fellow employees were upset and shocked and simply did not know what they would do. They were devastated. We all felt, at least momentarily, blindsided and walking through a Hell that was created by the decision of the owners.

We certainly felt, at the time, we were walking through a situation not of our choosing. The owners certainly did not think through the position they were putting their staff in. For if they did, they would have given everyone time to purchase supplies, set up their accounts, and notify clients of the changes.

The owners had built a wonderful salon and the staff was appreciative. We had created an alignment with each other that appeared to be working for everyone. Until it wasn't. Dropping this massive change without any time to react created misalignment instead. And it turned out to be a huge mistake for them.

Most of the staff had never owned their own company. We certainly had to scramble to purchase products for our clients and make sure we had enough cash on hand to give our clients change if they needed it.

Within the week, many of the stylists had moved to other salons in the area, which completely devasted the owners' bank account. Sadly, they did not think ahead and thought that the stylists would simply stay, and all would be fine. In this situation it was anything but.

As a business owner, I can understand them wanting to keep the books in good balance. What they neglected to pay attention to was the requirements that W2 employees are completely different from 1099 contract employees. Employers can require their employees to keep the salon clean, answer the phones and take money. They can require them to work certain hours. As contract workers none of those requirements are allowed.

It was a costly lesson for these owners. They should have taken the time to talk with each employee and figure out how they could assist them in transitioning over to the new system. It would not have been difficult and it would have been valuable to the employees. I believe most would have been happy to stay if they only knew how.

Instead of working with everyone and figuring out the best outcome for each person, this owner was only looking out for themselves and ended up losing everything.

It is a lesson that I have carried with me for a long time. Whenever we are asking people to switch how they do something or change, we need to make sure that it works as well for them as it does for us. The best way to accomplish this is to either take the time to see how it can be good from their side as well as your own or to simply have a conversation filled with questions.

A life lesson learned was that God gave us two ears and one mouth. For me, this equates to listening twice as much as speaking. Of course, there are times when we are the main person speaking so this would not hold true. If you want to have a lasting impact on people, there are certain traits you need to learn. This is one of them.

Each of us has been guilty of saying something at the wrong time or to the wrong person. The other person may have interpreted it incorrectly, or we simply may have run our mouth without enough knowledge of the subject. Three small words that are important to learn as early as possible in our life are, "I am sorry."

Admitting to causing harm to another human being is a lesson each person should learn how to do. Admitting you are sorry takes courage. But if you were wrong, you need to own up to it quickly. We all know how difficult it can be to realize we were wrong. But the sooner you admit it, say you are sorry, and move on the better. For when we hurt someone, whether unintentionally or not, we have done damage.

An analogy I like to share is to look at a beautiful clean, smooth piece of parchment paper. It is perfect with no imperfections. Take that piece of parchment and crumble it up in your hands, perhaps put it on the floor and step on it so it is not only wrinkled and torn but is now dirty as well. Now try to smooth it back to its pristine perfection. What happens? You cannot take it back to what it was before the damage was done to it.

The same goes for friendships, co-workers, and people we meet along this journey called life. When we do harm, even saying we are sorry will never bring things back to how they were originally.

Whenever we find ourselves in a situation that won't move forward, we need to decide whether the argument is worth winning. Sometimes, you simply must walk away or allow the other person to feel like they won. This is called taking the "high road." It simply means that losing a friend or a client is not worth winning an argument that really isn't meaningful enough to fight for.

Whenever I receive a call from a client who is upset over something, I give them time to explain the situation from their point of view. I allow them to share with me as many points of contention that they may have. The main reason I do so is because allowing them to verbalize their frustration, to someone who may be able to help, is huge in diffusing the situation. Once I allow them to share, I can be in a better position to offer guidance and help. If I jumped in and tried to cut them off without hearing everything they had to say, it would quickly turn into an impasse. Sometimes you need to listen with both ears to the full story and then share the options available.

As the saying goes, "You win more friends with honey than you do with vinegar."

"Just as your car runs more smoothly and requires less energy to go faster and farther when the wheels are in perfect alignment, you perform better when your thoughts, feelings, emotions, goals, and values are in balance."
~ Brian Tracy

SALLY WURR

About Sally Wurr: Sally Wurr is an international speaker and multi-book author.

Sally is known as the "Storm Whisperer" because her message is about how to prepare for life's storms. Each person has trials and tragedies, but it is how we react to those events that help us grow and survive in our business and personal activities.

By sharing her expertise with stories, she teaches you how to embrace change and how to face life's struggles head-on. Simply put, she likes to teach others how to problem solve.

Sally embraces the knowledge that those who can must be the ones that do. She shares her stories so that others can find their true purpose.

In addition to writing and speaking, Sally is the President and Founder of SW Insurance Corp. She has helped thousands of CEOs develop employee benefits programs to attain and retain employees. It is her problem-solving and attention to detail that have made her successful in this arena for many years.

Author's Website: *www.SallyWurr.com*

Book Series Website: *www.TheBookofInfluence.com*

SARAH LEE

THE IMPORTANCE OF ORGANIZATIONAL ALIGNMENT

Let‘s begin by really, really understanding the value of the word Alignment:

Alignment is 1) an ***arrangement in a straight line, or in correct or "appropriate relative positions" or a position of agreement or alliance.***

I want to focus for a minute on the term "appropriate relative positions" and what that really means.

Achieving success is a violent act. Let me explain why. Let's look at these words.

Appropriate = suitable or proper in the circumstances OR

Appropriate, the same word, pronounced differently—meaning, take (something) for one's own use (typically without the owner's permission).

This is an entirely different understanding of "what's appropriate" in a group setting, now isn't it?

Relative**: **considered in relation or in proportion to something else, usually higher or lower.

Position: a place where someone or something is located or has been put, and placed in an intentional way.

So, just by those definitions alone, Alignment is intentional, (maybe sometimes) taking of someone else's position intentionally for one's own use. It is also being "in line" with a goal or a value of another or a group.

This authors group is a type of alignment, where we all have a common goal and purpose, and we AGREE to follow a certain set of rules and morals to be here and take part in it. We get support based on "agreement."

If you are reading this, you too are most likely aligned with the goals, hopes, wishes, and desires of many in this group, and wonder how this all works.

Let's discuss it.

Tony Robbins—who I have studied, crewed, and helped run the 14,000 person events for the last eight years—teaches, correctly, that the thing that people defend most in their lives is their identity. Identity, of course, being one's self-image and their idea of themselves to others.

Each of us define ourselves in a very specific and unique way. The way we define ourselves is complex but is primarily determined by 1) our experience, 2) inputs we got from other people often, but not limited to, as a child 3) and the MEANING we attached to those items, events and outcomes.

Most of the Programming was unintentional, and most of us have attached significant meaning to things that do not have that meaning intrinsically by definition.

This is our lives and actually how we actually create our destinies.

If you take that further, most, if not all, have then "acted on that belief and understanding" and are willing to fiercely defend their position, never really understanding that most if not all of what you see in life is a construct.

Construct meaning: ***an idea or theory containing various conceptual elements, typically one considered to be subjective and not based on empirical evidence.*** This means what you "know to be true" is almost never true for others. And the only way to move in a group is to all share an illusion of what "something means" and see if you can find or create others who agree with you. That is how one leads and that is how one achieves success. But knowing this, ***it is amazing that anything at all gets done in this world, much less gets done as a group.***

So, in order to have alignment, one must have something to align to and align with, and usually that is **shared goals and or shared values.**

Now, being that I am an expert on this topic, where we align in this group is that we all want to have an impact on the world, and we all want to be known as multiple time Best-Selling Authors (a dream I had since I was a kid), with the hope and idea that people will respect and listen to our opinions, and know us better. We will leave a record for future Generations, and find the people who are looking for more guidance around this message from someone with some experience in Success and Success Management.

Much of what I just said is taught either in psychology, psychiatry, or by a few very high level and famous coaches and speakers, like Bob Proctor, Tony Robbins, or Wayne Dyer. And if one does not deeply understand this, it will be much, much harder for you to align with an organization, or group and be successful. Especially because, without a why, and even with a strong why, it is very hard for most people to put their ego (read: ***identity*) *aside*** in order to achieve an easier result, unless they know, and believe with their whole heart, this information.

In the US and in Capitalism, we are taught that our identity is the most important possession we have in the WORLD and that we have rights to express it, but that is not taught in most countries in this world.

So, where we love the idea of being a unique individual, and having our voice heard by others (and feeling like it matters), many of us miss out on the power of organizational alignment, because often people do not want to give up their individual impact for the good of the group, if the group is not also returning the favor, yet there is more power in a group of people moving in the same exact direction than there is in one individual voice.

This is the dilemma of success, and of building a success mindset.

When I was a kid, my mom would say often to me: "You have to know when to hold them, know when to fold them, know when to walk away, know when to run. You never count your money when you're sitting at the table; there will be time enough for counting when the deal is done."

(And yes, that is Kenny Rogers, and, yes, it's still wisdom.)

So now, I've outlined the problem pretty clearly and, for me, this is why I enjoy coaching, training, counseling, influencing, and mentoring other people. Because, not understanding this deeply is a common success blocker to many people. This affects even those who believe that they are aligned with their goals, and we know this, because they will defend their position even when its weak, flawed or, when very few others can see it, by their actions, or lack thereof.

So, what to do?

I pointed out in the first paragraph what is alignment is, especially in terms of a group.

The reality is that, no matter what, in a group, someone is going to take Center Stage—someone will be smarter, more experienced, tougher, kinder, more likable and more relatable, and often that person will be looked to for influence, AND often *that someone* might actually "displace someone else when they do it" because that is *ironically* the exact nature of *alignment*. That displacement is often mistakenly identified as **competition,** a word I hate in business, and competition or the idea of it, naturally leads to the idea of **conflict.**

I outline this for you because it is the basis of teaching the science of achievement and those that understand this are going to have a much easier time, "temporarily" or "permanently" at times, making themselves "smaller," so they can fit in with the organizational alignment of the group of people, especially if everyone in the group are all trying to achieve the exact same result.

So, a few questions you can ask "yourself" now, that are "self-impactful" when trying to achieve any goal:

First, do I really understand my goal and can I clearly outline the exact steps that a reasonable person would need to take to achieve that exact goal?

Second, do I know or can I identify the exact people that I need to "align myself with" to achieve that same result?

Thirdly, am I ready to do the actual work it takes and change my habits and or beliefs to match the person who achieves what I want?

Fourthly, have I defined and accepted the things that I need to give up, either temporarily or indefinitely, in order to be the person who can achieve the thing that I want to do, and how I want to be perceived by others?

If you cannot answer yes to these basic questions, what I teach my students and mentees is that you're probably not ready to start on the journey towards whatever your goal is quite yet.

The reason that some people achieve goals much more easily than others is, in part, because achievers understand the ***science of achievement*** and this is one reason we revere people like Napoleon Hill, William Waddles, Ong Mandingo, Earl Nightingale, and the great Florence Stovall, who, in their day, were the people who taught the Principles of Success to others.

Those people inspired people like Jim Rohn, Zig Ziglar, Bob Proctor, and Wayne Dyer, who then inspired and informed people that I have worked with and studied with and spoken on stage with: living legends like

Robert Kiyosaki, Tony Robbins, Doria Cordova, and Laurel Langmeyer, who I am most similar in business to.

When it comes to influence, business, financial literacy and mindset, some others that come to mind are Eric Zuly for marketing; Eric Swanson, Forbes Riley, JT Foxx for branding; Marcia Weider for Enrollment; Bill Walsh, John Shin, Ed Mylett, Wharton, UCLA and SF State and Cal State Fullerton for business, events and speaking; Dr Sandy Rosenberg, Byron Katie, Dr. John Demartini, UCLA, UCI and USC for psychology. And the list of who I have learned from goes on and on and on.

My favorite influencer and business mentor/coach of that group is Anita Gross, who is not well known but she was my first trainer and teacher and mentor in the subject and she is as good or better than many of these people forementioned, and she happens to be my mother as well.

Each Giant stands on the Shoulders of the Giant before them and no one makes a large impact without standing on the shoulders of Giants, so that should be the first understanding of how you yourself can achieve even more influence and success. You can't just want it, you have to know what you want, what you will give up for what you want, and the exact steps a reasonable person would take to achieve that result.

It helps to have people that will Mentor you that have been there before. It helps to have people that will support you on your journey as well, but you don't *need those people* to do anything—having them, that's a bonus. But you can achieve any result that you choose to, with or without a group, if you know what you want, what you will give up for what you want, and the exact steps a reasonable person would take to achieve that result, and then do the work.

There is literally never a shortcut to doing the work yourself.

It is who you will become, from making these decisions and doing the hard work when no one is looking, that will determine how successful you are and how you are remembered. In the end, controversial as it is, *you* need to be aligned with your goals, more than you need to be aligned with people, as people will all "steer you in different directions if you let them," but you will take something from every person you work with to achieve your result, else you will not know how to stand on the shoulders of giants and no one will see you how you actually see yourself!

That's my time for today. Thank you for listening. Carry on... to the next! See you soon.

SARAH LEE

About Sarah Lee: A brilliant educational psychologist and leadership expert by education, Sarah Lee is the innovative author of "Rock Soup - An Innovational Idea in Leadership." By profession, Sarah has been teaching financial literacy for the last 15 years using her own firm as a platform. She is a full-service financial advisor and manager of her own Securities Branch of a national firm.

In addition, she networked with 100 Brokers all over the US. Sarah has an MBA in Finance and Social Impact and is 14 months shy of a Ph.D. in Educational Leadership. She is also the founder of multiple other companies and brands; some sold for profit, some she learned from, and some she consulted on other businesses. She is now mostly currently focused on her production company with her husband, MONEY MENTOR, LLC™ .

She has been advocating and speaking on large issues like financial literacy, literacy, mindset, clean water, and service to the world (hunger, water issues, poverty, and literacy) for her entire life. She is the child of a public servant. Her father was a writer (he wrote textbooks on risk and insurance practices), a city councilman in a small town who taught Sarah civic duties, service to the public, and how the national political system works. She learned how to serve others, run a nonprofit volunteer group, and make a community impact. That led to an opportunity to be "on TV (not streaming) weekly as a host" as a nine-year-old. The opportunity became more interesting when they asked Sarah what she would like to produce for Kids-4 TV.

She said, "I would like to host a consumer reports show, where I would interview local business owners and see how I could highlight them while giving them ways to give back and make a difference." She was nine. That led to a life of public speaking, running endowments, and working with local universities on educational issues. She developed her world-famous business philosophy during this time: "Business is just like Rock Soup…"

Learn more about Sarah Lee, MBA, and follow her on FB: @coachmeSarahLee, @moneymentormethod; Instagram: @moneymentorcompany, @coachmeacademy. For Money Tips, you can text the words "MONEYMENTOR" to 55444 for a free gift or visit our webpage: linktr.ee/MoneyMentorMethod.

Author's Website: *www.MoneyMentorFreeGift.com*

Book Series Website: *www.TheBookOfInfluence.com*

STEPH SHINABERY

CREATING ALIGNMENT THROUGH CONNECTIONS & REFLECTIONS

In influence and relationships, creating alignment is a beacon, guiding toward understanding and mutual respect. As I've discovered, the journey to alignment is intricate and enlightening, filled with lessons from personal experiences and a deep-seated belief in the power of connections.

Influence and relationships are like a delicate dance; creating alignment is a guiding light, illuminating the path toward genuine understanding and fostering mutual respect. Through my encounters, I have realized that the pursuit of alignment is a profound and enlightening voyage, enriched by the wisdom gleaned from personal interactions and steadfast faith in the transformative power of genuine connections.

Each step taken on this journey deepens our bonds and broadens our perspectives, leading us closer to a harmonious state of unity and shared purpose. Let us embrace this journey with open hearts and open minds, for in the realm of alignment; we discover the true essence of meaningful connections and the beauty of authentic relationships.

The Double-Edged Sword of Judgment & Understanding

It's an intriguing paradox that our era, while marked by unprecedented connectivity, often sees us hastening to judgments. We're quick to decide whether someone aligns with our worldview, sometimes even before giving them a fair chance. Yet, this readiness to judge is a double-edged sword. On one hand, it signifies a strong sense of self and a keen awareness of what we seek in relationships. On the other hand, it risks closing doors prematurely, missing out on potentially enriching interactions.

I've found that true alignment in relationships is about seeking balance. It's about understanding that disagreements or differences don't necessarily mean a lack of harmony. Instead, they can be the foundation for building stronger connections based on mutual respect and understanding.

It's important to remember that no two individuals are exactly alike, which makes relationships fascinating. Embracing diversity of opinions and perspectives can lead to growth and enrichment. When we approach disagreements with an open mind and a willingness to listen, we create space for meaningful conversations and opportunities for genuine connection. This kind of alignment fosters a deeper bond built on acceptance, empathy, and a shared commitment to growth, both individually and together. So, instead of fearing differences, let's celebrate them as the colorful threads that weave a beautiful tapestry of connection and love.

Personal Stories of Connection & Discovery

From unforgettable bike rides to immersive hikes and encounters in far-flung destinations, I've collected stories that testify to the power of openness. Each adventure and exchange taught me the value of genuinely pausing to connect with those around me.

One such memory takes me back to a winding trail, the crisp air filled with the scent of pine, and the person beside me, a then-stranger, sharing their perspective on a world so different from mine. In that moment of sharing and listening, I understood alignment isn't about sameness. It's about finding common ground, appreciating differences, and moving forward with a shared purpose.

It was a profound realization that transcended words and connected our hearts in a way that only understanding can. As we continued our journey through the winding trail, the colors of the forest seemed more vibrant, the birdsongs more melodic, and the sunlight filtering through the leaves more magical. It was as if nature itself was celebrating our newfound connection.

In that shared experience, I learned the beauty of diversity and the power of empathy. Each step we took together was a testament to the strength of embracing different perspectives and finding unity in our shared humanity. Our conversation flowed effortlessly, weaving together stories, dreams, and aspirations, creating a tapestry of understanding and respect.

As we reached the trail's end, I realized that while our paths may diverge, the bond of mutual respect and shared purpose will always remain. That chance encounter with a stranger on a winding trail had turned into a lasting memory of connection, growth, and the transformative power of listening with an open heart.

The Essence of Alignment in Everyday Interactions

Alignment often manifests in the simplest interactions—a smile shared with a stranger, a conversation sparked by genuine curiosity, or a silent understanding between friends. In these moments, we realize the impact of our presence and the value of our attention.

Walking into work, exchanging smiles and eye contact, I'm reminded of the beauty of everyday connections. These brief encounters, though fleeting, carry the weight of genuine human interaction. They're a reminder that alignment, at its core, doesn't always require grand gestures or profound exchanges. Sometimes, it's as simple as acknowledging another's humanity and offering kindness without expectation.

It's fascinating how these small moments of connection can brighten our day and uplift our spirits. In a world that often feels fast-paced and disconnected, these simple gestures of acknowledgment serve as gentle reminders of our shared humanity. By being present in these interactions and offering kindness without expecting anything in return, we enrich our lives and contribute to creating a more compassionate and understanding world. So, let's continue to cherish these everyday connections and appreciate the beauty they bring to our lives.

Navigating the Complexities of Alignment

The path to creating alignment is nuanced and filled with challenges and opportunities for growth. It involves introspection, a willingness to confront our biases, and an openness to embrace perspectives different from our own. It's about recognizing that every individual we meet can offer a unique insight, a different piece of the puzzle that is our understanding of the world.

In my journey, I've learned that alignment doesn't mean agreeing on everything. Instead, it's about striving for mutual respect, a shared understanding that respects our differences while celebrating our commonalities. It's about building bridges, not walls, and recognizing that every thread has its place in the vast tapestry of human experience.

In this intricate, complex web of life, each thread weaves a unique story, bringing its color and texture to the fabric of our existence. Just as every thread is essential to create a beautiful design, every individual perspective is valuable in shaping our collective narrative. Embracing diversity enriches our lives, allowing us to learn from one another and grow together.

When we seek alignment through mutual respect and understanding, we open ourselves to new possibilities and broaden our horizons. By listening to different viewpoints and honoring diverse backgrounds, we strengthen the bonds that connect us and foster a culture of inclusivity and compassion.

Let us continue to bridge the gaps that divide us, reach out across divides, and extend a hand of friendship. Together, we can create a tapestry of unity reflecting our shared humanity's beauty.

The Continual Pursuit of Alignment

Reflecting on creating alignment, I'm reminded that it's an ongoing journey that requires patience, empathy, and a genuine desire to connect. It's about making space for those who bring us joy, challenge our thinking, and help us grow. And perhaps most importantly, it's about being present—truly present—with those we encounter along the way.

Creating alignment is more than a principle; it's a practice, a way of living that embraces the complexities of human relationships. It's a commitment to understanding, a pledge to listen more than we speak, and a promise to value the connections that shape our lives.

In sharing these stories and reflections, I hope to inspire others to embrace the beauty of alignment in their lives, recognize the power of connections, the value of diverse perspectives, and the profound impact of simple acts of kindness. In the end, it's through alignment that we find our most meaningful and enriching relationships, shaping a world marked by understanding and mutual respect.

STEPH SHINABERY

About Steph Shinabery: Steph Shinabery is The World's Best Possibility Coach, Nurse Anesthesiologist, Artist, Speaker and the Founder of GENIUS CODE ACADEMY.

After spending much of her life in a career that lacked the inspiration and fulfillment she knew was available to her, she began a journey to answer the question: "what is it I truly desire?"

Her journey led to creation of the Genius Identity Code™, a process for unlocking your gift, purpose and path, and helping people see, believe and execute their unique genius to achieve miraculous outcomes.

Steph works with creative experts, entrepreneurs and coaches to help them embrace their authenticity and create a life that gets them excited to jump out of bed every day!

You can find her talk, "Wake Up Your Genius Machine" on Amazon Prime Video's Speak Up: Empower Your Ideas, Season 4.

Author's Website: *www.StephShinabery.com*

Book Series Website: *www.TheBookofInfluence.com*

SUSAN CARPIO

CREATING ALIGNMENT THROUGH FLEXIBILITY

In the fabric of our professional and personal lives, the alignment principle operates as both a guiding light and a foundational pillar, shaping how we interact, influence, and ultimately lead. My journey, marked by profound loss, unexpected shifts, and the constant pursuit of balance, offers a unique perspective on the power of alignment.

From my personal experiences, it delves into the core concept of establishing alignment theoretically and as a practical, ongoing process.

Understanding the importance of alignment is crucial in various aspects of life. It involves harmonious integrating beliefs, values, and actions to achieve a sense of coherence and purpose. In theory, alignment provides a solid foundation for decision-making and goal-setting, ensuring that every choice and action aligns with one's core principles.

However, in practice, alignment is a continuous journey that requires reflection, adaptation, and perseverance. It involves regularly reassessing priorities, adjusting as needed, and staying true to one's authentic self. By actively engaging in the alignment process, individuals can cultivate a sense of clarity, integrity, and fulfillment in their personal and professional endeavors.

My understanding of alignment has been shaped significantly by two critical aspects of my life: my professional career and a deeply personal tragedy. Each has taught me that at the heart of alignment lies flexibility—a quality that, much like a river, carves its path through the landscape of life, adapting, adjusting, and always moving forward.

The Essence of Professional Flexibility

My career has offered a vantage point to observe and engage with the concept of alignment in action. In one memorable instance, during a comprehensive assessment with my team, it was revealed that I was the second most flexible person in a group of eighty. This revelation came as no surprise, considering my belief in the transformative power of adaptability in leadership and teamwork.

I recall working closely with a colleague who, in stark contrast to my flexibility, was the most inflexible member of our team. Despite our differing approaches, we fostered a remarkably effective partnership, achieving monumental outcomes for our project. This experience underscored a vital lesson: alignment is not about uniformity but finding harmony amidst diversity, leveraging our strengths to achieve a common goal.

In every successful collaboration, there is often a beautiful dance between contrasting styles and personalities. It's fascinating how our differences can complement each other, creating a dynamic synergy that propels us towards success. In the case of my colleague and me, our partnership was a testament to the power of embracing diversity and recognizing the unique contributions each individual brings to the table.

Of course, our journey together was not without its challenges. Our contrasting approaches sometimes clashed, leading to spirited debates and creative tension. Yet, through open communication, mutual respect, and a shared commitment to our project's success, we found a way to navigate these differences and channel them into productive outcomes.

Looking back, I am grateful for the opportunity to work alongside someone whose perspective differed from mine. It pushed me to broaden my horizons, think outside the box, and approach problems from new angles. Together, we uncovered innovative solutions, broke through barriers, and achieved results that surpassed our wildest expectations.

Ultimately, our partnership taught me that proper alignment is not about everyone thinking and acting the same way. It's about embracing diversity, celebrating each other's strengths, and working harmoniously to achieve a common purpose. It's about recognizing that our unique differences are not obstacles to overcome but powerful assets to leverage to pursue our shared goals.

Learning from Loss

Amid these professional revelations, my family faced an unimaginable tragedy. We lost my four-year-old grandson in a terrible accident, a heartbreak that no amount of professional success could ever offset—this period of profound grief taught me the importance of aligning with life's unpredictable nature, embracing flexibility not as a strategy but as a means of survival and healing.

The aftermath of the accident forced me to reevaluate my priorities, leading to a significant decision to relocate closer to my family. Though fraught with uncertainty and the discomfort of leaving behind a life I loved in Tucson, this decision was a testament to my commitment to aligning my actions with my heart's deepest needs.

In the weeks following the accident, as I grappled with the physical and emotional toll it had taken on me, I found solace in the unwavering support of my family. Their love and care became a guiding light, illuminating the path towards healing and renewal. During this reflection, I realized the importance of cherishing those closest to me and nurturing the bonds that truly matter. And so, with a mix of trepidation and hope in my heart, I boldly chose to uproot myself from the familiar streets of Tucson and embark on a new chapter closer to home.

The decision was a challenging one. It meant saying goodbye to friends who had become like family, to the comforting routine of everyday life in the desert city I had grown to love. But deep down, I knew this change was necessary for my well-being and my soul's longing for connection and belonging. And so, armed with courage and determination, I set out on the journey towards a new beginning, knowing that the love and support of my family would be my anchor in this sea of change.

The Power of Alignment in Leadership

The concept of alignment extends beyond personal adaptation to encompass leadership and influence within professional settings. Taking the helm of a team amidst a major organizational reorganization, I encountered the challenge of leading a group that had previously suffered from poor execution and lack of direction. My approach was rooted in the belief that proper alignment within a team begins with genuine care and investment in individual members.

By dedicating time to understanding each team member's aspirations, concerns, and strengths, I aimed to foster an environment of mutual respect and shared goals. This endeavor was about improving performance and creating a space where alignment was the natural outcome of a collective commitment to each other's success.

In doing so, I encouraged open communication and empathy within the team. By recognizing and valuing each member's unique contributions, we were able to tap into a wealth of diverse perspectives and ideas. This approach not only enhanced collaboration but also fueled innovation and creativity. As we worked together towards our shared objectives, our bond grew stronger, paving the way for greater achievements and a sense of fulfillment that transcended individual success.

Flexibility as the Foundation of Alignment

My lifelong journey of embracing flexibility, informed by the values instilled in me from a young age, has been a cornerstone of my ability to navigate the complexities of life and leadership. Growing up in a family of dairy farmers, where the day's demands started before dawn, I learned early on that flexibility was not merely a choice but a necessity.

This upbringing and my challenges and opportunities have solidified my conviction that flexibility is the essence of creating alignment. Whether aligning a team around a shared vision, adapting to unforeseen circumstances, or finding peace amidst personal turmoil, flexibility enables us to meet each moment with resilience and grace.

Embracing flexibility allows us to navigate life's ever-changing landscape with openness and adaptability. It empowers us to adjust our sails when faced with unexpected challenges, to pivot our strategies when necessary, and to approach each situation with a willingness to learn and grow.

Flexibility is not about compromising our values or goals but finding creative ways to stay true to our purpose while being open to new possibilities and perspectives. By cultivating flexibility in our interactions, decisions, and mindset, we can forge stronger connections, easily overcome obstacles, and embrace the beauty of life's unpredictability. Remember, being flexible does not mean being weak; it means being strong enough to bend without breaking.

Embracing Alignment as a Way of Life

Ultimately, alignment is more than a principle to be applied; it's a way of living. It's about how we respond to life's inevitable changes, how we support and uplift those around us, and the paths we take to lead with integrity and compassion. My story is one of many, each with lessons on the power of alignment. Through sharing these experiences, I aim to inspire others to explore the depths of their flexibility, discover the strength of adaptability, and embrace the profound influence we can exert when we align our actions with our most profound truths.

In this journey of life, where every turn brings new challenges and opportunities for growth, let us hold fast to the principle of alignment. By cultivating flexibility within ourselves and fostering it within our teams, we can navigate the most turbulent waters, reach new horizons, and achieve harmony that propels us forward together.

SUSAN CARPIO

About Susan Carpio: Susan has worked in the high-tech industry for more than 30 years, starting her career with an electrical engineering degree. Her experience encompasses deep technical roles in electronics labs, front-line project management, and senior-level leadership roles in the commercial, aerospace, and defense sectors. Currently, Susan is a technical business development manager for integrated test systems supporting aerospace and defense applications at Keysight Technologies based in Loveland, Colorado.

While working for technology companies, she also has an entrepreneurial spirit and heart. Her son, Jase, his wife, Shilo, and their three children are the light of her life, and watching that young family start on their own has created her dedication to helping young mothers find a sustainable income so they can stay home with their children.

Susan is a cancer survivor and a thriver for 10+ years. She attributes this to the mercy of Jesus Christ, the loved ones who surround her, and her heartfelt thankfulness for life!

Author's Website: *www.SusanCarpio.com*

Book Series Website: *www.TheBookofInfluence.com*

TEASHIA FRENCH

AUTHENTICITY, EMPATHY, & MUTUAL UNDERSTANDING

In my journey through various phases of my life and career, from navigating new schools as a child to ascending the corporate ladder and venturing into entrepreneurship, one underlying principle has been a beacon guiding my interactions and decisions: the power of creating alignment. This principle, deeply rooted in Dale Carnegie's teachings, has transformed my communication, leadership, and relationship-building approach. It is a testament to the strength found in authenticity, empathy, active listening, and the cultivation of likability—elements that are not just personal values but are, indeed, universal truths for fostering genuine connections.

Understanding and embracing the concept of creating alignment has been pivotal in my personal and professional growth. It has allowed me to build bridges with others in a classroom, boardroom, or networking event. I have fostered trust, inspired collaboration, and driven positive outcomes in various situations by aligning my actions and words with my values and intentions.

In practicing this principle, I have come to appreciate the importance of authenticity in all my interactions. Being genuine to myself has helped me gain respect from others and encouraged openness and transparency in communication. Moreover, approaching conversations with empathy and a willingness to understand different perspectives has enabled me to forge deeper connections and resolve conflicts more effectively.

Active listening has emerged as a cornerstone of creating alignment in my relationships. By truly listening to others without judgment or distraction, I have grasped their needs, concerns, and aspirations. This has strengthened my ability to connect with people meaningfully and paved the way for collaborative problem-solving and mutual growth.

Lastly, cultivating likability has played a significant role in nurturing genuine connections. I have created a positive rapport that transcends mere transactions or exchanges by showing kindness, appreciation, and a genuine interest in others. This likability factor has enriched my interactions and has also been instrumental in building a supportive network of individuals who share common values and aspirations.

In essence, the power of creating alignment through authenticity, empathy, active listening, and likability is a transformative force that has shaped my approach to communication, leadership, and relationship-building. It serves as a reminder that by staying true to oneself, understanding others' perspectives, and fostering genuine connections, we can navigate life's complexities with grace, compassion, and purpose.

Authentic Conversations as the Foundation

My life is intricately woven with threads of transformation—each move in my childhood, each career pivot, and each leap into the unknown underscored by the essence of authentic conversations. In my view, authenticity is not merely about being truthful or genuine; it's about embracing vulnerability, navigating the complexities of human emotions, and engaging in meaningful exchanges that transcend superficial interactions. In his timeless wisdom, Dale Carnegie championed the importance of genuine interest in others—a principle that has been my north star.

As I ventured into the world of medical devices and, later, into the realm of sales and entrepreneurship, the authenticity of my conversations became the bedrock upon which trust was built. In sales, especially where likability and trust are paramount, my willingness to engage in authentic dialogue and a genuine interest in understanding my client's needs and aspirations set the foundation for lasting relationships.

I learned that authenticity is not just a buzzword but a powerful tool that can pave the way for meaningful connections and successful ventures. By genuinely listening to my clients, acknowledging their concerns, and offering genuine solutions, I could establish a sense of trust and credibility that transcended mere transactions.

In the fast-paced world of sales and entrepreneurship, where competition runs high, and relationships are often fleeting, authenticity emerged as my secret weapon. It allowed me to differentiate myself from the crowd, connect on a deeper level, and create a bond beyond the confines of business.

As I honed my skills in understanding human nature and mastering the art of authentic communication, I discovered that the true essence of success lies in closing deals and building enduring partnerships. Through authenticity, I found my voice, purpose, and path to sustainable growth and fulfillment in my professional and personal endeavors.

Empathy: The Bridge to Alignment

Empathy has been my compass, guiding me through the intricacies of human interactions. The ability to step into another's shoes, view the world through their lens, and feel what they feel has allowed me to create alignment with those around me. This alignment goes beyond mere agreement; it is a deep, empathetic connection that fosters mutual understanding and respect.

Empathy has enabled me to navigate difficult conversations, whether discussing career aspirations with a supervisor or confronting the realities of a job that no longer aligns with my personal goals. Dale Carnegie underscored the importance of understanding others and advocating for a sympathetic grasp of their viewpoint. It is this empathy that allows for authentic communication to flourish, creating an environment where alignment is not only sought but achieved.

Empathy serves as a powerful compass in the intricate landscape of communication. It is the key that unlocks the door to meaningful dialogues and fosters genuine connections between individuals. When approaching conversations with empathy, we are better equipped to listen actively, comprehend diverse perspectives, and respond compassionately.

Empathy acts as a bridge in times of uncertainty or conflict, enabling us to traverse the gap between differing opinions and find common ground. By acknowledging and validating the emotions and experiences of others, we demonstrate respect and build trust. This foundation of understanding paves the way for constructive discussions, where mutual respect and empathy lay the groundwork for fruitful resolutions.

As we navigate the complexities of our professional and personal lives, let empathy be our guiding light, illuminating the path toward harmonious relationships and effective communication. Embrace empathy as a tool for transformation, allowing it to shape our interactions and cultivate environments where empathy reigns supreme and understanding prevails.

Active Listening: The Pathway to Mutual Respect

The act of listening, truly listening, has been a cornerstone of my approach to building relationships. We demonstrate respect and regard for others' opinions, ideas, and feelings through active listening. This practice is not merely about silence while another speaks but about engaging fully—mentally, emotionally, and with genuine interest. Dale Carnegie emphasized the power of being a good listener and encouraging others to talk about themselves as a path to winning friends and influencing people.

In my professional journey, listening more than speaking has been instrumental in creating alignment. It has allowed me to understand my clients' unique challenges, negotiate effectively, and build partnerships based on mutual respect and shared goals. Listening has been the pathway through which I have offered tailored solutions that resonate on a personal level, thereby cementing trust and likability.

Listening has also given me valuable insights into my client's needs and preferences. By actively engaging in attentive listening, I have been able to decipher underlying motivations, unspoken concerns, and subtle cues that have guided me in formulating strategies that truly address their specific requirements. This empathetic approach has enhanced the quality of my professional interactions and fostered stronger connections with those I collaborate with. Through the art of listening, I have honed my problem-solving skills and deepened the impact of my contributions in the professional realm.

Cultivating Likability: The Keystone of Successful Relationships

Likability, the subtle yet powerful force, has been a critical element in my ability to create alignment. Through likability, barriers are broken down, and genuine connections are forged. Being likable is not about curating a universally appealing persona but about being authentic, showing empathy, and actively listening. These traits engender trust and respect, facilitating alignment in both personal and professional realms.

My career, especially in sales, has been a testament to the power of likability. By being authentic, demonstrating genuine interest in my client's needs and aspirations, and engaging in empathetic listening, I have negotiated and closed deals that benefit all parties involved. Likability, rooted in the principles championed by Dale Carnegie, has been the keystone of my professional success and personal fulfillment.

Cultivating genuine likability through kindness, empathy, and respect has opened doors for me in my career and enriched my relationships. By following Dale Carnegie's timeless advice on building meaningful connections, I have found that people are more willing to collaborate, communicate openly, and support each other's growth. This approach has brought me professional success and provided me with a deep sense of fulfillment, knowing I am positively impacting those around me through authentic interactions. Embracing likability as a core value has been a transformative journey that continues to shape my path toward greater achievements and meaningful connections.

Creating Alignment is an Art

Creating alignment is an art—a delicate balance of authenticity, empathy, active listening, and likability. It is about understanding and being understood, about mutual respect, and about fostering connections that are deep and meaningful. In my journey, guided by the truths espoused by Dale Carnegie, I have found that creating alignment is not just a strategy for professional success but a blueprint for living a life rich in relationships and experiences.

Alignment fosters harmony and understanding in every interaction, workplace, or personal relationship. It involves more than superficial agreement; it requires a genuine connection based on authenticity and empathy.

Active listening is a critical component in this art form, as it allows us to hear and understand the perspectives of others truly. Listening with an open heart and mind shows respect and creates a space for meaningful dialogue and connection.

Likability also plays a role in creating alignment, as genuine warmth and positivity can help to build bridges and strengthen bonds with others. When we approach interactions with kindness and a willingness to connect, we set the stage for positive and enriching relationships.

Creating alignment is a powerful tool for personal growth and professional success. By embracing the principles of authenticity, empathy, active listening, and likability, we can cultivate relationships that are not only fulfilling but also contribute to a life rich in connections and experiences.

As I continue on my path, whether in business, design, or personal growth, the lessons I have learned and the principles I have embraced remain my guiding stars. I have discovered that creating alignment is not merely about finding common ground but building a shared vision anchored in the truth of our shared humanity.

TEASHIA FRENCH

About Teashia French: Teashia French, MBA is a seasoned professional with over 15 years of experience in the Medical Device and Pharmaceutical industry. She has held various leadership positions, including Marketing Manager and Regional Vice President of Sales. Teashia's dedication to her career is matched by her commitment to education. She holds a bachelor's degree in communication from the University of Washington and an MBA with a concentration in Finance from Washington State University. Additionally, Teashia has received a digital marketing certificate from Rutgers University.

More recently, Teashia has leveraged her passion for design and her expertise in marketing to start her own interior design business, Visceral Design. As the founder of Visceral Design, Teashia creates intentionally minimalistic spaces for busy women who want beautiful homes. She combines her eye for design with her marketing skills to create functional and aesthetically pleasing spaces for her clients.

When she's not working, Teashia enjoys spending time with her family. She is a proud mother of two beautiful children and is happily married. Teashia and her family reside in Paradise Valley, AZ, where they enjoy the sunny weather and outdoor activities. With her diverse background, education, and entrepreneurial spirit, Teashia is a true force to be reckoned with.

Author's Website: *linkedin.com/in/TeashiaNelson*

Book Series Website: *www.TheBookofInfluence.com*

TERESA CUNDIFF

A NO-WIN SITUATION

When my mom was living, I would sarcastically joke that we were going to put, "She was right!" on her tombstone. She would beat a point to death and have to have the last word. I will admit that when I began to recognize this trait in myself, I squashed it as best I could. I still have flare ups, but I try to be careful and not be a know-it-all! Sometimes my mind is moving too fast, and words fall out of my mouth that I don't intend. But I have never been confrontational with people as that brings a level of discomfort for everyone and rarely are things accomplished.

I remember the time when I thought everything my mom said was gospel, and she was happy to let me think that. I got into an argument once with a friend from church over the pronunciation of the word Ramada in Ramada Inn. My mom pronounced it Ramunda, so I thought that's how it was said and took my friends to task. She then spelled it out for me, and clearly, there was no N in the spelling.

That was the beginning of me realizing that my mom didn't know everything. And even though it was a tiny event, I would then start noticing that my mom was very critical of almost everything and that the way she thought something should be said or done was the only way to say or do it! And she never changed and lived 84 years thinking she was right! Or maybe this situation was so severe because I was her daughter.

So, I started very early on with my sons telling them that I didn't know everything because of the embarrassment I went through coming to grips with that fact with my mom. I never wanted them to feel that way about me. If I did know a thing or two about the subject, I would explain how I knew and maybe when I learned it. I had the best time doing algebra with my younger son, because I rocked algebra in school once I got the hang of it. Now, over-the-road trucking? Don't know a thing about it! How to run for office? Not even a clue about where to start! The rules to football? Damn skippy! I know the rules AND hand signals!

Avoiding an argument is the only way to win it, according to Dale Carnegie. "You can't win an argument. You can't because if you lose it, you lose it, and if you win it, you lose it." It's a No-Win situation. To this I say, it takes a supreme amount of confidence to not feel as though we must stick up for ourselves. We want to prove that we are right! It's so easy to be defensive about something so we don't come off looking dumb or embarrassed. It's okay to not know everything, and it's a strong, brave person who can admit at the outset that they don't. Sometimes it's a fine line, though!

I have always been a huge advocate for learning both sides of the story while bearing in mind that the person telling the story will slant things in their favor! This was especially true when listening to my two boys passionately explain their differing points of view on an incident. Of course, children have very little empathy most of the time as they want things their way. It's not until we mature that we understand more about Human Engineering 101! But even with maturity, we will still slant the story in our favor! Conscious or unconscious to that fact, it must be factored in when trying to authentically communicate…not be right!

It has usually been my practice to assume the posture of the one being in the wrong if a point is in dispute. To me, this was always the best way to avoid being confrontational. However, some may see this as me making a doormat out of myself. I will admit, I have been guilty of that simply because it was the path of least resistance. It really all depends on the desired outcome. If we can check our ego at the door and be more interested in resolution to a problem instead of being right that only MY solution will work, so much more can be accomplished!

Listening is so, so important when trying to understand another person. Rarely do people listen to understand. Most of the time people listen to respond. Many times, we "agree to disagree" because we each know that the other isn't going to change their mind. When family gatherings are approaching, there is always the "avoid politics and religion" policy, right? Those would be the two most polarizing subjects that can turn what was otherwise a pleasant party into name calling, insult hurling, and bad blood for a long time. And, when we know we're "right," it becomes difficult to disagree without being disagreeable! Who knew there were so many cliches around this subject?

One thing to bear in mind is that the other person may be right! Or, they might have some valid points we haven't considered before. The questions here is, do you allow yourself to adjust your way of thinking if the other person makes his or her point with convincing evidence? It's better to be forthright and admit that you are learning something that you hadn't previously considered than to keep hammering your point or act as if you knew it all along. Try to adopt the strategy that you will keep your mind open and hear everything before passing sentencing.

Think about a Mastermind where several people come together to solve problems or to support each other. You could even call a book club a Mastermind. My mindset when I am on a Mastermind call is to see what I can learn from the others. What nuggets of wisdom I will take away from the group? A lot of brainstorming takes place in a Mastermind conversation and so much good can be accomplished. Everyone is there to contribute and learn. No one would purposefully be argumentative during a MM call. It's the perfect place for minds to come together in a kind of "group think" and tackle problems and share solutions. The leader of on MM group I'm in poses a question earlier in the day for us all to think about and be ready to discuss on the call that night. And we are all encouraged to submit our topics/questions to him to put before the group. It's an hour a week that I truly enjoy!

Do the best you can to keep yourself out of No-Win situations and preserve your friendships. Don't offer yourself up as a sacrifice, mind you, but have the eyes to recognize when a conversation is beginning to spiral and simply excuse yourself. It will help your peace of mind and your stress level to just avoid the people you know will push your buttons. How many conversations have you wished you had walked away from to preserve the friendship or your sanity or both. Be on the lookout (BOLO) for them and remain calm!

TERESA CUNDIFF

About Teresa Cundiff: Teresa hosts an interview digital TV show called Teresa Talks on Everyday Woman TV. On the show, she interviews authors who are published and unpublished—and that just means those authors who haven't put their books on paper yet. The show provides a platform for authors to have a global reach with their message. Teresa Talks is produced by Wordy Nerds Media Inc., of which Cundiff is the CEO.

Cundiff is also a freelance proofreader with the tagline, "I know where the commas go!" Teresa makes her clients' work shine with her knowledge of grammar, punctuation, and sentence structure.

Teresa is a 21x #1 best-selling contributing author. Of which, three are in the Library of Congress.

Author's Website: *www.TeresaTalksTV.com*

Book Series Website: *www.TheBookofInfluence.com*

THOMAS MALAGISI

GETTING INTO ALIGNMENT

Often times people may think that they're in balance with what is happening around them. But, they seem to struggle through everything that happens. Struggle is a large clue that something just is not right. When we struggle, we look for ways of stopping the struggle, but we are remiss in knowing how to do so. This misalignment causes us to begin to blame outside influences. It's that person, it's that group, or it's the government. It's… fill in the blank.

Misalignment and the struggle can be proven to cause health issues. This has been sighted in many psychological and health journals. Start to observe others and you will quickly see this in their facial expressions. The droop in their face. The way they walk and talk. Then, when you find a person who is aligned, you'll find them cheerful. People will think, what's the matter with him/her? Well, nothing is the matter, they are aligned. That's the point.

Alignment with the laws of nature. According to the internet, there are seven laws of nature. (*insidedestiny.com/the-seven-laws-of-nature*) I remember when I studied Engineering that the laws of nature were described somewhat differently. Energy can neither be created or destroyed. With every action, there is an opposite and equal reaction, etc. So, how does this apply to creating alignment? When aligned it's like a fish swimming with the current. (but not salmon when they're spawning). We hear the term often of going with the flow. That to me is creating alignment. Now there are times when we see or are brought into situations that don't align with our wonderful character. When that occurs, we simply remove ourselves from that conversation or situation. We don't have to change with each and every situation. We have the ability to pick and choose.

Alignment with the group you surround yourself with has been stated in various different ways throughout the ages, but it is true. "Want to know how much you'll make, look at your five best friends and see what they earn." That will tell you what your potential is. Criminals have been cited as falling into crime due to their surroundings. Those they associate with have influence. When first encountered, they don't like it, but become accustomed to it. Likewise, those who give and are charitable find it hard at first, but then due to those they surround themselves with, find it easy. So, creating alignment with those you associate with is an important step. You have a choice. Pick and choose wisely. You have the ability to do so.

Alignment with what you wish to become is a difficult thing for many. This is difficult due to the things we hear, the things we see, and the items that are allowed to enter our conscious mind.

Ever listen to music? Of course, you have. You sing along and like the rhythm of the beat. Ahhhh but do you know what the words are affirming? Repeating the song time and time again is affirming this to yourself. The lyrics may be inspiring or detrimental. Ever think of that?

It used to be said, that we become what we read. It may now be; that we become what we watch. Watching television is similar to singing that song. It's either building or tearing down. You have a choice, leave it on, or turn it off. Select what you desire to watch.

So, how does one create alignment with what the person wishes to become? Not having idols or people to look up to can cause some difficulty. But there are the greats. These people that have accomplished, become, or done something that resonates with you. They may have lived hundreds of years ago or are currently alive. We can play a game and ask ourselves, what would they do, how would they think, and how would they respond to a situation. Placing yourself in their persona is a thing that you'll probably not speak of to others, but you can try it out. See if it makes a difference in the direction of your life. Often, you may have heard this as I am. Your I am ness is just that. Affirmations that create your own alignment.

Alignment with the Things You Desire

Desiring things is not bad despite what cultures attempt to instill in populations. Desiring things is a result of growth. Growth without things is creating of storehouse of useless inward gathering for no good. Growth with things is outwardly benefitting others. After one has all that one desires; the clothes, the cars, the house, the whatever, it then shifts towards an outer expansion for others.

Although the car has to have nuts and bolts, metal, and other materials, those have to be made. That takes those who build machines, and people to run those machines and care for them. These are jobs for others. Cloths, create jobs for seamstresses, cotton growers, fertilizer manufacturers, etc. Perhaps you create jobs for others. Perhaps you give to charities. Perhaps you give of yourself to others to teach them something for their growth.

Alignment with yourself. Oh wow… that's tough. We're not all the same. That's great. How you think, how you feel, and how you act, are key to knowing if you're aligned with yourself. Everyone will say that they are aligned with themselves, but few probably are. Imagine if everyone was. Give this some thought please. **Think, Feel, Act (TFA)**. Will you score high with these three?

It's probably easy to get the think and feel. Action, are the actions reflective of what the thought and feel is all about? Let's take two of the greats. Let's start with the master inventor of things. Whatever the thing is. It may be the lightbulb. It may be the best social media. Are you able to think in the way that the master inventor has done. Maybe so, and it may take some time to form.

Can you feel what it would be like to create as the master inventor did? You probably can: an adrenaline rush, a great feeling, or a gush of pride. How about the action? Are your actions affirming what that master inventor would have gone through? Let's take another. A master chef.

The Cordon Blu instructor. You pick who it is. Can you think as he/she would think while going through the creation? How about the feeling you'd get when your company sampled and tasted your creation? Just like the inventor, you probably can. So, now for the action. Are your actions practiced enough to support and affirm what your thoughts and feelings were?

Look around, most people give up after one attempt or don't even get that far. It takes practice. Practice, practice, practice. Each time getting better and closer to what you think and feel.

THOMAS MALAGISI

About Thomas Malagisi: Thomas Malagisi, BSME, MBA, has over 30+ years of Manufacturing and Business experience. Thomas enjoys working with teams in many capacities. He thrives on accomplishing that which previously was thought of as something that couldn't be done. He celebrates the achievements of those types of goals. Thomas loves building upon group and individual strength through leaders and teamwork. Thomas utilizes Development-of-Management skills when leading groups and teams. He is also focused on employee retention for companies as well as the growth of individuals. Thomas holds his standards to world class business skills.

Thomas is a 3x Best-Selling Author in the new hit series, *The Principles of David & Goliath.*

Book Series Website: *www.TheBookofInfluence.com*

TYLER ERICKSON

THE ART OF ALIGNMENT

In personal development, alignment emerges as a concept and a vital catalyst for influence and change. The legendary Dale Carnegie once emphasized the creation of win-win situations and the power of understanding and empathizing with others as foundational to building solid and influential relationships. Yet, as we delve deeper into the 21st century, the essence of alignment demands a more nuanced exploration. The layers of alignment, positioning it as the cornerstone of influence, can ignite change and foster profound connections among people.

The Power of Alignment

The hypothesis, "Never underestimate the ability of a small group of people to change the world; indeed, it's the only thing that ever has," serves as a beacon, illuminating the transformative power of alignment. It challenges the individual's self-imposed limitations and societal doubts, encouraging a belief in the collective power of focused, aligned effort. This principle underscores the essence of influence—not as a solitary journey but as a communal expedition towards shared aspirations.

In a world where individualism often takes center stage, the notion of collective impact can feel revolutionary. Yet, throughout history, small, dedicated groups of people have sparked monumental change. The essence of this hypothesis lies in recognizing that when individuals come together with a shared vision, remarkable transformations can occur.

Imagine a group of diverse minds and talents converging towards a common goal, each contributing their unique strengths to the collective tapestry. This synergy creates a ripple effect, amplifying the impact of each individual's actions. In this harmonious symphony of collaboration, the true power of aligned effort emerges.

As we navigate the complexities of our modern world, let us remember the profound truth embedded in these words. The ability to effect change rests not solely on one person's shoulders but on the unity and determination of a united front. Together, we can defy the status quo, challenge the norm, and carve a path toward a brighter, more inclusive future.

Alignment as a Journey

Understanding alignment as a journey rather than a destination offers a liberating perspective. It's a dynamic process, evolving with our goals, dreams, and the paths we choose to follow. The essence of alignment lies in its ability to direct our focus, unite our efforts with others, and steer us toward a common goal. Yet, this journey is fraught with challenges, notably the ease with which we can drift off course. The clarity of our goals, or the lack thereof, directly influences our ability to achieve or lose alignment. Thus, the journey towards alignment begins with setting a clear, compelling destination.

As we embark on this journey towards alignment, it's crucial to remember that the path can sometimes be straight and smooth. Just as a ship adjusts its course to navigate rough waters, we must be adaptable and resilient in the face of obstacles. Embracing flexibility allows us to make necessary course corrections without losing sight of our ultimate destination.

Moreover, alignment is not a solitary endeavor. It thrives in the collaboration and support of like-minded individuals who share our vision and values. By surrounding ourselves with a supportive community, we can draw strength from each other and stay motivated on our collective journey toward alignment.

In moments of doubt or uncertainty, we must remind ourselves of the purpose behind our pursuit of alignment. Reconnecting with our innermost desires and aspirations can reignite the passion and drive needed to stay on course. Remember, alignment is not just about reaching a destination; it's about the growth, learning, and transformation that occur along the way.

So, as we continue on this profound journey of alignment, let's embrace the challenges as opportunities for growth, the setbacks as lessons in resilience, and the victories as milestones of progress. Let's forge ahead with determination, unity, and unwavering commitment to aligning with our true selves and shared goals.

The Role of Conflict in Alignment

Ironically, the pursuit of alignment often navigates through the waters of disagreement and conflict. It's a reminder that alignment does not equate to uniformity but thrives on diversity and the richness of differing perspectives. Disagreement becomes inevitable and necessary, challenging us to refine our goals and strengthen our convictions. The true essence of alignment lies not in the absence of conflict but in pursuing a common purpose despite our differences.

In this dynamic journey towards alignment, we embrace the beauty of diversity and the power of inclusivity. Each dissenting voice becomes a valuable puzzle piece, contributing to the mosaic of ideas that shape our collective vision. We discover new angles, uncharted territories, and innovative solutions as we engage in healthy debates and respectful disagreements.

It is the harmonious symphony of contrasting opinions and unique viewpoints that propels us forward, propelling us toward a shared destination despite our paths. Just as the colors of a rainbow blend seamlessly to create a breathtaking arc, our diverse perspectives blend harmoniously to create a tapestry of unity and progress.

So, let us welcome disagreement as a catalyst for growth, a beacon of change, and a testament to our unwavering commitment to a common purpose. In the tapestry of alignment, every thread, no matter how different, weaves together to create a masterpiece of collaboration, understanding, and, ultimately, success.

Personal Alignment and Change

At the heart of influence is alignment within oneself—the harmony between one's values, beliefs, and actions. This internal unity is the foundation upon which external influence is built. Yet, achieving personal alignment is an ongoing challenge, a reflection of our evolving nature as human beings. Our opinions, values, and goals shift over time, necessitating a continuous reevaluation of our alignment. Recognizing and embracing this fluidity is crucial to maintaining authenticity and influence.

Recognizing the need for continuous self-reflection and adjustment is critical to staying true to oneself while also being able to impact others positively. By consistently revisiting our values, beliefs, and actions, we can ensure that we always align with our true selves. This authenticity serves as a beacon to those around us, allowing our influence to be genuine and impactful. Embracing the ebb and flow of personal growth and evolution empowers us to adapt and grow as individuals and as influencers in the lives of those we touch. Remember, staying true to yourself is your most potent influence.

Strategies for Creating Alignment

Creating alignment, whether within oneself or among groups, requires intentional effort. It begins with empathy, the ability to see the world through others' eyes and to understand their motivations and challenges. Communication is the bridge that connects differing perspectives, enabling the co-creation of a shared vision. Finally, establishing common goals guides the collective journey toward alignment.

When individuals or groups strive for alignment, they embark on a journey of understanding and collaboration. Empathy lays the foundation for genuine connection, fostering a sense of mutual respect and trust. Through open and compassionate communication, diverse viewpoints can be acknowledged and synthesized, leading to the emergence of innovative solutions and shared perspectives. With shared goals serving as a guiding light, the collective efforts of all involved can be directed towards a harmonious and purposeful path forward. Creating alignment is a profound unity, cooperation, and shared growth exercise.

Case Studies & Examples

The annals of history are replete with examples of leaders and movements that have harnessed the power of alignment to effect change. From social reformers who galvanized communities around shared causes to business leaders who united diverse teams toward a shared vision, these stories underscore the transformative power of alignment. Through their journeys, we glean insights into the strategies that foster alignment and its impact on the world.

I recognize it as an ever-evolving, dynamic force. It is not a state to be achieved and maintained but a continuous process to be engaged with. Alignment is about movement—towards oneself, towards others, and towards the broader aspirations that unite us. This movement's influence is born, nurtured, and unleashed to create change.

As we stand at the crossroads of our journeys, the concept of alignment challenges us to reflect on our paths. It invites us to consider our direction, align our steps with our deepest values, and join hands with others who share our vision. Let us embrace the art of alignment, recognizing its power to transform our lives and the world.

TYLER ERICKSON

About Tyler Erickson: Meet Tyler Erickson, the Managing Director at The Erickson Coaching Company, a business coaching and consulting firm that has a mission to impact ten thousand businesses in the next 5 years. With a diverse background in mining and resources , hospitality management, and frail aged nursing, Tyler brings unique experience and that help business owners and their teams thrive. Thanks to his successful work in various industries, world travel, and solid country upbringing, Tyler is equipped to help businesses solve complex problems and tackle challenges head-on. At Erickson Coaching Company, applying expertise to empower businesses helping them reach their goals and achieve their full potential.

As an accomplished business coach, Tyler has logged over 4000+ hours of coaching clients and facilitating sessions. He has helped entrepreneurs and small business owners develop meaningful strategies and implement growth plans, resulting in more successful and fulfilling businesses. His expertise is further reinforced by his studies in business pursuing an MBA.

In addition to being an accomplished business coach, Tyler is also an author, sharing his knowledge and expertise on leadership, entrepreneurship, and business strategy. He is keenly aware of the challenges that business owners face, and his writings offer valuable insights and practical

Author's Website: www.EricksonTraining.com.au

Book Series Website: *www.TheBookofInfluence.com*

WILLIAM GOOD

AGREEMENT...OR ALIGNMENT?

"Action springs out of what we fundamentally desire. . . and the best piece of advice which can be given for would-be persuaders is: First, arouse in the other person an eager want. He who can do this has the whole world with him. He who cannot walks a lonely way."
~ Dale Carnegie quoting Harry A. Overstreet

Finding the Better Way

Dale Carnegie speaks on a topic of great significance and utility here, the possibility and practice of "Creating Alignment" between people. The publishers and all 33 authors who share in this collaborative literary reflection are aligned over the importance of. . . *well*. . . alignment—especially now, in this age so deeply marked and marred by misalignment bred in contention and disharmony.

Notice I said we are "*aligned*," not that we are "*agreed*." And that's an important distinction. . . but we'll get there in a bit.

Let me start our conversation with a car story—perhaps something of a parable, if you will.

But first, courtesy demands I ask a question here: Is that okay? ***Are you aligned?*** After all, you paid good money for this book.

I once owned a 1997 Eagle Vision automobile. This was a really fine car created by the American Chrysler Corporation from distinctly European aspirations. It was a beautiful and responsive machine, part sports car and part luxury sedan, finely detailed and deeply satisfying to own.

My otherwise admirable Eagle only had one particularly egregious shortcoming: all four wheels simply refused to keep rolling in the same precise direction at the same time. It was as if each of them was possessed by a wrench wielding demon with a singular mind and goal all its own.

If you've ever driven a car in which the wheels were out of alignment, you know what I'm talking about here. When all four wheels are not harmoniously cooperating to move the vehicle forward in a concerted, unified, and parallel direction your driving experience advances from vaguely unpleasant to utterly intolerable in rapidly succeeding stages.

At slower speeds in which variances are less critical, you experience a slight shimmy in the steering wheel and a correctable tendency for the car to veer afield from your desired line of travel. However, as speed increases, so do consequences. That annoying but innocuous shimmy transforms into a frighteningly rabid shake as the car threatens to pull itself apart trying to run at the multiple and simultaneous instruction of each of its four contending wheels. The faster you go, the worse it gets as you careen haphazardly down the highway with minimal control and even less comfort. This was—sadly—the case with my otherwise finely engineered Eagle.

In addition to the obvious mortal danger, this failure of alignment had additional consequences of a secondary dimension—my rogue Eagle consumed its overstressed and misdirected tires at a furious rate, literally tearing them into (expensive) pieces. It was as if the very soul of the poor disorderly vehicle had been reincarnated from a previous life as an automated teller machine.

The challenge was, however, that repeated attempts to mechanically correct the situation proved repeatedly unsuccessful. I almost gave up on the car.
So, "What's the point?," you ask. Why am I spinning my wheels with this car story?

Simply this: Creating alignment—while not necessarily a simple process—is always critical to a smooth journey. Especially when it comes to a group of people struggling to embrace and move forward toward a common goal.

Our American worldview—as our democratic political system inherently testifies—places a high value on consensus. In fact, we have long celebrated this as "the American way." We teach it in schools, stress it in our homes, and profess it in all sorts of social contracts. Unfortunately, this perspective often misinterprets consent as agreement and mistakes capitulation for support. And then we wonder why our society is so fraught with anger and contention.

Here's the thing. . . groups of people often resemble those misaligned wheels on my Eagle. While they may share an ostensible goal, more often than not, their vision for getting there dictates vastly different directions of travel. As a result, the process of navigating agreement almost inherently involves the application of a certain undue and undesirable pressure. Pressure which frequently begins as uncomfortable harmless arm twisting, but which ultimately builds to painful and soul-damaging bullying.

This inherently coercive process may generate something *resembling* consensus, but all too often leaves behind a divisive residue of resentment and disharmony. Just like my struggling Eagle, it may get you where you want to go; but it certainly tears up a lot of valuable tires along the way. I suspect most—if not all—of us can testify to the truth of this.

Dale Carnegie points us to a better way—a way which bypasses this damaging process of negotiating agreement in favor of a healthier one: "There is only one way under high heaven to get anybody to do anything," he says. "Yes, just one way. And that is by making the other person want to do it." And the only way to do this, he insightfully suggests, "is to talk about what [others] want and show them how to get it." In essence, Carnegie sees that the way to realize a successful and fulfilling concurrence on anything is by seeking a reciprocal alignment of desires grounded in recognition and satisfaction of mutual self-interest.

Unlike agreement, reaching alignment isn't initially focused on the goal —the *"where;"* it's focused instead on the participants—the *"who."* It involves creating a shared vision by honoring and acknowledging the other person's point of view. It's about **creating a vision** that is both **comprehensive** and **compelling**. It seeks to *"arouse that eager want"* that both Harry Overstreet and Dale Carnegie recognized as the critical component to success.

Contrary to what you might suppose, this process is really quite simple and not nearly as demanding as the manipulative maneuverings involved in reaching agreement. It vests itself in plain old common sense wrapped around humble curiosity and careful listening.

It all starts with seeing through the eyes of others. Here are the basic steps:

- Recognizing and honoring the other person's point of view
- Identifying mutuality of interests
- Locating points of common desire; then
- Casting vision that embraces these shared interests and desires.

With this information at hand, you now have the tools to enroll the other person in a collaborative vision by helping them see how it will satisfy *their* wants, achieve *their* goals, and benefit *their* interests. Alignment succeeds, not by being manipulative as with agreement, but by being responsive. "The best way to motivate someone to do something for you," says Dale Carnegie, "is to show how it would benefit them as well."

In short, creating alignment thrives on getting what **you** want by getting what **they** want. And you arrive there with all your tires intact.

"By the way. . .," you ask, "whatever became of your poor, misguided Eagle?"
A happy alignment was ultimately achieved; but, only after a number of visits to the Dealer's Service Department when one particularly visionary

mechanic finally put the car up on the hoist, removed a few pieces, and looked closely at the steering mechanism from a whole new point of view. This fresh perspective quickly revealed a disharmonious culprit lurking in the form of a previously unnoticed but critical component which had been malformed in the pressure of its hot metallic conception.

Replacement ultimately created possibility for a truer and more durable alignment which, in turn, potentiated a delightfully harmonious relationship amongst the four previously dissonant wheels. (Think turning a Metallica rant into a Billy Joel ballad here.) It was a smooth ride from that point on.

I'm glad you asked.

You see, this new reality in my Eagle was brought into being only after an investment of considerable time, focused attention, and a fresh perspective open to possibility. And, therein lies the final lesson here.
Creating alignment—especially alignment amongst people—requires similar devotion, even as it opens the door to similar congruence. It truly provides a better way.

So, let me ask you: Are you ready to try something new?

Are you aligned with me?

WILLIAM GOOD

About William Good: Bill is passionately committed to bringing together the message of Jesus Christ with the methods and vision of Transformational Leadership. In his life, his teaching, his coaching, and his writing, his deepest desire is to bring about world change through interpersonal reconciliation and relationship recovery.

Bill holds a Master's in Divinity degree from Fuller Theological Seminary and recently retired as Pastor at Fountain Hills Presbyterian Church. He teaches at Grand Canyon University, guiding college students to develop their own worldviews and purpose.

His online ministry features devotionals and virtual biblical and spiritual curricula, which can be found on the Uncommon Community Facebook page. He is also CEO and Senior Counselor of Path to Peace, a ministry providing conciliation services to individuals and organizations seeking to overcome trauma and find reconciliation.

Bill holds advanced certifications in Christian Reconciliation and Peacemaking from IC Peace, and is a graduate of the NextLevel Masters in Leadership program.

He is currently engaged in writing two books for publication, *Between Sundays*, a practical study of Jesus' reconciliation ministry, and *From Here to There*, a collection of autobiographical essays on spiritual development. He'd love to hear from you at:
facebook.com/uncommoncommunity419 or via email at
Uncommoncommunity@gmail.com.

Author's Website: www.facebook.com/UncommonCommunity419

Book Series Website: *www.TheBookOfInfluence.com*

WILLIAM BLAKE

UNLOCK THE POWER IN LISTENING: ILLUMINATE

"If you only ask general questions, you'll only give general advice."
~ William Blake

Everyone Communicates no Matter Where They Work

Most conversations initiate with two unconscious behaviors. One, preparing a response without listening to the other person. Or two, listening with the intent to converse and reply based on what the other said. As you'll discover later, master communicators, expert entrepreneurs, and high performers all practice the skill of listening with intent to converse. Why? Because they know if they want to effectively communicate, it's more important to stay with what the other is interested in rather than push their own agenda.

Let's recap the first two skills in the power of listening.

In the previous two books of The Book of Influence, I shared two skills needed to unlock the power of listening. The first is preparation. Preparation is the ability to shape your mindset into a belief of being a lifelong student and the wisdom of realizing you don't know everything. Another way to see it is practicing humility. The second is discovery. This is the ability to quietly observe and listen. You observe through your ears, eyes, and mind as you hear what they say, see how they react, and read in between the lines. Life coaches, teachers, psychiatrists, interrogators, therapists, doctors, and many other jobs use these skills to communicate. Can they do it without it? Of course. However, they are subpar compared to the other professionals in their field focused on mastering communication.

However, there's more to it than discovery and being prepared…

You also must learn what it means to illuminate a conversation. Imagine you went to your doctor's office. After waiting, the doctor walks in and starts asking you what's been going on. You begin to tell them. After listening to you for 5 minutes, the doctor stands up and leaves the room. Would you feel satisfied? Was that worth the money you spent to go to their office? Absolutely not! You'd complain!

So, even though they listened to your problems, something was missing.

Now imagine you're back in the office with the same doctor. They sat down and listened to your issues. But this time, they asked questions about your health, family, illnesses, surgeries, etc. They recommend what steps you should take next and walk out. Sounds like a regular doctor now, right? Now being more satisfied with the result, you recognize the only difference between the two was the doctor's ability to ask questions and give answers.

That's what it means to illuminate.

Illuminate means to bring light to necessary information in a conversation. It's to ask questions to continue to unveil information that might be crucial to know. As a doctor, asking about a patient's medical history can unveil many answers needed to diagnose them properly. As a salesperson, asking questions reveals more about the customer that the sales rep can use to help close the sale. From lawyer to business owner, from introvert to extrovert, asking questions is crucial in mastering the skill of listening and communication.

What about my ability to offer advice/solutions?

The doctor's example offered a great view that it's not only about asking great questions but offering great advice too. However, offering advice and solutions is the fourth skill in unlocking the power of listening. It is called *Evaluate*. Before we get ahead of ourselves, we will leave that for the last book in this series. Because to offer great advice and solutions, one must learn how to ask the right questions first. If you only learn to ask general questions, you'll only give general advice. Let me teach you about asking the right questions first so by the time we get into offering advice and solutions, you'll be ready.

Back when I was a young college student…

I was asked the same questions by EVERYONE:

- How are you doing?
- What are you majoring in?
- What is your field of study?
- Where are you going to use your degree?
- Any prospects for marriage lately?

And each of those questions lead to my robot answers of:

- Doing good…
- Business Management…
- Business with marketing…
- Some type of business stuff…
- Nope but still trying…

And they became so repetitious!

I felt my head would explode if I had to tell one more person how mundane my life felt. And it wasn't mundane! I felt I had a lot going for me with connections I'd made, things I was learning, and challenges I overcame. But the continuation of uninteresting questions made me feel like I had to answer showing myself in a vanilla flavor kind of life.

Then one day, a stranger came up to me.

Knowing he was just another person; I prepped my answers to his questions. He then looked at me and asked, "What are you passionate about?" Shocked, I had to ask him what he said again because I wanted to make sure I heard him right. He asked again, "What are you passionate about?" Stumbling over my words, I began to share things I liked to do and felt passionate about. Then out of left field, he asked another question, "Willie, what is your story?" Energy flowed through my body for the next hour and a half as I told this guy my life story. It blew my mind that I had so much to say and so much inside of me…and all it took was two questions to get it out. Not only is that stranger one of my closest friends today, but he taught me an important lesson.

I knew I could never ask questions the same way again.

So I started using those questions with people I met. I would ask them, "What are you passionate about?" and "What is your story?" Every interaction became an explosive game as I saw people who I thought were shy and timid release an energy I could only compare to when I was first asked these questions. It was exciting to get to know much more about a person than what general questions only gave. And the best part, most of these interactions left with a deeper connection than I believed possible. I became so delighted about all this that I started creating my own deep questions. My favorite one of all time (one I call my golden question) is this. "If you had no limits on time, money, resources, or connections, and didn't care what other people thought about you…what would you do?" This question alone has opened so many different avenues for people and opportunities. So you see, simply asking a different question or rephrasing a common one connects you more with a person than any general question would. General questions get general answers. But deep questions build deep relationships.

It's time to level up your questioning skills.

This doesn't mean you have to change who you are. You simply make a mind shift on how you go about asking questions. Instead of asking:

- How is your day?
- What's your degree in?
- What have you been up too?

Level it up! Ask:

- What are 3 new things you've done this week?
- What goals are you aiming for this year?
- How have you failed this week and what lesson did you learn?

Caring a little more about how you ask questions changes EVERYTHING.

The best part about this is the alignment you share with another individual. You create alignment from two strangers talking together to two people getting to know each other. When you listen and observe what they say, you understand more from where they come from. They begin to like you and surprisingly, you begin to like them! And just like that, a few golden questions create a long-lasting relationship. Whether in a personal conversation or a professional manner, powerful questions create alignment.

If you don't know where to start… just start.

I started by asking those two questions someone shared with me. Then as I got more experience, I created my own questions. And that's how you can start. Ask people you come by, "What are you passionate about?" and "What is your story?" Then as you get more comfortable, ask different unique questions. You'll find your conversations will become livelier. Connections and relationships will grow deeper. And your ability to communicate will be sharper and more professional.

Preparation, Discovery, Illuminate…

Three skills so powerful within themselves that taking one will improve your communication dramatically. But put them together, you're pretty much unstoppable. Now there is one last skill needed to master and unlock the full power in listening. That is the ability to Evaluate. This is where interpretation, offering advice and solutions, and becoming an expert comes into play. The final skill for mastery.

Unlock the full power of listening by learning this final skill and jumping over into the final book in *The Book of Influence* series.

WILLIAM BLAKE

About William Blake: William is a speaker and motivator. He focuses on the skill sets of learning, listening, and observing to help people access new avenues of success and solutions. What might seem like regular everyday skills that most overlook, William teaches people how to find creative ways of accessing those skills.

William Blake is a stalwart professional in the world of organization, strategy, and methods. Being diagnosed with Dyslexia at a young age and struggling with reading and speaking, William is an example that through perseverance, any challenge can become a superpower.

William spearheads a dynamic coaching and speaking venture, empowering dyslexics to harness their unique strengths and embrace a world of boundless possibilities. He is also one of the chapter team leaders and corporate associates at Champion Circle Networking Association founded by Speaker Jon Kovach Jr.

From speaking to youth to being a camp counselor at Idaho Diabetes Youth Programs, William loves volunteering and helping children and teens believe in themselves and their unlimited potential. And of most importance to William is his love for his family. With his wife, he is dedicated to raising his daughters in a world of greatness, happiness, and unlimited belief.

Author's website: *www.WilliamBlakeLight.com*

Book Series Website: *www.TheBookofInfluence.com*

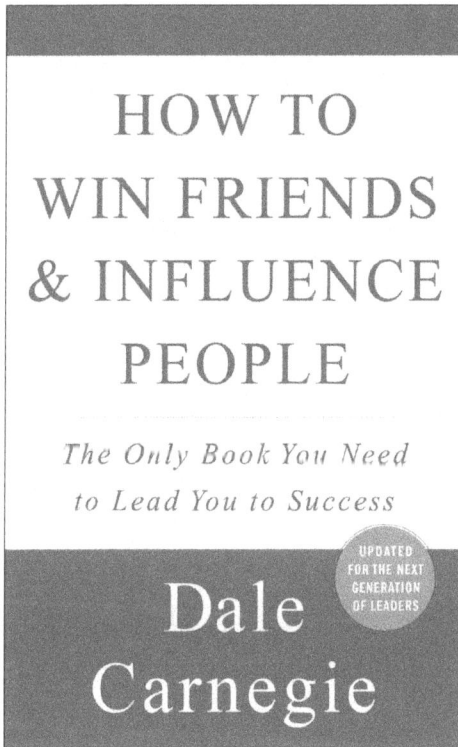

Habitude Warrior Mastermind

Join a team of

AWESOME

Entrepreneurs, Coaches, Business Owners, and Leaders to support you in your journey of success!

Be one of my personal guests for a session!

www.MastermindGuestPass.com

HABITUDE WARRIOR & INTEGRITY PUBLISHING EDITORIAL TEAM

Habitude Warrior International and Integrity Publishing take great pride in our editorial team who put their sweat, tears, and heart into each and every project and national bestseller! Thank you team!

JON KOVACH JR.
Team Manager

Jon Kovach Jr. strives to assist every author and every team member in the process of self-development for ultimate success.

PAT MINTON
VP of Operations

Pat Minton has been with the Habitude Warrior International team for over 20 years getting her start with Brian Tracy & Erik Swanson.

JILLIAN KOVACH
Editorial Manager

Jillian is a vital team member of Habitude Warrior & Integrity Publishing bringing her expertise managing our Editorial Department.

FATIMA HURD
Editorial Team & Photographer

Fatima is our Professional Photographer for Habitude Warrior as well as one of our members on the Proofing Department team.

LAUREN COBB
Editorial Team Member

Lauren Cobb is part of our Proofing Department for Habitude Warrior & Integrity Publishing as well as one of our authors.

To inquire about joining our team please send us an email to Team@HabitudeWarrior.com

www.ingramcontent.com/pod-product-compliance
Lightning Source LLC
Chambersburg PA
CBHW051255020426
42333CB00026B/3223
* 9 7 8 0 9 8 9 4 1 3 6 9 5 *